Digital L2 Writing Literacies

Frameworks for Writing

Series Editor: Martha C. Pennington, SOAS and Birkbeck University of London

The series offers books focused on writing and the teaching and learning of writing in educational and real-life contexts. The hallmark of the series is the application of approaches and techniques to writing and the teaching of writing that go beyond those of English literature to draw on and integrate writing with other disciplines, areas of knowledge, and contexts of everyday life. The series entertains proposals for textbooks as well as books for teachers, teacher educators, parents, and the general public. The list includes teacher reference books and student textbooks focused on innovative pedagogy aiming to prepare teachers and students for the challenges of the twenty-first century.

Published:

Academic Writing Step by Step: A Research-based Approach
Christopher N Candlin, Peter Crompton, and Basil Hatim

Arting and Writing to Transform Education: An Integrated Approach for Culturally and Ecologically Responsive Pedagogy
Meleanna Aluli Meyer, Mikilani Hayes Maeshiro, and Anna Yoshie Sumida

Creativity and Discovery in the University Writing Class: A Teacher's Guide
Edited by Alice Chik, Tracey Costley, and Martha C. Pennington

Creativity and Writing Pedagogy: Linking Creative Writers, Researchers, and Teachers
Edited by Harriet Levin Millan and Martha C. Pennington

English Composition Teacher's Guidebook: How to Survive (and Even Thrive) as an Adjunct or Part-Time Instructor
Tom Mulder

Exploring College Writing: Reading, Writing, and Researching across the Curriculum
Dan Melzer

Investigative Creative Writing: Teaching and Practice
Mark Spitzer

Reflective Writing for Language Teachers
Thomas S. C. Farrell

Tend Your Garden: Nurturing Motivation in Young Adolescent Writers
Mary Anna Kruch

The "Backwards" Research Guide for Writers: Using Your Life for Reflection, Connection, and Inspiration
Sonya Huber

The College Writing Toolkit: Tried and Tested Ideas for Teaching College Writing
Edited by Martha C. Pennington and Pauline Burton

Understanding the Paragraph and Paragraphing
Iain McGee

Writing Poetry through the Eyes of Science: A Teacher's Guide to Scientific Literacy and Poetic Response
Nancy S. Gorrell, with Erin Colfax

Digital L2 Writing Literacies

Directions for Classroom Practice

Ana Oskoz
Idoia Elola

SHEFFIELD UK BRISTOL CT

Published by Equinox Publishing Ltd.

UK: Office 415, The Workstation, 15 Paternoster Row, Sheffield, South Yorkshire S1 2BX
USA: ISD, 70 Enterprise Drive, Bristol, CT 06010

www.equinoxpub.com

First published 2020

British Library Cataloguing-in-Publication Data

A catalogue record for this book is available from the British Library.

ISBN 978 1 78179 692 4 (hardback)
978 1 78179 693 1 (paperback)
978 1 78179 694 8 (ePDF)

Library of Congress Cataloging-in-Publication Data
Names: Oskoz, Ana, author. | Elola, Idoia, author.
Title: Digital L2 writing literacies : directions for classroom practice / Ana Oskoz and Idoia Elola.
Description: Sheffield, South Yorkshire ; Bristol, CT : Equinox Publishing Ltd, 2020. | Series: Frameworks for writing | Includes bibliographical references and index. | Summary: "Two experts in the field offer an up-to-date view of digital writing research and practice with a focus on the teaching of second language, foreign language, and heritage language students"-- Provided by publisher.
Identifiers: LCCN 2019057393 (print) | LCCN 2019057394 (ebook) | ISBN 9781781796924 (hardback) | ISBN 9781781796931 (paperback) | ISBN 9781781796948 (ebook)
Subjects: LCSH: Composition (Language arts)--Computer-assisted instruction. | Composition (Language arts)--Study and teaching. | Second language acquisition--Computer-assisted instruction. | Social media in education.
Classification: LCC P53.27 .O85 2020 (print) | LCC P53.27 (ebook) | DDC 418.0071--dc23
LC record available at https://lccn.loc.gov/2019057393
LC ebook record available at https://lccn.loc.gov/2019057394

Typeset by S.J.I. Services, New Delhi, India

Contents

Dedication

Nire amari

Ana

Nire amari y, a ti, Curtis

Idoia

Series Editor's Preface

Collected in this important book is a wealth of professional knowledge and insight gleaned from years of practice in language teaching and curriculum design for writing and digital literacy, summarized with examples and recommendations, by two of the leading educators and researchers in the field. It is an authoritative and timely work, providing an up-to-date overview of digital writing in L2 contexts, with reflections on its specific applications and potentials as an environment for development of communicative skills and personal expression, and on how digital media have expanded the options for teaching language and writing in particular. It is a learned and highly original work, extensively referenced, showing wide-ranging knowledge of the relevant literature and offering cutting-edge theoretical perspectives on multilingual, multimodal composing. It is also a reader-friendly book, well written and designed to be of value to researchers and teachers working with multilingual students in second language, foreign language, and heritage language classrooms.

The main chapters are structured to provide the necessary background of definitions, descriptions of practices, and key research findings, along with detailed sample learning projects and ideas for reflection and discussion that those involved in L2 writing should find interesting and relevant. The authors begin with a wide-ranging review of digital tools and environments and how these are influencing communicative modes and written genres. They address how those tools and environments are encouraging interactive and collaborative writing in online environments, innovative multimodal forms of composing such as digital storytelling, and new avenues and modes for expression of multilingual writer voice and identity. They further discuss how feedback, revision, and assessment practices for L2 writing must change to reflect the changing processes and products of digital composing. The content of the book is summarized in a model of theoretical and pedagogical factors impacting digital L2 writing and in a future-oriented discussion of L2 writing and digital practices in the 21st century, making for a stimulating set of implications and take-away messages to ponder.

For those who are on the fringes as well as those who are at the center of digital practices, the book provides much in the way of continuing education and food for thought. As the most comprehensive and current state-of-the-art treatment of its subject matter, *Digital L2 Writing Literacies: Directions for Classroom Practice* is simply the must-read book for all those with an interest in L2 writing and language teaching.

– Martha C. Pennington
Series Editor, Frameworks for Writing

Acknowledgements

We have always enjoyed writing, especially writing together. We have written in all the languages that we have learned or studied as a second, third, or even fourth language. It thus makes sense that we have devoted our first book to the teaching of digital second, foreign, and heritage language writing.

This contribution is the result of years of investigating and writing articles and chapters on second language writing and technology. Throughout these years, we have worked together numerous times. Often over Skype, in sessions that ranged from a few minutes to 9 hours – thinking aloud, sharing ideas and silences – while both of us worked on a text at the same time. This type of collaboration and compromise that we have exhibited and shared during all these years of working together has made us look, according to family and friends, like twin sisters, a married couple or life partners, who finish each other's thoughts. When the time came to give author credit for this book, we thought of hyphenating our last names (Oskoz-Elola or Elola-Oskoz) or of creating a new last name that could represent the totally collaborative nature of our work! In the end, we abandoned our radical ideas for signifying coequal collaborative coauthorship and ended up with one of us going first. Our next contribution will be the other way around. Undoubtedly, and worth mentioning, we believe that the beauty of this partnership has primarily been the academic growth that has been part of our learning process as researchers, as presenters, and as writers.

None of this would have been possible without the support of our institutions, Texas Tech University and the University of Maryland,

Baltimore County (UMBC). The Texas Tech Women Faculty Writing program – in particular, Elizabeth Sharp – provided time and space to develop many ideas in the book. The College of Arts, Humanities and Social Sciences (CAHSS) Research Fellowship for 2017–2018 at UMBC provided invaluable months for the final push to complete the first draft of this book. A special thanks to the team at the Dresher Center for the Humanities at UMBC. Jessica Berman, La Atwater, Natalia Panfile, and Rachel Brubaker, you were great companions and models as we were working on the book. We also want to show our gratitude to our former chairs, Omar Ka and Erin Collopy, who have been nothing but supportive through the years that we have worked with them. There are also many colleagues and friends who have accompanied us in the development of this book: Ana Maria, Marta, Nicoleta, John, Ariana, Marta T., Josh, Diego. También queremos darles las gracias a nuestros estudiantes, con los que hemos ido aprendiendo a lo largo de los años y sin los que no podríamos haber escrito este libro. And we want to also thank all of the researchers and authors we have included in this book because without your previous work, our book would not have been possible.

We also would like to acknowledge Martha Pennington, the series editor, who has believed in this book and worked closely with us in the last stages of writing and editing. We want to show our deepest gratitude as well to our long-time editor, Valerie Mobley, who for more than a decade has constantly inspired and forced us to become better writers in English, our third language. And last but not least, to our mentors at the University of Iowa, we owe much for forming us into the researchers we are today.

Eskerrik asko gure familiei: Aitxa, Iñaki, Salbador, Lidia, Eli, Reme, Marisol, Luis, Concha, Ayem, and Ibai. To Nestor.

Introduction

Opening Digital Horizons in the L2 Writing Classroom

Our first collaborative writing experience dates back to 2006; soon after graduating from our Ph.D. programs, we thought of how to combine our strengths and collaborate on our first project. One of us was in a study-abroad program in Seville, Spain, and the other one was teaching in the United States. The natural endeavor was to connect the study-abroad students with those in the United States. Based on the cultural topics discussed in the class, the U.S. students reflected on topics and asked the study-abroad students reflective questions about their experiences in Seville. Students in Spain answered the questions and added their own reflective questions for the U.S.-based students. Through a series of prompts in their group blogs, students collaboratively enhanced their cultural knowledge of their first and second languages. Students further explored the topics by responding to each other's posts with their questions and answers. At that time, our decision on the use of blogs for this collaborative project was based on the type of digital tools our students were already beginning to use as a means of communication in their daily lives.

What we did not realize then was that we ourselves were also engaging in collaborative writing. While working on our first article together, we jointly drafted our literature review using Microsoft Word (no, we did not use Google Docs). When the six-hour difference did not allow us to work at the same time, we provided feedback to each other using the "Comment" function in Word. We text-messaged each other to schedule online meetings. On Skype, we spent long hours discussing every single sentence that we wrote in our Discussion section. When the audio failed us, we made use of the Skype written chat function. We should have recorded our interactions and analyzed our own work!

Given the benefits that we had experienced in our initial collaboration, it was only natural that we wanted to share our experience to help our Spanish second language (L2) and heritage language (HL) students achieve the type of composition that represents the times in which we live. Yet, like many other instructors throughout the years, we have pondered how the inclusion of digital tools such as wikis, blogs, Google Docs, Twitter, and/or Instagram can more effectively address the diverse needs and challenges (i.e., academic, literate, and cultural) of our traditional L2 students, who learned the language in the instructional context, and our HL and generation 1.5 students, who had different degrees of academic and non-academic knowledge of their heritage language.

Before we move on, we have a small confession to make. As L2 writing instructors we freely admit that the integration of digital tools in the L2 writing class has been a difficult challenge, although an interesting one. When we implemented the use of wikis for first time, chaos appeared all over the place: students could not understand the need to write collaboratively in a wiki; colleagues were puzzled by the integration of digital social tools in an academic writing class. Yet, we were swept up by the promise and power for collaborative learning that wikis could bring to the classroom. Following sociocultural approaches, we firmly believed in the benefits of students collaborating to produce wikis in a scaffolding process – that this innovative tool would almost magically help students to improve their writing skills significantly. But to start with, we were still largely unaware of the full potential of this digital tool, and so we just replicated the traditional argumentative and expository essay genres commonly taught in advanced

L2 writing classes. We were still following the view of "writing as a linguistic modality, or standalone linguistic skill" (Belcher, 2017, p. 80) that privileged the five-paragraph essay (Casanave, 2017). At that time, our eyes were not opened to the full range of affordances that social digital tools could offer. We had yet to learn that wikis could help us to expand the repertoire of writing tasks to more relevant and engaging communicative purposes. Soon enough, however, as we discovered other digital tools and introduced them into our classes, we began to question our own assumptions about writing. We recognized that the L2 writing class is not merely the place where learners become aware, learn about, and practice writing conventions, but it is also the place where we, as researchers and educators, could and should provide students with access to the digital literacies they need to succeed in today's world. We became gradually convinced that today L2 writing is not just a vehicle for language practice, but an enabler that shapes multiliterate and multilingual writers and communicators in a dynamic digital world.

This book is specifically intended for those who are interested in the inclusion of digital tools in their L2 classes. Throughout the text, particularly in Chapters 2 through 6, we provide a detailed examination of the implementation of different tools, backed up by a comprehensive literature review, and practical recommendations in the form of detailed project ideas for the L2 classroom. Our hope is that this book will continue the conversation regarding the inclusion of digital tools – the current ones and the new ones to come – based on sound instructional practices informed by systematic research.

During the past few years, we have observed how many L2 instructors still dread the introduction of digital tools because they believe they do not help, or even impede, L2 development. They are not alone. As Casanave (2017) pointed out, many instructors are concerned that the integration of digital tools in the classroom will supplant the traditional art of writing, limiting students' capacity for academic growth, their ability to read and write in an academic register, and their development of thinking skills. We should respect these concerns; however, there are at least five reasons why the advent of digital tools in the L2 classroom should be welcomed rather than dreaded.

First, written language is not likely to disappear in today's technological age: indeed, as Yi (2017) pointed out, it is likely to continue "to be the most powerful mode of formal learning" (p. 90) in the foreseeable future. If we look back into history, we see that the invention of writing is itself a type of technological development that expanded the "possibilities of human expression" and provided "a means for knowledge to be recorded and accumulated" (Chun, Kern, & Smith, 2016, p. 65). Over time, the development and complexity of human expression has spurred a continuous expansion of our formal and informal literary practices, an expansion that has allowed us to move beyond the use of written text[2] to the incorporation of the visual and aural modes.

Second, as Belcher (2017) points out, we should not be talking only about developing writing but "facilitating composing, that is, creating and communicating meaning" (p. 81). Today the process of composing text can access a large semiotic toolkit which offers writers a complete range of color, sound, and still and moving images to complement the written word. It is therefore a natural consequence of society's technological advances that people will want to use the tools and semiotic resources available to them, to assist communication in writing. While the concept of multimodal literacy in the L2 classroom is not new (Miller-Cochran, 2017; Yi, 2017), the novelty in our view resides in the inclusion of digital multimodal literacy in our L2 students' writing. Ultimately, multimodal literacy is reshaping our understanding of the meaning of genre and changing our conception of academic knowledge and practice (Bowen & Whithaus, 2013).

Third, what it means to be literate in the world today (Bowen & Whithaus, 2013) has shifted from the acquisition of the decoding and encoding skills necessary to read and write, to being able to participate and communicate in a multimodal, multimedia, multicultural, and multilingual society (Cope & Kalantzis, 2015; Kern, 2015; Pennycook, 2001). As the New London Group (1996) pointed out, multiliteracies, which include new communication technologies, are representations of (multi)cultural and (multi) linguistic diversity. Since that statement was made, there has been a movement to introduce "multimodal texts, and particularly those of the new digital media, into the curriculum and classroom" (Cope & Kalantzis, 2015, p. 3). This inclusion calls for the need to teach with new and emerging computer-mediated writing tools and genres (Thorne & Reinhardt, 2008). A new sense of hybridity (on a continuum from traditional genres to new ones) is changing our fixed notion of genre in a way that offers our students a new understanding of what multiliteracy could represent.

Fourth, it is clear that technology and digital composing are here to stay, so it is vital that we include multimodal forms of communication in the L2 classroom to prepare students for their future lives in a "digitally mediated world" (Hafner, 2015, p. 487). Introducing digital tools in our classrooms also entails the closing of the so-called digital divide – a gap that persists despite the deceptively ubiquitous presence of mobile devices (Belcher, 2017) – by providing both privileged and deprived groups in the population with the functional literacies required to succeed in today's world (Ortega, 2017).

Fifth, within the broad scope of multiliteracies, there is also an area for multilingual and translingual expression. Although these two terms are used interchangeably, in this book multilingualism or plurilingualism refers to the acquisition of two or more autonomous languages in an additive manner but separated from one another (García & Li Wei, 2014). Translanguaging, on the other hand, refers to how students make meaning using their linguistic repertoires in a dynamic and integrated manner (Li Wei & Ho, 2018). We need to see both manners of expression as valid and respected forms of communication, challenging prescriptive, monolingual thinking that sees each language as a unique and separate system (Kramsch, 2014). Taking into account such forms of expression entails the need to consider L2 students' linguistic experiences outside of the academic context as we bring multilingual and translingual practices into the L2 classroom.

The increased understanding of multiliteracies has also helped us realize that the myth of our students being "digital natives" (Prensky, 2001) has been debunked. It is true that their extensive exposure to new media strengthens their confidence in navigating those media. In the L2 learning context, a great proportion of our students are undeniably "digitally wise" (Prensky, 2009) in that they appear to properly employ technological innovations not only to supplement their learning strategies but to compensate for certain cognitive limitations. That said, as DePalma and Alexander (2015) recognize, "the extent to which these literacies have prepared students to *produce* rhetorically sophisticated texts is a different question altogether" (p. 184). As L2 instructors, we can help instill the social dimension of digital wisdom – the conscious decisions students make to exploit technological advances – that comes "*from* the use of digital technology to access cognitive power beyond our innate capacity," and is seen "*in* the prudent use of technology to enhance our capabilities" (Prensky, 2009, para. 2). This social dimension also alludes to "real-world" (i.e., non-institutional) situations and enriches students' experience by connecting them with an audience beyond the classroom, moving beyond the established institutional roles and identities that are linked to being a language student in a local context (Lam, 2004; Sykes, Oskoz, & Thorne, 2008; Thorne & Black, 2007).

Students gain a sense of authorship and empowerment that permeates their identities as language users when they position themselves as communicators, not just in the local, but also in the global digital interactive context (Ushioda, 2011). Further, as our L2 students' backgrounds become more culturally and linguistically diverse, the line between first-language (L1) and L2 writing becomes more and more blurred (Canagarajah, 2013a). In the case of digital writing, the existence of this blurring affects students' developing sense of self across different languages and registers of expression. They have a natural desire to communicate, whether in academic or non-academic registers, and digital tools offer them the flexibility to use different language varieties as part of academic writing. As Kayi-Aydar (2018) points out, participation in virtual worlds helps students to position themselves as language users with evolving multilingual identities who interact in complex ways as they begin to influence one another.

Implementation of digital social tools for writing is undoubtedly challenging, not least because these tools are constantly changing. To become successful writers who can develop digital writing literacy, students need to recognize that the value of writing goes beyond the classroom and the maintenance of social connection through texting and other messaging media. They need to be aware of the importance of preparing themselves "for the increasingly complex and interconnected global society in which they live and work" (Moore, Fowler, & Watson, 2007, p. 46). Thus, the goals of any educator should first be to raise students' awareness of the value of working with digital writing tools and then to teach them to use these tools effectively to create meanings and interpret the texts created by others.

The idea of this book is to showcase the most pertinent areas of research and practice for educators who are seeking a deeper understanding of L2 digital writing.[3] We want to advocate for the development and implementation of digitally mediated instructional practices in the light of theoretical and pedagogical perspectives. In this context, we describe in some detail the development of classroom tasks that will support students' growing multiliteracies. These examples could provide insights for those who wish to engage in research or to study instructional methods that could not only guide their own practice, but also help them modify instructional and curricular practices in their institutions, including language teachers, university academics, educational administrators, and tertiary students who have not yet had the opportunity to practice digital writing professionally. We see this book as an exploratory journey into L2 digital writing, one which is based on our own research and that of other scholars and which reflects the exciting challenge of teaching in this digital age.

The Soul of This Book

In *Digital L2 Writing Literacies*, we address digital writing literacy as a condition inherently associated with L2 instructors' and students' growing familiarization with the use of digital tools in the classroom and elsewhere. We also explore the new communicative possibilities and concerns that the introduction of digital tools brings to the writing classroom in relation to local and global contexts. Our explorations are supported by updated and carefully selected references from L2 writing research that reflect how technology (especially in the area of digital social tools) is changing writing practices and has allowed new writing genres to emerge. In the book we describe how digital social tools are revolutionizing the area of L2 writing, because they challenge the notion of text as people have traditionally known it. We discuss the nature of these new texts and provide examples of how instructors and students can incorporate them in interesting ways into their L2 courses. The purpose of the book is to share with other practitioners the insights we have gained from our own study and application of digital media in our classes.

In the first of seven chapters, we present the overarching theoretical and pedagogical frameworks that inform our practice. The coverage of each succeeding chapter includes an introduction to the chapter topic, a review of current work and recent directions in the area of the chapter topic, pedagogical and practical considerations and suggestions for applications that can be used in L2 classes, and further ideas for individual or group reflection and discussion by L2 practitioners. An original feature of the book is the inclusion in Chapters 2–6 of detailed specifications for L2 classroom projects involving digital media that have been developed based on our own practice.

In Chapter 1, *Digital Literacies: Definitions, Theoretical and Pedagogical Frameworks*, we discuss the challenges that L2 writing faces in the 21st century and discuss the implications of emerging digital literacies which become apparent from the interface of tools and modes in text creation. After defining the notion and function of digital literacies in the L2 writing context, we consider some of the challenges of the qualitative changes that social tools bring to the writing process. It then analyzes contemporary notions about digital literacies and how they relate to emerging digital genres; discusses the relevance of social tools in L2 writing and the need to recognize their differing affordances; and presents theoretical and pedagogical frameworks, such as the genre-based approach (Hyland, 2001), bridging activities (Thorne & Reinhardt, 2008), the task-based approach (González-Lloret & Ortega, 2014), and Learning by Design (Cope & Kalantzis, 2015) – all of them useful pedagogical frameworks that can help L2 researchers and educators to develop robust research and instructional practices in the area of digital literacies for writing.

In Chapter 2, *Transforming L2 Writing: New Writing Tools, New Genres, New Ways of Writing*, we focus on the new digital tools that can be applied to L2 writing and how they are opening up new digital genres. New and emerging digital tools have led to a proliferation of multimodal genres that, because of their social nature, require a deeper understanding of the target language's sociolinguistic and cultural norms. The inclusion of these tools and genres raises the question of how to address digital multimodality in the L2 context and how to equip L2 writers with the appropriate linguistic and rhetorical knowledge to enable their successful participation in a wide range of new and distinctive discourse practices. L2 educators/writing professionals need to incorporate multimedia, multimodality, collaboration, and hybridity into our curricula and make flexible use of available and emerging digital tools and genres. Instructors need to understand the affordances of the different tools, such as blogs or wikis, and what effect they have on the writing processes and interactions that L2 writers have with their audience; how do they affect the development of content and, importantly, how do they support linguistic development? The chapter provides some practical examples to illustrate how to incorporate new tools and their corresponding genres into courses. Following a task-based approach and the bridging activities framework, we describe the integration of a blog and Google Maps into an L2 history and culture class; this is an example of how students can work with digital literacies and how new genres for writing can be introduced to them.

By their very nature, digital social tools have transformed writing from an individual to a collaborative act. In Chapter 3, *Collaborative Writing in the L2 Classroom: Making the Most of Digital Social Tools*, we argue that the advent of digital social tools – which has to some extent blurred the lines between reading and writing – has also emphasized "collaborative forms of textual composition and interpretation" (Blyth, 2014, p. 204) and redefined literacy practices as both collaborative and public. After defining what collaborative writing means and arguing for its central role in the L2 classroom, we examine current research on L2 collaborative writing, which has been informed mainly by sociocultural and activity theories. Following a task-based approach, we provide an example of collaborative writing in which students use online forums, wikis, and chats to engage in learning about the topic and then collaborate on developing the content, structure, organization, and accuracy of the essay.

In Chapter 4, *Developing L2 and Multilingual Students' Identities as Writers: Acquiring a Voice*, we focus on the issue of identity. L2 students face challenges as well as opportunities as they develop their identities as writers; some are bilingual or multilingual, and they come from a wide range of social and economic backgrounds. We examine here ways that students can express and develop their own sense of identity through writing. To date, there is limited knowledge of incorporating digital literacy into the teaching of languages to multilingual (or translingual) speakers, a gap which indicates an area for future research and the need to develop new guidelines for pedagogical methodology. This chapter, following a sociocultural perspective, explains how contextual factors (such as linguistic background, dialects, and mixed populations in the same classroom) enrich our writers' socialization and identity development. It shows how students' self-perceptions might change from initial feelings of inadequacy as they grow in confidence and discover their own voices as L2 writers (King, 2015; Sauro, 2014). After discussing the value of digital literacies for supporting students' writing practices, the chapter examines how our understanding of literacies influences pedagogical and practical considerations in educational settings. Following a Learning by Design approach, we show how a task for HL students can allow them space to explore their identity while giving them agency to use their own voices in the creation of a personal digital story. The example demonstrates that students' opportunities for linguistic development and identity construction can coexist.

In the Chapter 5, *Becoming Digitally Literate: Rethinking Feedback and Revision*, we move on to examine the influence that digital tools have had on the area of feedback and the revision process in L2 writing. Text composition in the context of digital multimodal genres requires careful thinking about what type of feedback might be most appropriate for students – not only in terms of linguistic aspects of the composition, but also in terms of non-linguistic aspects, such as the use of still or moving images and sounds. At the same time, the use of digital tools to provide feedback, such as Screencast recordings or the track changes function in Word, allows instructors to provide (and learners to receive) multimodal feedback. After analyzing current research and applications on technology-mediated feedback for L2 writing, which mainly stem from interactionist and sociocultural theory, we focus on the impact that various digital tools have on L2 writing development. We look at different media for provision of feedback, including digital and non-digital. As such, we include face-to-face feedback that students can provide to each other in "circles" during the process of developing a multimodal narrative because we believe that feedback for digital multimodal text can be well served by traditional face-to-face feedback techniques. That is, in this chapter we explain how we can combine face-to-face and digital feedback to guide students in the development of a multimodal artifact.

In Chapter 6, *Assessing Digital L2 Writing: Challenges with New Tools and New Genres*, we focus on the linguistic and non-linguistic factors of assessment in the context of digital literacies and their implications. As Belcher (2017) points out "perhaps more challenging to digital pedagogy newcomers than how to implement digital writing projects is how to assess them" (p. 83). Traditional assessment practices that have primarily targeted L2 writers' linguistic development – in terms of accuracy, complexity, fluency, and vocabulary selection – may need to change with the inclusion of digital genres and literacies. Traditional evaluation practices fall short on delivering a comprehensive assessment of student writing that may now reflect the nuances and possibilities of digital genres and tools. Therefore, we emphasize the need to examine both linguistic and non-linguistic components of, for example, collaborative work in wikis, the expected impact on the audience from blogs, the use of hashtags in Twitter, and the selection and integration of sounds and images in digital stories. Collaboration with others, engagement with the audience, involvement with the community, and intermingling of images, sound, and text are all factors that will demonstrate learners' growing skill in how to convey meaning. We argue for the need to include students in the development of assessment criteria from the beginning stages of the writing task. Asking students to think rhetorically in this way helps them to reflect about relationships within and across modes (Kress, 2003; Odell & Katz, 2009; Sorapure, 2006) as well as about the audience, the genre, and issues of authorship and ownership. Following a task-based approach we present a digital story as an example, and we show how, after analyzing several digital stories, students themselves create grading criteria that reflect the integration of multimedia and the manipulation of semiotic resources within the various modes to convey meaning.

In Chapter 7, *Coming to Terms with 21st Century L2 Writing and Digital Literacy*, reflecting on current digital tools (but also anticipating new and unknown ones), we restate what we believe are the most significant points of the book. The aim of helping L2 students to become successful communicators remains unchanged. Yet we also encourage L2 instructors to address issues of identity, the educational possibilities of digital social tools, and also the need to close the digital divide that reflects current social inequality. To guide L2 instructors reflecting on their pedagogy, we present some questions that are designed with the idea of moving from abstract concepts to more tangible and practical applications. The chapter also highlights the interface of theoretical and pedagogical knowledge which continues to create new meanings about our notions of text and which provides a sound framework for the gradual adoption of digital literacies and multilingual practices.

We are aware that tackling collaborative writing, the introduction of multimodality, and moving to student-based assessment can seem, in combination, like an overwhelming task; and so we conclude the book with a model of practice to show how these areas can be successfully integrated. Our hope is that this model will help L2 practitioners to develop new instructional tasks for a more interconnected, globalized (but still localized), and more digitally multimodal world. The final chapter calls for a view of what a new language practitioner will look like in a future of digital literacies and technologies and it concludes with questions for reflection.

In the *Concluding Remarks*, we highlight the need for L2 educators and researchers to recognize the rapid social and technological changes that are taking place in this era. We also highlight several areas of possible future research; these can inform and advance our own L2 instructional practices and will help the L2 instructor of the future to explore as yet unforeseen instructional approaches with an open mind.

Notes

1. We want to acknowledge that throughout the book we use the abbreviation *L2* for reasons of economy but that we also have written this book with foreign language (which identifies specific instructional contexts) and heritage language (which is definitionally a native language that does not conform to monolingual standards and that is generally the least dominant language in academic settings) students in mind as distinctive groups.
2. *Text* in this book refers to written text in conjunction with other semiotic resources.
3. In this book, we use the term *writing* as an umbrella term that includes the composing of multimodal texts (which incorporate text, visuals, and sound).

Chapter 1

Digital Literacies: Definitions, Theoretical and Pedagogical Frameworks

Digital Social Tools in the L2 Classroom

The introduction of social tools in the second language (L2), heritage language (HL), and foreign language (FL) classrooms in the United States has inspired a renewed interest in writing as an essential part of the curriculum – an element perhaps somewhat neglected in recent times as communicative approaches have focused more on oral communication. Today we can acknowledge that the use of digital social tools (e.g., wikis, social networking, blogs) as learning tools is clearly influencing the teaching of writing away from its traditional focus on linguistic development. The advent of these social tools has multiplied our learners' writing practices in ways that were unthinkable a decade ago, opening up multiple communication channels and experimentation with exciting new digital genres. Research into technology-based L2 writing has emerged in the last decade (Blattner, Dalola, & Lomicka, 2016a, b; Kessler, 2009; Lee, 2010a, b; Oskoz & Elola 2016a, b; Reinhardt, Warner, & Lange, 2014). However, many educators still stick to familiar instructional approaches and teach to conventional academic genres – perhaps sporadically trying out, for instance, the use of wikis for the development of expository essays or experimenting with blogs for learners to practice native-like written discourse.

As we have previously pointed out (Elola & Oskoz, 2017), we do not advocate the discarding of conventional approaches to L2 writing, many of which have firm roots in L1 and English as a second language (ESL) research and pedagogy. However, in this chapter, we argue for the need to question and redefine the pedagogy of L2 writing: that is, to call for a redefinition of literacy, writing genres, and associated instructional practices within L2 learning theories. First, we acknowledge the profound shift in thinking that occurs when we embrace digital literacies. As we expand our definition of literacy to suit a digital age, we are seeing the emergence of new writing genres that integrate a rich suite of modes, modalities, and media – moving beyond accepted L2 pedagogies that are confined to the textual (what is on the page), to embrace new perspectives that also consider non-linguistic sources, such as social-semiotic theory (Kress, 2003, 2009). This is a challenging but essential shift in thinking if we are to recognize what the act of writing means and can mean in our L2 classrooms. This chapter goes on to define digital literacies and then to address the integration of multimodal texts in the digital context, to acknowledge the affordances of social tools for writing and the existence of new digital genres, and to suggest how learners can achieve digital literacy as they develop their digital identities. We then refer to some theoretical and pedagogical frameworks underpinning the discussion which contextualize pedagogical guidelines for L2 educators and administrators who want to foster L2 writing in an increasingly digital age. As we see it, instructors and students will need to become familiar with the semiotic affordances of different media and modes, experiment with new genres, and ultimately master digital literacies. Remaining open to change will be the key to success in tomorrow's language classrooms as we create digital texts in ways that we could not have imagined a few decades ago.

Digital Literacies: Understanding Literacies as Social Practices

Literacy and *literacy learning* have been defined as the acquisition of a series of decoding and encoding skills necessary to read and write, using a foreign alphabet or writing system in the context of unchanging, rule-governed, monomodal, and static linguistic elements (Pennycook, 2001). Yet given the internet revolution and the proliferation of digital tools, we need to redefine *literacies* as "social practices that are fluid, sociocultural, multimodal, and dynamic" (Chen, 2013, p. 143), that are exercised "by individuals as parts of larger groups" (Reinhardt & Thorne, 2011, p. 259), and that support the goals of writers and audiences and the social relationships between them (Hafner, Chik, & Jones, 2013). Viewed from a sociocultural perspective, the concept of literacy sits within broader social, institutional, and historical domains, and may be described in the context of user practices in particular media (Barton, 2007). The term *digital literacy* primarily applies to internet- and technology-mediated learning (Chen, 2013), and it intersects with other literacies related to communication skills. For example, *computer literacy* is the competence to use and make use of technology; *information literacy* is the ability to find and evaluate information; and *media literacy* is critical awareness of media representations and their ideological purposes (Dudeney & Hockly, 2016; Hockly, 2012). Digital literacy is therefore much more than skill with the technology itself – it relates to "the ideas and mindsets, within which particular skills and competencies operate" (Bawden, 2008, p. 19) and reflects the practitioner's agency in "the myriad social practices and conceptions of engaging in meaning making [...] via digital codification" (Lankshear & Knobel, 2008, p. 5). Consequently, it involves the development of a particular way of thinking. That is, developing digital literacies in the L2 class implies not only learning how to use a tool for a specific instructional goal, but how to become active users of technology in everyday life.

Incorporating digital literacy into the curriculum is therefore important for two reasons. First, as argued by Ortega (2017), the integration of digital literacy in learners' lives is a matter of social justice. It becomes a way to narrow the gap between the haves (with a wider access to technology) and have-nots (with more limited access). As educators, it is our responsibility to develop "know-how skills" (Ortega, 2017, p. 301) and competencies to help L2 learners from the full range of cultural and economic backgrounds to engage in socially empowering uses of technology– that is, features of technology that relate to economic success for individuals as opposed to recreational activities. As L2 language educators, we must remember that engaging with travel blogs, digital storytelling, or adding a Wikipedia entry have a value beyond immediate learning goals: in the long term we are helping learners to become dynamic members of an increasingly technological society (Lomicka & Lord, 2011, 2016). Second, as we pointed out in the Preface, the myth of "digital nativeness" (Prensky, 2001) – the assumption that current learners come born with technological competency – has been long disputed; learners are not always aware of all the possibilities, especially for educational purposes, that digital tools provide (Marsh, 2016). Developing an L2 curriculum that places digital literacy at its core means recognizing learners' digital literacy learning needs as well as their language learning needs (González-Lloret, 2014). Applying these twin goals will allow us to impart the capital-enhancing technology that will help close the digital divide. So engaging with digital literacy in our L2 classroom is not a luxury or an add-on to the regular class, but a must if our learners are to measure up in a digitally transformed world.

Digital Literacies: Integrating Multimodal Texts

No longer viewed in isolation, text is now often a complement to, or complemented by, other ways of communicating meaning. As Crystal (2011) writes:

> In a multimedia world, it is not possible to focus exclusively on the spoken or written element, treating everything else as marginal – as non-linguistic extras. All the elements combine in a single communicative act, and their joint roles need to be considered. (p. 139)

Within the world of multiliteracies, we need to build a detailed understanding of constructs such as mode, modality, and media that must be effectively integrated when constructing a digital text (Kress, 2003, 2009). According to Guichon and Cohen (2016), *mode* may be defined as the semiotic representation (textual, aural, visual) used to present information, whereas *modality* refers to the "semiotic realization of one mode" (p. 510), or the specific way the information is encoded; for example, the visual modality of videoconferencing is realized through the webcam image. Modalities can be asynchronous, when production and reception take place at different times (e.g., the writing of a blog post which is read later on by a reader), or synchronous, with simultaneous production and reception (e.g., two writers composing in Google Docs or using the chat to plan an essay). *Multimodality*, then, refers to the use of different modes in an integrated fashion to communicate meaning (e.g., text and visual combined in a blog). Lastly, *media* are "the technological means of inscription and production that shape the ways any message is conveyed and accessed" (Guichon & Cohen, 2016, p. 510). In a digital story, for instance, a learner would combine the visual mode (images), the aural mode (the sound, spoken word, music) and the textual mode (e.g., subtitles or additional text) through digital storytelling software (the tool or medium). The integration of these different modes, which has transformed the (printed) text as we knew it, requires a new understanding of the often multimodal text and the different modes involved in the act of composition.

Working in the context of multiliteracies, L2 practitioners and researchers must make decisions "about how what is to be represented should be represented: in what mode, in what genre, in what ensembles of modes and genres and on what occasions" (Kress,

2003, p. 117). According to social-semiotic theory (Kress, 2003, 2010), when immersed in producing a text, the author makes use of *semiotic resources* (an alternative term for grammar) to sit within a *frame* (or *genre*) in which several types of *modes* (e.g., written, oral) are used in the production of a text. This means that learners should become active designers who need to arrange and rearrange the presentation of a message by selecting and mingling semiotic resources according to the intended meanings to be conveyed (Yang, 2012). Therefore, when composing with multimodality, we need to integrate multimodal resources (such as images, sounds, or text) in a process called *synaesthetic semiosis* (Kress, 2003), or multimodal creation, the inclusion of oral, aural, and written modes, often in an intertwined manner when developing a text, "within which writers understand not only the role played by the mode of representation as a design element but also the effects of both the absence and the existence of design elements on readers' responses to the multimodal text" (Shin & Cimasko, 2008, p. 378).

The process of synaesthetic semiosis occurs in two forms during the construction of a multimodal text (Kress, 2003, 2009): First there is *transformation*, the actions that reorder and reposition semiotic resources within a particular mode, and second *transduction*, the reorganization of semiotic resources across modes. Thus, when developing a digital story, transformation is the process of reconstructing the syntax or structural complexity of sentences from a narrative (written) story into a digital story script. Transduction, on the other hand, involves converting written narration into spoken language and incorporating images, music, and sound. However, neither transformation nor transduction are easy concepts for learners to grasp. A key way to work with these processes indirectly is for learners and instructors to become fully aware of the particular affordances provided by every available digital tool and mode.

Digital Literacies: Understanding Affordances

Affordances, a term coined by Gibson (1979), refers to the possibilities for action that an environment "provides or furnishes [a learner], either for good or ill" (p. 127). Although affordances are only attained "in the interaction between organisms and objects in the environment" (Baerentsen & Trettvik, 2002, p. 52), the affordance of an object (e.g., a digital tool) is not altered based on whether the learner "may or may not perceive or attend to the affordance" (Gibson, 1979, p. 139) or whether they have the capacity to comprehend the possibilities of that object. For affordances to be operationalized, they have to "be perceived by the observer, who must possess the required physical or mental capacities to enact them" (Blin, 2016, p. 48). To be exact, even though the tools' affordances might have been consciously engineered by computer-assisted learning designers, such technologies do not possess self-sustaining value in themselves (Blin, 2016). Their affordances derive from their users' perceptions, motivation, and capacity (Gibson, 1979; van Lier, 2000). In L2 classroom contexts, then, the potential of affordances will be dependent on the traits of particular learners and learning environments (Blin, Jalkanen, & Taalas, 2016). Learners need to be taught the potential of digital tools and how to make use of them most effectively. In the language learning environment, the affordances of digital technologies "become reality through activities that are contextualized and purposefully planned" (Blin et al., 2016, p. 232) within the goals of communication (Dudeney & Hockly, 2016). Therefore, tools might be selected and used differently according to learners' skill levels and preferences. For example, when working on collaborative essays, learners can use online forums to develop the content (Oskoz & Elola, 2014), or they can use the comment feature in Google Docs to comment on each other's work (Pai & Liou, 2009; cited in Liou, 2016), or debate grammatical discrepancies in the chats (Grosbois, 2016). All these social tools share the potential to support writing; however, learners appropriate and adapt the affordances of the tools to suit their own communicative and linguistic purposes.

Digital Literacies: New Digital Genres

In line with Bakhtin's (1986) view of language as dialogic, Hyland (2011) notes how "writing reflects traces of its social uses because it is linked and aligned with other texts upon which it builds and which it anticipates" (p. 27). Written genres are therefore regarded by Hyland as "parts of repeated and typified social situations, rather than particular forms, with writers exercising judgment and creativity in responding to similar circumstances" (p. 27). The term *genre* has been defined as the grouping of texts that represent how writers use language to reply to recurrent situations (Swales, 2004). Although different schools of thought provide their own definitions of *genre* (Heyd, 2016), genre has been defined as "staged, goal-oriented social processes" (Martin, 1992, p. 505) that are recurrent configurations of meaning which enact the social practices of a given culture (Martin & Rose, 2008) and of a particular discourse (Maingueneau, 2010) and that vary according to which particular tool is used and how the story is conveyed to a wider community (Gebhard, Shin, & Seger, 2011).

In the present century, the definition has expanded to include other types of texts that respond to literacy demands or situations that were non-existent just a few decades ago. Some of these new texts that are being used in the L2 classroom context include: travel blogging (Ducate & Lomicka, 2008), encyclopedia entries in Wikipedia (King, 2015), Twitter postings (Blattner et al., 2016a, b), and online fandom participation (Sauro, 2014, 2017). Although the term *text* traditionally "was used to refer primarily to print-based, linear, fixed, written communication" (Vandergriff, 2016, p. 69), the emergence of the digital communication age has compelled us to think about texts and literacies in flexible, creative ways (Hattem,

2014). Unlike printed text, the dynamic nature of the digital context means that texts can be altered, moved, or even deleted at any time; are often linked to a network of texts through hyperlinking; and are frequently not text-only communication but a combination of different modes (Vandergriff, 2016). Hence, the expansion of social contexts and associated semiotic-linked activities in which individuals participate will ultimately result in the creation of new genres that we cannot conceive of today.

For L2 educators working with digital literacies, the multimodal genre can refer to the written text combined with images (as in blogs, Twitter, or digital story-telling), which offer diverse linguistic and non-linguistic repertoires and flexible pathways for co-representing meaning (Domingo, Jewitt, & Kress, 2016). In this view, genre encapsulates aspects of a social situation and depicts them in semiotic forms (Bateman, 2008).

Digital Literacies: New Opportunities to Develop L2 Writers' Identities

It has been frequently discovered that in digital contexts, L2 learners use their own voices and develop their own identity, or as Norton (2000) puts it, "how a person understands his or her relationship to the world, how that relationship is structured across time and space, and how the person understands possibilities for the future" (p. 5). In the technology-enhanced language learning world, this relationship has been investigated most extensively in fan fiction communities, where writers re-imagine their identities to gain the recognition and status that their formal educational contexts do not grant them (Black, 2006; Lam, 2000, 2006). As Sauro (2017) pointed out, in online environments fans use "digital tools and communication technologies to discuss, share, create, or otherwise respond to a public performance" (p. 132) that can include, for example, graphic novels, plays, television or film series. In many instances, these are extramural "activities that learners come in contact with or are engaged in outside the walls of the [language] classroom, generally on a voluntary basis" (Sundqvist & Sylvén, 2014, p. 4). Research in this area has found that, because of their engagement in fan pages (either for their technical or cultural knowledge or out of personal interest), learners considered to be low-achieving were able to develop their skills in English composition and also showed evidence of identities more empowered and capable than the formal educational structures they were exposed to allowed (Black 2006; Lam, 2000, 2006).

Given the potential of such extramural activities for linguistic and identity development, it is not surprising that they are being incorporated in the formal classroom. The challenge is, as Sauro (2017) points out, how best to integrate those extramural digital writing practices in the L2 classroom. Thomas and Stornaiuolo (2016), for example, encourage and provide guidelines for incorporating "bending" projects, in which fans critique and write themselves into the source text by changing the ethnicity or race (*racebending*) or gender (*genderbending* or *cisswapping*) of the characters; these ideas are incorporated as a way to help learners write themselves into less accessible mainstream texts or to explore perspectives and experiences different from their own. Sauro (2014) provides descriptions of fan practices and teaching ideas which, among others, include collaborative threaded word games or the creation of a fan wiki to document information about characters, plots, events, and objects in a story or movie. However, the issue of introducing and integrating new literacy tools and practices, such as fan fiction, to the classroom might backfire because it is precisely learners' agency in their own creativity that is crucial (Lin, 2015; cited in Sauro, 2017). It is also the case that, despite the emergence of multilingual practices (Leppänen, 2007; 2008; Zhang & Cassany, 2016), English has been the prominent language in these online fandoms. Nonetheless, there is no reason why the potential benefits of these recent digital practices cannot be transferred to other language contexts, in particular to the L2 classroom.

Digital Literacies: Challenges for Instructors

Digital genres can be an elusive concept for many instructors, given that technology-enhanced language learning is an open, evolving, and changeable environment and given these genres' non-traditional structures and diverse forms of hybridity and semiotic systems (Luzón, Ruiz-Madrid, & Villanueva, 2010). There is a need to develop helpful pedagogical frameworks that focus on the instructors' "awareness of semiotic affordances of media and modes and their subsequent ability to design appropriate technology-mediated tasks for language learning" (Guichon & Cohen, 2016, p. 517). Instructors therefore must understand which communication tools (e.g., blogs, wikis, online forums) and modes (textual, aural, and/or visual) are most appropriate to meet their teaching and learning objectives. Instructors also need to ensure that the inclusion of these media and modes are not beyond learners' cognitive abilities, while at the same time allowing them "the possibility to extend their multimodal competence" (Guichon & Cohen, 2016, p. 518). The inclusion of media and modes for instruction needs to reflect the smooth continua of the process: "from one mode to a combination of modes; from static to dynamic, to interactive media; from little to total control over the use of modes; from familiar to less familiar cultural codes" (Guichon & Cohen, 2016, p. 518). The process can include the introduction of the various tools progressively, so as not to confuse or frustrate learners (Guth & Helm, 2010), and it should always emphasize the benefits that digital tools bring to the composing process. At the same time, we must acknowledge learners' expressions of frustration or confusion and invite them to be part of the process. The inclusion of students in this learning process could translate into offering students the advice that text and audio chats are useful when designing the overall structure of the essay, while wikis can help them develop the internal organization of paragraphs, thus facilitating the flow of ideas (Elola & Oskoz, 2010a, b). Acknowledging the role of digital tools is the first step in digital instructional practices. Full integration entails the instructor understanding and applying the theoretical and pedagogical frameworks that underpin digitally enhanced learning.

Digital Literacies: Second Language Acquisition Approaches

Pedagogical and Theoretical Frameworks

Digital literacies require a person to "possess a wide range of abilities and competencies" (The National Council of Teachers of English, 2003, para. 1),[1] and pedagogical frameworks will change as we adjust our previous notions of writing in the light of current multimodal practices. Addressing language-related technology without an understanding of how language is acquired would be short-sighted (Blake, 2013). Some second language acquisition (SLA) theories "suggest differing degrees of importance concerning the role of instruction/practice and, by implication, the use of technology in the classroom" (Blake, 2013, p. 15). L2 practitioners therefore need to have a strong theoretical background to judge how the use of a particular tool might best promote learners' linguistic[2] and writing development, including for instance, the value of collaborative writing in that context. Social tools provide a useful springboard for exploring many tenets of SLA (such as scaffolding), which also align with the current interest in collaborative writing and its potential to develop linguistic competence.

Recent SLA research illustrates that cognitive and sociocultural theories feature prominently in discussions about the applications of technology. Perhaps because of the collaborative nature of digital tools, most studies of L2 digital writing follow either sociocultural theory (SCT), which frames the writer's co-construction of knowledge or, to a lesser extent, activity theory (AT), which illuminates the relationships between all facets (e.g., subject, community, rules) of the learning context. However, it is useful to examine the relevance of other approaches – such as the process approach, which focuses on discrete writing processes, or the interactionist approach, which confirms the importance of feedback (e.g., direct vs. indirect). So it is clear that existing linguistic theory will inform us as we design new instructional approaches to L2 writing. Below, we provide brief summaries of theoretical frameworks as they relate to L2 writing and digital literacies; they will be further expanded in later chapters.

Cognitive Perspectives

Cognitive approaches have provided insights about the nature of writing and how it can be taught: writer-oriented models, such as the process approach, and reader-oriented models, such as the interactionist approach. These cater for any difficulties that L2 writers may encounter at the macro level (e.g., the complexity of the writing tasks or the application of writing process sequencing) and also at the micro level (the effect of corrective feedback in instructor–learner or learner–learner interactions).

Process Approach

Although a process approach has been widely adopted in the L2 classroom (Ferris & Hedgcock, 2013), research examining the integration of social tools is still scarce. According to Flower and Hayes (1981), becoming a better writer involves the application of a staged and sequenced approach, which includes processes such as planning (e.g., outlining the composition), drafting (composing text), revising (deleting, adding, or rewriting at the word, sentence, or paragraph level), and editing (e.g., correcting spelling and punctuation). Oskoz and Elola (2014), for instance, used a process-oriented approach to motivate L2 learners to develop digital writing skills. Using previously established processes of planning, drafting, receiving feedback, revising, and publishing to an audience, they found that learners prioritized different processes depending on whether they worked collaboratively or individually, which tools they employed, and the chosen writing genre.

Interactionist Orientation

Whereas the process approach helps us to focus on and identify the different stages of writing, an interactionist orientation emphasizes the role of feedback. When applying an interactionist orientation to writing, Polio (2012) noted that input (re-reading a corrected or reformulated version), output (rewriting a corrected essay), and feedback (written correction) all have the potential to improve learning. In the context of L2 digital writing the effect of input, output, and feedback have been examined in written synchronous or asynchronous computer-mediated communication. In online chats and discussion boards, for example, L2 learners can see their interactants' contributions, which might trigger the provision of alternative linguistic models and awareness of knowledge gaps. The interactional adjustments that can take place "are seen as tools for facilitating comprehension and for triggering cognitive processes (e.g., noticing the gaps and uptake[3]) deemed essential for L2 development" (Sauro, 2011, p. 380). This theoretical orientation has been applied to examine feedback types and errors in the L2 classroom (Ducate & Arnold, 2012; Fernández-García & Martínez-Arbelaiz, 2002; Morris, 2005) and in telecollaborative encounters (Vinagre & Lera, 2008; Vinagre & Maíllo, 2007; Vinagre & Muñoz, 2011; Ware & O'Dowd, 2008).

Social Perspectives

Grounded in the idea that writing is an inherently social, "transactional process that entails mediational activity involving writer, reader, text, and context for writing" (Ferris & Hedgcock, 2013, p. 70), the theoretical frameworks that best inform writing in the 21st century are perhaps those of SCT and AT. Both theoretical perspectives conceptualize writing as a holistic activity in which key elements (e.g., participants, tools, outcomes) interact dynamically.

Sociocultural Theory

The two central tenets of SCT relevant to L2 writing with digital tools are *mediation* and *scaffolding*. In regard to mediation, SCT argues that higher forms of mental activity, such as attending, predicting, planning, monitoring, and inferencing, are mediated mental activities whose sources are external to the individual, and in which the learner participates through dialog (Vygostky, 1978). The mediation of these cognitive functions occurs through the use of psychological or semiotic tools, such as numbers, symbols or language; and physical tools or artifacts, such as blogs, wikis, or digital story-telling software. Another key construct in SCT is that of scaffolding, a construct introduced during learner–learner dialogic interactions to assist the development of more complex meaning (Wood, Bruner, & Ross, 1976) in what has been called the "zone of proximal development." The incorporation of digital social tools has undoubtedly brought a qualitative change to how L2 writers mediate and scaffold collaboratively as they write. Studies in digital tools for L2 writing have examined how, through collaborative dialog, learners assist each other with content development (Arnold, Ducate, & Kost, 2009; Kessler, 2009) and focus their attention on linguistic forms (Adams & Ross-Feldman, 2008; Lee, 2010a). Applying the Wood et al. (1976) scaffolding model, Oskoz and Elola (2014) examined how L2 learners marked discrepancies, controlled frustration, and pursued the goal – all actions enabled by the scaffolding process.

Activity Theory (AT)

The dynamic nature of the interrelationships between the elements of the writing process (author, audience, tools, tasks) is aptly illuminated by AT (Leontiev, 1981), which holds that cognitive development has cultural and social roots (Lantolf & Thorne, 2006). *Activity* has been defined as "a collective complex systemic formation that has a complex meditational structure" (Engeström, 2008, p. 26), and as "a form of doing directed to an *object*" (Kuutti,

1996, p. 27). An individual's actions are classified as both automatic processes (unconscious acts), and conscious processes (planned actions directed to the achievement of a defined goal). These actions occur within a collective system at the nexus of three factors: the available tools and artifacts (e.g., computers, languages, and tasks); the community and its understood rules (e.g., between instructor and learners in a classroom); and the division of labor in those community settings (e.g., instructors structuring lesson units). Blin and Appel (2011), who highlighted the essential role of artifacts used and created by L2 learners in mediating their collaborative online writing practice, found that their learners' goal-oriented actions were mediated by the provision of supporting artifacts. Yet even when the instructor and learners share the same goal – the completion of the writing activity – how they go about it might differ and might create contradictions or "structural tensions within and between activity systems" (Engeström, 2001, p. 137), which "manifest themselves as problems, ruptures, breakdowns, [or] clashes" (Kuutti, 1996, p. 34), or as disturbances, "actions that deviate from the expected course of regular procedure" (Engeström, 2008, p. 27). It is not unusual, for example, to find that learners react with disbelief or even rejection when surprised by unexpected classroom methods or events, such as the introduction of gaming as a stimulus for writing (Reinhardt et al., 2014).

Digital Literacy and Pedagogical Approaches in the L2 Writing Class

The judicious use of digital tools, such as social networking sites, blogs, and digital story-telling software, has brought about "aesthetic and stylistic shifts in communicative contexts, purposes, and genres of language use associated with new media [which] necessitate a responsive and proactive vision of foreign and second language instruction" (Thorne & Reinhardt, 2008, p. 560). Yet even with their increasing use and their growing body of associated research (e.g., Ducate & Lomicka, 2008; Oskoz & Elola, 2016a, b; Reinhardt et al., 2014), these new media literacies are still problematic for instructors because they require not only an understanding of communication theory in general (Thorne & Reinhardt, 2008), but also knowledge of the linguistic and rhetorical conventions associated with particular digital genres (Oskoz & Elola, 2012). Digital literacy is not only about the acquisition of a discrete set of skills, such as knowing how to use Facebook or Twitter; it is also about recognizing the purpose of communication as "to build a community of like-minded individuals and to use that community for professional and personal development" (Dudeney & Hockly, 2016, p. 117).

The central question faced by L2 instructors and researchers is how best to adapt to "the changing qualities, purposes, and contexts of [digitally] mediated language and literacy use, and specifically toward the challenge of deciding which emerging literacy practices to include in instructed educational curricula" (Thorne, 2013, p. 208). In the digital context, mastering diverse media and semiotic resources means that L2 writers will need to be able to negotiate a complex set of skills, be digitally competent, and be aware of literacy in general. They will need to (a) communicate using various methods; (b) cooperate with others in web-based interactions; and (c) create information in different forms (Erstad, 2011). To achieve all this, L2 learners need to acquire "multimodal competence" (Kress, 2003) or, as the New Media Consortium (2005) defines it, "the ability to understand and use the power of images and sounds, to recognize and use that power, to manipulate and transform digital media, to distribute them pervasively, and to easily adapt to new forms" (p. 2). To reach this digital competency, several frameworks, such as bridging activities (Thorne & Reinhardt, 2008), genre-based frameworks (Hyland, 2001), task-based approaches (González-Lloret & Ortega, 2014), and Learning by Design (Cope & Kalantzis, 2015) have been proposed.

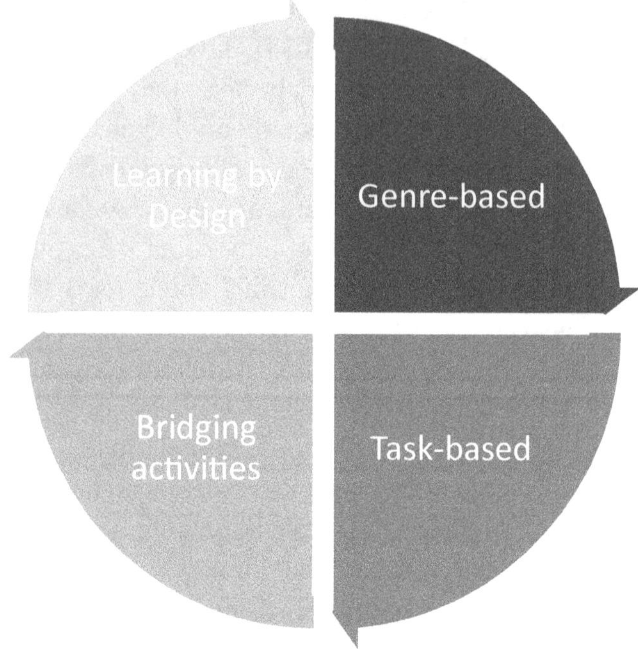

Figure 1.1. Pedagogical Frameworks

Bridging Activities Framework

The bridging activities framework stems from the idea that "advanced FL learning can be served by combining the best of the analytic traditions of schooling with the life experiences and future needs of today's foreign language students" (Thorne & Reinhardt, 2008, p. 562). Thorne and Reinhardt (2008) pointed out that in comparison to traditional genre counterparts, new media literacies practices are to some extent elusive. Moreover, because community-specific genres of communication are continually expanding as new tools, communities, and purposes emerge, digital literacies and genres are especially challenging to identify and teach. Following the New London Group, Thorne and Reinhardt (2008) argued the need for schooling "to take account of the multiple channels of communication and media now in popular use" (p. 562). They also acknowledged "the increasing salience of multiple cultures and linguistic diversity and, concomitantly, the strategic displacement of conventional notions of 'language' by contingently and thoughtfully assembled semiotic fragments and repertoires in everyday contexts of communicative activity" (p. 562). With these arguments in mind, Thorne and Reinhardt advocated the use of a teacher-mediated language awareness framework. The ultimate goal of this model, the bridging activities model, extends beyond high-level FL proficiency "to include intercultural and symbolic competence as part of an increasingly plurilingual, multiliterate global citizenry" (p. 562). This model, in which contributions from students are at the forefront, addresses the concern of how L2 instructors can select and teach digital genres that are themselves rapidly transforming and may even be transitory. The purpose behind this model, which raises the agentive possibilities for L2 students, is to raise learners' awareness of grammatical and lexical selections that encompass a text, so they can critically reflect on how these linguistic choices merge to operationalize different textual, social, and ideational meanings in situational and cultural settings. This goal is accomplished by a mix of contrastive analysis, data-driven learning, and qualitative discourse analysis methodologies applied to the texts, relevant to their current or likely future communicative needs and interests, searched for and brought by the students themselves.

The bridging activities model proposes to integrate vernacular, technology-mediated practices situated in learners' L1 primary discourse in such a way that they might form a bridge to new practices in the L2 (both vernacular and academic), thus fostering critical awareness, metalinguistic and analytical skills, as well as personal agency and relevance (Thorne & Reinhardt, 2008). As Thorne and Reinhardt (2008) propose, these outcomes can be achieved by (a) raising learners' awareness of the linguistic choices (grammatical and lexical) that comprise a text, and (b) considering "how these linguistic choices combine to realize different textual, interpersonal, and ideational meanings in situational and cultural contexts" (p. 563). Whether it is analyzing a blog, a threaded discussion board or a social networking site, the key to this three-phase model is "learner involvement in selecting the texts for treatment, which ensures relevance and builds motivation" (Reinhardt & Thorne, 2011, p. 270). In the first stage, *observation and collection*, learners identify their own interests and collect digital texts and practices that illustrate them. In the second stage, *exploration*, learners analyze a selection of texts that vary in social and lexico-grammatical aspects. In the third stage, *creation and participation*, learners produce their own texts, share them, and reflect on their reception. Following a slightly different model, Ducate and Lomicka (2008), in their two-part study with German and French learners, first asked their students to familiarize themselves with the uses and features of various blogs before working on their own. In the second (exploration) stage, learners analyzed both content and linguistic aspects of a range of blogs. Third, learners maintained their own blogs, applying discourse strategies (agreeing, disagreeing, complimenting, etc.) that they had previously learned in the first stage. Although Ducate and Lomicka found that the effective application of culturally appropriate markers was cumbersome and restricting at times, the three-stage process of observation, exploration, and creation and participation helped learners to achieve the level of digital literacy to successfully perform in their L2.

Genre-based Theoretical Perspectives

The genre-based approach has been applied specifically to L2 written digital literacies (Hyland, 2001); it entails seeing all writing as an attempt to communicate with an audience and identifying the particular language patterns of coherent and purposeful prose. For New Rhetoricians, genre allows an exploration of lexico-grammatical forms and rhetorical patterns and sits happily within social, cultural, and institutional contexts (Johns, 2011). Within this understanding, the text created by the writer presents characteristics that need to be socially understood in order to recreate them successfully. Despite the inherent characteristics that distinguish them from print-based genres, digital genres still respond to set regularities and conventions, and are also regarded as "flexible, plastic and free" (Bakhtin, 1986, p. 79), due to their dynamic qualities and intricate variations (Hyland, 2007a). That is, rather than considering and evaluating texts as fixed and structured genres, we should view them as multimodal, process-based activities that are artifact-mediated (Prior, 2007). The emergence of digital social tools forces us to think of texts and the notion of sentences/utterances (Hattem, 2014) in flexible and creative ways. This new paradigm has been described as "the awareness, attitude and ability of individuals to appropriately use digital tools and facilities to identify, access, manage, integrate, evaluate, analyze, and synthesize digital resources, construct new knowledge, create media expressions, and communicate with others, in the context of specific life situations, in order to enable constructive social action; and to reflect on this process" (Martin, 2005, p. 135). The expanding social contexts and associated semiotic activities in which individuals participate will ultimately construct new genres. For instance, narratives vary according to which particular tool is used and how the story will be conveyed to a wider community (Gebhard et al., 2011).

As we become more aware of digital genres, we need to help L2 students recognize that genres are socially situated and culturally embedded (Bawarshi & Reiff, 2010) as well as flexible and evolving. This broader notion of genres will encourage students to reconsider ideas about the nature of text they may have formed in previous writing contexts (Johns, 2011). The revised understanding of genres parallels a renewed pedagogical emphasis on genre-based writing instruction and raises questions about how writing assignments should be set in the classroom, and how online resources could be exploited to support essays in the rhetorical modes (Johns, 2011). Students can be led to enrich their existing notions of texts with the understanding that genres can be socially and culturally situated and can illustrate "the beliefs, values, and ideologies of particular communities and cultures" (Bawarshi &

Reiff, 2010, p. 195). Achieving such enriched notion of texts will require them to build an understanding of the communicative purposes and cultural norms and expectations of the digital genres. Genre therefore becomes "an ongoing, dynamic accomplishment of people acting together with shared tools, including – more powerfully – writing" (Russell, 1997, pp. 508–509). In our context, the result becomes a dynamic integration of digital tools, new social contexts, and flexible definitions of text that allow for old literacies to coexist with the needs of today's students.

Given that digital genres are highly relevant to the contemporary world, we need to pose the question of how to distinguish digital literacies and genres from traditional forms of literacy, which are still, of course, taught in our classrooms (Reinhardt et al., 2014). Following a New Rhetorical approach, for instance, students might understand that genres not traditionally related to learning, such as gaming (script writing for a fun activity), can be indeed relevant to class learning goals. This approach may serve to broaden students' familiarity with writing genres and demonstrate "communicative and symbolic practices as a negotiation between the familiar and the contested" (Reinhardt et al., 2014, p. 171). Yet, the integration of digital genres does not require L2 students to disregard traditional genres. Rather, students should be encouraged to develop awareness of both traditional and new digital genres and to view them as evolving, so they can apply their existing knowledge and past experience of genre to a new one, such as digital stories (Willingham, 2009). Within this new understanding of literacy, the text created by the writer presents characteristics that first need to be understood to recreate them successfully.

Task-based Language Teaching Approach

Tasks have been defined, among other definitions, as "the hundred-and-one things people do – identifiable as bounded, recurring activities that people engage in – in order to reach real-world (and very often non-linguistic) ends, and for which they need to use language" (Van de Branden, Bygate, & Norris, 2009, p. 6). More relatable to the classroom experience, tasks have been defined as "holistic activity which engages language use in order to achieve some non-linguistic outcome while meeting a linguistic challenge, with the overall aim of promoting language learning, through a process or product or both" (Samuda & Bygate, 2008, p. 69) or as "an activity in which a person engages in order to attain an objective, and which necessitates the use of language" (Van de Branden, 2006, p. 4). Common to these definitions is a non-linguistic goal or objective for which the use of language is required. The existence of such a non-linguistic objective is an essential feature of a task-based language teaching approach (TBLT), which aims to teach language through the accomplishment of tasks and which fosters the learning of the target language by working through meaningful activities that reflect what students might be involved in outside the classroom context (Long & Crookes, 1992).

The task-based teaching approach subscribes to the philosophy of learning by doing – that is, learning about the process of digital writing by producing a written composition that has been engineered by means of a sequence of interconnected steps that together make the process more accessible and visible. Within a task-based approach to L2 digital literacy, there are additional aspects that need to be considered. First, in the context of L2 learning, language is both a means and an end. In the L2 classroom, pedagogic sequencing can address the linguistic aspects of composing a digital text (e.g., grammar, vocabulary, structure, images) and can familiarize students with the process writing approach (e.g., planning the task, composing drafts, providing feedback). Some of the process stages toward that outcome might entail the support and mediation of other tools (e.g., blogs, chats, wikis) that foster language processes which might include: sharing information, negotiating the topic, understanding the rhetorical style of the chosen genre, evaluating joint writing decisions, negotiating revisions based on feedback, and editing and publishing the final written essays. We could say that the first outcome is the written product submitted to the instructor. The second outcome is the student's acquisition of digital literacy skills by progressing through the stages of planning, composing, receiving feedback, revising, and publishing.

The use of such real-world online tasks in the language classroom is not new (Blake, 2000; Hanna & de Nooy, 2003; Sauro, 2001, 2014). However, although a task-based language teaching approach has been extensively applied in the L2 classroom (Nitta & Baba, 2014; Norris, 2009), its relationship to computer-assisted language learning has been tenuous (González-Lloret & Ortega, 2014). In their aim to highlight this relation and maximize the potential for language learning, González-Lloret and Ortega (2014) distinguish three requirements that respond both to "TBLT as a language education approach and to the transformative nature of new technologies" (p. 5): (a) to include a TBLT definition of tasks that takes into account the characteristics of new technologies, (b) to be cognizant of the implications of new technologies in language learning, and (c) to acknowledge the role of the curriculum into the forefront of task and technology integrations.

With regard to the first requirement, González-Lloret and Ortega (2014) suggest five key definitional features of a task that realize technology-and-task integration:

- a primary focus on meaning, in which there is both a pre-planned and incidental language learning goal;
- goal orientation, which includes a communicative purpose and an outcome resulting from the task completion;
- learner-centeredness, in which learners' linguistic and non-linguistic (e.g., digital skills) are addressed by the task;
- holism, which takes into account the real-world processes of language use; and
- reflective learning, which involves both learning through direct experience and opportunities for reflective higher-learning.

Regarding the second requirement, an awareness of the profound implications that the integration of new technologies into educational design brings to any kind of learning, there is a need to remember that the addition of new technologies is never neutral, affecting people, language (in our case our learners' language), and their personal knowledge and relations (Crystal, 2008; Jenkins, Clinton, Purushotma, Robison, & Weigel, 2009; Walther, 2012). We do not use the same type of language and interactions when writing an email, participating in a fandom, or playing in immersive environment and multi-player online games. That is, as soon as the technology design mediates the task, technology is not "just a vehicle of instruction or delivery," but rather technology "spearheads a set of new demands and actions which in and of themselves become target tasks – and hence part of the curriculum" (González-Lloret & Ortega, 2014, p. 7).

The third requirement, bringing the curriculum into the forefront of task and technology integrations, requires the need to explain clearly how tasks and new technologies are articulated and integrated into any given programmatic context. Although tasks are the salient organization units in any programmatic context (González-Lloret & Ortega, 2014), a task-based approach is not just about tasks or even just about the sequences of tasks (Norris, 2009), and when integrating technologies, the relationships between task and new technologies have to be clearly articulated in ways that are optimal for language learning. As González-Lloret and Ortega (2014) eloquently put it, "The development of pedagogic tasks should take full advantage of chosen technology to do what cannot be done in the classroom with paper and pencil" (p. 8). For instance, a necessary analysis of tasks that involves technology would take into account not only the language skills needed but also the affordances of the technological tools and the learners' and instructors' digital literacies. Similarly, an approach that aims to integrate technology and tasks should consider that the technologies employed will necessarily shape the assessment rubric (Nielson, 2014; Winke, 2014).

Learning by Design

Learning by Design is a pedagogical approach that follows the New London Group's (1996) redefinition of the term *multiliteracies* to embrace the flexibility and contingency of communication in the current globalized times, in which multiliterate communicative practices are shaped by new technologies and multimodal text construction. Such a definition allows for a shift in how we conceptualize discourse community and literacy practices (Samaniego & Warner, 2016). In this new view, literacies are seen as society's ways of designing meaning, for which instructors provide students with text designs that mirror real-world performances and help them position themselves as creators of meaning. Design of meaning implies creatively arranging resources with respect to purposes, contexts, and former discourse to generate texts (New London Group, 1996). The idea is that the reconfiguration and reshaping of available texts lead to a redesign of a text. Texts, furthermore, are not only reconstructed by the designer, but also by the audience through experiencing, conceptualizing, analyzing, and applying pedagogical principles while making use of available resources that form the distinct texts and the meaning that needs to be communicated (Zapata, 2018). The notion of texts with their corresponding genres as a socially situated linguistic practice implies a sense of flexibility and transformation that defies traditional (academic) structures. The process of design and redesign is fashioned by two types of contexts: the immediate context (i.e., encompassing the designer's intentions, identities, resources, and site) and the social and historical environment (e.g., ideologies, values, and cultural practices) (Kern, 2015). Thus, the design is shaped by the individual and by social and material resources. This way of seeing multiliteracies requires a pedagogical shift that opens the space for critical awareness of how a writer/designer occupies one's space in new types of communication (Samaniego & Warner, 2016).

Cope and Kalantzis (2015) conceptualized the notion of multiliteracies into a Learning by Design approach that follows the New London Group's curriculum components:

- *Situated practice*: This involves degrees of mastery in practice, by being immersed in a community in which students participate in authentic versions of such practice. There are however limitations in what can be learned through such community immersion and participation, such as practice not being the same for all students or not leading to conscious control and awareness of what one knows and does, or students not being able to foster critical analysis of what they learn or being unable to put knowledge into practice (New London Group, 1996, p. 84). Therefore, situated learning needs to be supplemented by other components, such as overt instruction, critical framing, and transformed practice.
- *Overt instruction*: This implies active involvement on the part of the instructor and other experts that support learning activities within a community of students, allowing the student to expand their explicit knowledge and to employ and build on what the student already knows and has achieved. This kind of instruction creates an atmosphere that brings conscious awareness and control over what is being learned.
- *Critical framing*: The objective is to guide students to operationalize their evolving mastery in practice (situated learning) in order to achieve deliberate control and comprehension (overt instruction) in connection to "the historical, social, cultural, political, ideological, and valued-centered relations of particular systems of knowledge and social practice. Instructors need to denaturalize and make strange again what they have learned and mastered" (New London Group, 1996, p. 86).
- *Transformed practice/applying*: This refers to the development of ways in which students can show that they are able to design and perform, in a thoughtful way, new practices

> rooted in their own goals and values. They should be capable of demonstrating that they can apply concepts obtained via overt instruction and critical framing in practices that help them simultaneously to implement and revise what they have learned in other contexts and cultural sites (New London Group, 1996).

Although these four instructional foci can be present in other pedagogical models, Learning by Design provides equal weight to each of these curriculum components. Through the experiencing process, the student can connect what they have seen in class with their own life experience; it is subdivided into experiencing the known (what the students brings as knowledge, emotions, etc.) and the new (the new connections students make based on the theme or topic being taught, a new way of seeing an experience). The *conceptualizing* process pushes the student to go a bit deeper into the design components of a text. Students learn to conceptualize by naming (e.g., organizational and structural elements in a particular text) and then they conceptualize by theorizing, which helps them make connections between concepts and how a particular text functions. The next step is *analyzing critically*, in which students are expected to interpret and make inferences about the text, taking into account their social knowledge and looking critically at different perspectives, including their own, to comprehend the social purpose behind the various perspectives (Zapata, 2018). The last curriculum component is the application: *applying appropriately* and *creatively*. *Applying appropriately* refers to the students' creation of a text that represents a specific genre, whereas *applying creatively* refers to students being able to be more inventive based on knowledge being transferred from a previous task to the new one they are carrying out. Studies like Samaniego and Warner's (2016) looked at these four curriculum components while Spanish heritage language students worked with television advertisements to illustrate how this approach can be carried out in the classroom. Similarly, Zapata (2018) worked with Spanish heritage language students on analyzing a novel, using *Glogster* (multimedia interactive posters) and reflection pieces.

Supporting Digital Literacy with All Four Frameworks

We would like to conclude this section by suggesting that rather than being exclusive and competing, these four frameworks can all be used in one educational setting, and can work well together. It is essential to apply flexible instructional approaches, whether bridging activities, task-based language teaching, genre-based learning, or Learning by Design. These approaches allow learners to acquire not only textual literacy, but also multiliteracies, through multimodal expression. In this way, learners will become digitally literate and able to operate skillfully and creatively in dynamic and ever-changing future professions (Liou, 2016).

Conclusion

Although prediction of new approaches and goals in education is an uncertain science (Kern, 2015), the movement to redefine literacies is important to our understanding of what L2 writing in the 21st century may come to look like. In our L2 instructional context, digital literacies need to be understood by researchers and educators as "an acknowledgment of language learning as emerging from, and thus inseparable from, language use in socially meaningful contexts" (Reinhardt et al., 2014, p. 161). This redefinition of digital literacies implies focusing on writing processes; recognizing the writers' struggles in an unfamiliar domain; including the reader as an assistant; selecting the right tools to suit each task; and recognizing the relevance of the "written" text for wider audiences (Kern, 2015). Thus, the selection of genres and tools, which are themselves rapidly transforming or transient (Thorne & Reinhardt, 2008), becomes a vital pedagogical decision that needs to be continuously revisited. At the same time, it is also important for learners to master the particular linguistic and other resources required in the use of these newer genres. That is, working with digital stories, blogs, wiki entries, or fan fiction will require non-traditional sets of linguistic and semiotic competences that will need to be taught.

When considering the new genres and tools (with their various affordances), rather than focusing on them in isolation we need to consider them within the bigger picture. We must think about how new digital genres and tools mediate between language, social context, and medium of expression; introduce into our teaching discourse a certain level of abstraction in order to encourage critical awareness about the role of languages in communication (Chun et al., 2016); and reflect on how to promote digital literacy in diverse educational contexts. Additionally, we need to continue examining L2 learners' writing practices by considering different social, cultural, and cognitive perspectives, as well as multiple contextual factors that enable social interaction and meaning making (Zhung & Warschauer, 2017). Such awareness might bring about the acceptance and expansion of technology and a more sophisticated approach to L2 writing in the language curriculum.

In the remaining chapters of this book, we will examine and provide theoretical frameworks and practical applications for the integration of digital writing literacies in the L2 classroom, ranging from collaborative writing, to the production of multimodal texts, to the development of identity, and to new assessment practices. But we must keep a sense of perspective: to really master multi-literacies, despite the present emphasis on digital literacies, the spawning of these new forms of communication does not imply a rejection of, but rather a co-existence with, traditional and well-established forms of written language (Kern, 2015). With that proviso, it is clear that we are living in an exciting time for the L2 writing curriculum. Our intention with this chapter has been to identify pertinent theoretical and pedagogical frameworks that can prepare learners not only to use "technologically mediated forms of expression effectively" (Kern, 2015, p. 232) when working with diverse literacies, but also to base writing practices on sound theory and pedagogy. In the following chapters, we will share ways in which instructors can apply the relevant frameworks productively and judiciously to make teaching writing in the 21st century both productive and enjoyable.

Notes

1. This website is no longer available.
2. We use the term *linguistic* here as a general term to include L1, L2, and L3 as well as multilingual and translingual development.
3. These essential cognitive processes involve noticing the differences (gaps) between the learner's intention and actual performance (in this case, what has been written) and the incorporation of newly apprehended information in performance (uptake).

Ideas for Reflection and Discussion

1. The chapter has presented several pedagogical frameworks useful for L2 writing (bridging activities, genre-based, task-based approaches, Learning by Design). Choose one framework and suggest why you would use, or do use, this framework. If you have already used one of these frameworks in your practice, what have been the teaching or learning outcomes?
2. Think of three different tools (e.g., blogs, wikis, Twitter, Facebook) and examine the affordances that those tools might bring or have brought to the act of writing in the classroom, or to your own writing. Explain how the multimodality allowed by your selected tools affect and modify the traditional understanding of the written text.
3. The introduction of digital tools has given place to either modified genres (e.g., the travel blog, the encyclopedia entry) or to new ones (e.g., tweets, Facebook posts). Choose two genres,

one modified and one new; analyze and explain the linguistic resources and communicative features that characterize those genres.

4. Thinking about multimodal literacies, analyze the role of each mode (e.g., visual, textual, oral) in your L2 learners' digital written texts (e.g., developing a blog, Facebook post, or digital story). Explain how those modes can be integrated in the development of such texts.
5. Reflect on and discuss the challenges for instructors seeking to introduce multimodality and multiliteracy into the L2 classroom.

Chapter 2

Transforming L2 Writing: New Writing Tools, New Genres, New Ways of Writing

The Changing Landscape of Written Communication

In a radical change from only a few decades ago, most of the writing in our personal and professional lives is now performed online (Chun et al., 2016). The written text remains a key form of communication but we now have a variety of digital writing tools (e.g., blogs, wikis, Twitter) that can accommodate the inclusion of other semiotic resources, such as images and sound. For example, someone might create a travel blog to collate their research before going on a trip; then they might document their travels during the trip, afterwards adding photos and videos. Twitter is popularly used for commenting, and this platform can also incorporate images. Without doubt, the use of digital tools is altering our previous notions about writing as a form of communication.

Despite the ubiquity of social tools in our L2 students' daily lives, and despite the exponential increase of research on technology-assisted L2 writing (Arnold et al., 2009; Arnold, Ducate, & Kost, 2012; Elola & Oskoz, 2017; Kessler, 2009; Lee, 2010a, b; Oskoz & Elola, 2016a, b; Reinhardt et al., 2014), many L2 instructors still struggle with the challenges of integrating digital social tools and working with multimodal texts in the classroom. Instructors need to appreciate the essential shift in literary practices that digital tools bring to the L2 classroom and their application to writing

(Elola & Oskoz, 2017). They need to move beyond traditional pedagogical perspectives that focus on the textual component of students' assignments and start to incorporate visual and aural modes as well (Nelson, 2006; Oskoz & Elola, 2014, 2016; Yang, 2012). That is, instructors need to integrate the changing view of literacies and validate them in the educational context (Reiss & Young, 2013). To some extent, these changes require L2 instructors to "confront and reevaluate our professional identities" (Ellis, 2013, p. 48), and to alter the expectations of students who often have been trained in print literacy and do not see "the need to add on multimodal composing" (Bump, 2013, p. 131). L2 instructors might be reluctant to introduce digital genres into the writing classroom, but successful mastery of pre-digital academic genres is no longer sufficient for today's students. Rather, digital literacy knowledge, which includes the use of multiple digital genres, is "a requirement for full participation in societal practices" (Vandergriff, 2016, p. 71). To be successful writers, L2 students "will need a wide repertoire of writing skills and genre knowledge, from applying the appropriate language register when participating in social media, to ensuring language is grammatically correct in writing formal reports" (Godwin-Jones, p. 1, 2018). This shift in literacy understanding is gaining digital tools and digital genres a valid place in the language education curriculum.

L2 researchers and educators are now considering how one selects, and then teaches, digital genres that are themselves rapidly evolving, or that may be transient or quick to pass out of vogue, within L2 instructional settings (Thorne & Reinhardt, 2008). In this chapter, we will therefore examine the idea that to validate our L2 students' literacy practices "the classroom should somehow imitate learning in informal ways" (Lehtonen, 2017, p. 57). In introducing digital contexts and modes of instruction into our L2 classrooms, we will need to revise our current practices to reflect certain aspects of informal learning that have proven to be motivating and effective (Cole & Vanderplank, 2016). We will need to find an appropriate balance combining traditional-type assignments with participation in online communities (Godwin-Jones, 2018), one that encourages digital practice and addresses L2 instructors' concerns about integrating digital tools and new genres into their classrooms. We will address the distinctions between digital genres and tools, which have sometimes been confusingly used as synonyms, and then we will discuss the process of integrating digital tools and genres into the curriculum and the classroom. We next consider a number of digital tools that can be useful in the L2 writing class in terms of their affordabilities and their relevance to L2 writing. We conclude with the suggestion of a practical application in the L2 classroom and with questions for further reflection.

Distinguishing Tools and Genres

It is clear that new digital tools and interfaces are altering our notions of genre (Guichon & Cohen, 2016), as text, image, and sound appear to converge, sometimes within a limited physical space (e.g., Twitter) or time (e.g., digital stories). Although *tools* and *genres*, as terms and concepts, have sometimes been used interchangeably, it is important to distinguish between them. Tools have been defined as "the technological means of inscription and production that shape the ways any message is conveyed and accessed" (Guichon & Cohen, 2016, p. 510). Genre, on the other hand, refers to the "abstract, socially recognized ways of using language" (Hyland, 2007b, p. 149), in specific types of communicative events, each with a specific communicative purpose (Swales, 1990) in a "staged, goal-oriented social process" (Martin, 1993, p. 121). Digital tools can then be seen as the physical means people employ to express meaning and communicate, while genres are the linguistic means people employ to express meaning and communicate – more precisely, the recognized and distinctive uses of language that are related to specific forms of communication (Hyland, 2007a, b). Different genres are therefore distinguished by specific forms of language and communicative functions.

Demarcating the relationship between genre and tool or medium has often been problematic (Müller, 2011), and sometimes the terms *medium* or *media* and *genre* have been used interchangeably. As Yates and Orlikowski (1992) noted some years ago:

> The concept of medium has often been confused with that of genre. Confusion arises when researchers compare genres of communication (e.g., memos or bulletins) with communication media (e.g., electronic mail or fax). (p. 310)

It can be noted that some genres are associated with a particular medium (e.g., tweets with Twitter) and also that the same medium or tool can be utilized for different genres (e.g., wikis to write encyclopedia entries or formal reports). For instance, as Chun et al. (2016) explain, writing an email is very different from writing a blog, which is also very different from writing a text message; and yet all of them can take place using the same digital device. Kern (2015) further reminds us that even various media associated with the broad category of electronically mediated writing (i.e., email, chat) "cannot be unambiguously associated with particular genres" (p. 191). As Kern elaborates: "Email messages, text messages, and tweets are all electronic forms of writing, but they involve unique genre constraints, and how they are written will vary widely according to audience and purpose" (p. 240). Leaving aside the discussion of whether the definition of genre rests on a matter of form or functionality (Askehave & Nielsen, 2005; Müller, 2011), when distinguishing between digital genres and digital tools, what is important is that a digital genre embodies a "communicative action in a specific social context" (Müller, 2011, p. 187) – that is, the particular social function and cultural context of a given act of communication – while a digital tool is that which enables the means of production, distribution, and reception of texts. Over time, it often happens that the nature and evolution of digital genres are influenced by the digital tools used in their production.

Reconsidering Writing in L2 Digital Learning Contexts

Integrating Semiotic Resources in L2 Learning

The advent of technology and digital tools in our daily life has highlighted how language (whether written or oral) interacts with other semiotic modes (Kern, 2015). In our current digital environments, although "written text is not at risk of disappearing, [it] will increasingly share the semiotic stage with other players" (Kern, 2015, p. 209). The existence of a wealth of semiotic resources suggests that both instructors and students should welcome new and different modes and appreciate them for their inherent value in the creation of meaning. Integrating a blog or a digital story with an eclectic range of semiotic resources should be seen as more than a way to offer light relief in the classroom. Multimodal writing is not only reshaping genre boundaries but is also changing what it means to be a literate individual in today's society. L2 instructors need to understand that "the shapes and forms of academic knowledge within undergraduate writing are undergoing transformations" (Bowen & Whithaus, 2013, p. 4). If text-based literacy means "privileged words, their sequencing, and rules of usage as the primary organizing system for articulating experiences as texts" (p. 5), the diverse range of semiotic resources supporting the digital texts requires a new set of conventions and rules which go beyond the written word.

Integrating semiotic resources requires breaking the traditional rules and developing new ones as "part of the experimentation process inherent in multimedia composing as well as the development of individual students' writing skills" (Bowen & Whithaus, 2013, p. 6). The integration of new tools and genres, with their own set of conventions, challenges students and instructors (Ball, Bowen, & Fenn, 2013; Nelson, 2006). It is common "for someone to be quite literate in certain mediums [and genres] but not at all in others" (Kern, 2015, p. 240). Integration of semiotic resources and use of tools that produce dynamic texts, often collaborative and with distributed authorship structures, requires a reconsideration of the "new *basics* in communication and education" (Lotherington & Sinitskaya Ronda, 2012, p. 122) and their meaning in L2 learning contexts. The creation of dynamic texts implies moving from the traditional *three Rs* of modern education – *Reading, wRiting,* and *aRithmetic* – to the *four Rs* for a digital era (Sinclair, 2010; cited in Lotherington & Sinitskaya Ronda, 2012). These are: *Reuse* (backup or the right to use content in a wide range of ways); *Revise* (adapt, adjust, modify or alter the content itself); *Remix* (combine the original or revised content with other material to create something new); and *Redistribute* (share copies of original, revised or remixed content with others).

In the creation of digital texts, it is important to avoid adding digital elements as an afterthought, which then "are not fully valued by either students or teachers" (Whithaus, 2005, p 131). We should recognize the power that the inclusion of multimedia and diverse modes of expression brings to the creation of texts, especially when they are developed collaboratively (Lotherington & Sinitskaya Ronda, 2012). L2 instructors therefore need to think broadly when developing new curriculum content, remembering to incorporate multimedia, multimodality, collaboration, and hybridity into their use of available digital tools and genres.

Multimedia

The term *multimedia* refers to the mediating technologies used to develop writing. As a note of caution, no-one expects L2 students, nor their writing instructors, to be technical experts in digital production; rather, L2 students and teachers need to understand how different media and different tools work together. As Jones and Hafner (2012) point out, when "mixing two or more tools together [...] the constraints of one tool are cancelled by the affordances of the another, opening actions which neither of the tools alone could have made possible, as people do when they create remixes [the combination of two or more works together] and mashups [the process of altering aspects of an existing work]" (p. 101). Rather than thinking about media in a "simple, 'one-to one' way, L2 instructors are to think of digital tools and themselves "as parts of systems of actions and activities, meanings and thoughts, social organizations and identities" (Jones & Hafner, 2012, p. 10). That is, the use that we make of the affordances of the tools, the meanings that we create, and the actions that we take might have "profound and unexpected effects on the relationships and identities we might form in the future" (p. 10).

Today it is becoming difficult to use one medium exclusively within digital communication. For example, many bloggers also use Twitter and Instagram. The latter use is often connected to Facebook. When communicating on a platform like Facebook, users have the ability to like, create their own posts and comment on others', and communicate via messaging or chat, which can be described as "one multi-faceted genre repertoire" (Heyd, 2016, p. 96). This potential to merge genres is currently known as *digital genre ecology*, an environment in which "various conversational genres are interdependent and act – in a variety of ways – to support the functioning of a system as a whole" (Erickson, 2000, p. 8). In the L2 classroom, the blended use of different digital genres and tools is common. For instance, to enhance the collaborative nature of wiki writing, it is not unusual to combine wikis with other digital tools, such as written or spoken chats (Elola & Oskoz, 2010a), blogs (Stickler & Hampel, 2011), or to mix forums and blogs (Miyazoe & Anderson, 2010).

Multimodality

Multimodality, which refers to the "practice of combining multiple modes [aural, gestural, oral, visual, written]" (Jones & Hafner, 2012, p. 50) to co-create meaning, has increased in our daily lives with the inclusion of new digital media and tools. Given its acceptance, we should consider how users can draw on semiotic resources to create multimedia texts. For instance, as Jones and

Hafner explain, the written mode allows for a linear and sequential logic, while the visual mode involves a more spatial and simultaneous one. The question is how to combine and create relationships between those modes. For example, how we can reinforce each other's messages in different situations: when both the textual and visual information concur or complement each other; when text and image present slightly different information or conflict with each other; or when text and image present opposite meanings, often with a critical message. We need to help students orchestrate and direct the semiotic resources they employ, both in terms of coherence and meaning creation.

Connectivity

Connectivity is the acknowledgment that the existence of an audience informs the multimodality and content of the texts. When developing multimodal texts using digital tools, L2 students engage with a wider audience than just the instructor and participate in local or global issues of their interest to produce real-world outcomes (Lotherington & Sinitskaya Ronda, 2012). In keeping with critical pedagogy, which encourages students to become active participants in their own learning, L2 writers use both linguistic resources and digital tools for critical reasoning and for fostering independent learning in meaningful interactions.

Collaboration

Collaboration describes how L2 textual creation/learning is distributed. In the digitally mediated world, single authorship is an option but is not the only form of knowledge contribution.The introduction of digital tools that emphasize connection to community has made room for digital genres that move writing into a social context rather than remaining focused on the individual approach to writing (Kurek & Hauck, 2014). Writing a Wikipedia entry, for example, accommodates multiple authorship with ease when more than one writer creates and edits a document. Even when blogging, writers are influenced by readers' postings, emphasizing the blurry line between the writer and reader in what Allen (2003) has termed "wreading." Multimedia learning supports collaborative authorship, an activity in which content, as would happen in a wiki, is democratically created and collaboratively edited by a group of users (Lotherington & Jenson, 2011). By collaborating in the pursuit of communicative objectives, knowledge building is distributed among participants. While still valuing individual contributions, in this digital collaborative context we value "collaborative knowledge competence" rather than individual cognitive competence (Cope, Kalantzis, McCarthey, Vojak, & Kline, 2011, p. 83).

Hybridity

Hybridity refers to the mixing and remixing of old and new content, semiotic resources, genres, media, and/or cultural materials to create new meanings (Lotherington & Sinitskaya Ronda, 2012; Thorne, Black, & Sykes, 2009). Hybridity takes place because easy access to the internet allows writers to produce new types of digital texts or artifacts that include and adopt the works of others (Jones & Hafner, 2012). Remixes and mashups should not be confused with copying because "they require a creative re-working of the source material so that when it is placed in the new context and merged with texts from other sources, it takes on a new meaning or significance" (Jones & Hafner, 2012, p. 46).

These practices of mashing and remixing raise philosophical and practical questions. In the digital context, originality comes from the combination and juxtapositions of images and utterances in novel ways with one another, reminding us "that creativity is not just an individual trait, but also a socially distributed and collaborative practice" (Kern, 2015, p. 195). Unlike in traditional written texts, originality does not stem from original or borrowed images or utterances employed, but from the particular associations created by the novel use of those images and utterances. This contextualization of work created in partnership implies that creativity is not solely an individual feature but is socially distributed and a collaborative praxis (Kern, 2015). As Jones and Hafner (2012) and Kern (2015) remind us, it is not as if we have never before used the words of others. Every time we quote, for instance, we incorporate the words of another person into our text; and as Bakhtin (1986) pointed out, texts are "filled with other's words, varying degrees of otherness or varying degrees of our-own-ness" (p. 89). In the digital age, however, these recontextualizations bring up two issues: plagiarism and text ownership, "intellectual property and copyright, especially in relation to commercial, pop culture texts like movie-clips and songs" (Jones & Hafner, 2012, p. 45). Although as Kern (2015) points out, "authentication and citation is not part of mash-up culture" (p. 196), they become an issue when the mash-up is removed from its native (i.e., original) material and social ecology and is incorporated into a non-native (i.e., new, or non-original) medium or used for a non-native purpose.

Fortunately, as Dudeney, Hockly, and Pegrum (2013) point out, many educators have fair use or fair dealing laws on their side. It is also possible to make use of works which are in the public domain or works that have been placed under Creative Commons licenses. When working with digital media, L2 instructors should explore all of the free and available options while also ensuring that they themselves as well as their students abide by the law and the policies of their institution. L2 instructors might also consider that, "as timely as the wider war against the excesses of copyrights may be, the classroom probably isn't the place to play out its battles" (Dudeney et al., 2013, p. 38). The constant and ever evolving discussion about privacy and copyright laws in the national and international spheres will likely have an impact on users, including on L2 writers and on students' use of the mixing and remixing of old and new content when creating their own original compositions.

The Interface between Digital Tools' Affordances and L2 Writing

When thinking of digital tools, it is tempting to see them forming a continuum, from more traditional tools to more innovative ones. However, it might be more productive to think of these tools in terms of their *affordances*, the qualities of an object or an environment that allow a writer to perform an action in terms of (a) individual or collaborative writing, including the role of the audience, which can sometimes become a (co-)author; (b) the integration of different semiotic resources to create meaning; and (c) the genres that the writer and audience are likely to encounter. This view suits today's classrooms, where new orthographic and discourse practices are flourishing, where authorship is moving from the individual to the collaborative, and where genres such as games can offer multifaceted literacy practices (Lotherington & Jenson, 2011). The characteristics of these tools, as summarized in Table 2.1, might make them more conducive to developing either local (vocabulary, editing, grammar) or global (content, structure, organization) aspects of students' L2 writing.

Digital Storytelling Software

Digital storytelling software allows users to create storylines that integrate text, images, and sounds in an online environment. Although digital stories are often used for personal narratives (Lambert, 2012), current educational uses also include historical documentaries or stories designed to inform or instruct viewers on particular concepts or practices (Robin, 2006), or sociopolitical themes (Gregori-Signes & Pennock-Speck, 2012). When working on a digital story, students generally engage in a mix of traditional skills (e.g., research, writing, interviewing) and new skills (e.g., creation and development of graphics, animation, music) to convey a story, allowing an expanded definition of storytelling (Gregori-Signes, 2008). As opposed to traditional forms of

Table 2.1. Digital Tools, Modes, and Genres in the L2 Classroom (adapted from Elola & Oskoz, 2019)

Tools	Description	Genre	Modes	Linguistic/Rhetorical Component
Digital storytelling software	Asynchronous tools that attract the attention of the audience through personal storytelling	Digital storytelling that can include scripts based on narrations	Textual, visual, and aural	Content, grammar, structure, and organization
Online forums	Asynchronous tools that encourage the development of lengthy written texts	Fan fiction, debates	Mainly textual	Creativity, content, persuasion and argumentation
Blogs	Asynchronous tools that allow the development of lengthy written texts	Blogging (travel blogs, financial blogs, news blogs), fanfiction, etc.	Mainly textual and visual, sometimes aural, resources	Creativity, content, persuasion and argumentation
Social networks (e.g., Facebook)	Asynchronous tools that encourage fast and immediate responses from users and followers	Opinion pieces, summaries, fan fiction, Facebook, amalgam of opinions, commentaries	Mainly visual and aural, with some textual resources	Vocabulary, grammar, spelling, fluency
Twitter	Asynchronous tool that incites fast and immediate responses from users and followers	Tweets	Mainly textual and visual	Vocabulary, grammar
Instagram	Asynchronous tool that incite fast and immediate responses from users and followers	Posts and comments	Predominantly visual, accompanied by textual resources	Vocabulary
Wikis and Google Docs	Asynchronous and synchronous tools that provide space for collaborative writing	Argumentative or expository essays, reports, Wikipedia entries, etc.	Textual, sometimes with visual resources	Rhetorical organization, coherence, grammar, content

knowledge distribution, which are commonly related to narrative, expository, or argumentative genres, digital stories involve "narratives with ordinary people's stories, digitalized and displayed on publicly available websites and made through cultural institutions in society" (Alcantud-Díaz, Ricart Vayá, & Gregori-Signes, 2014, p. 188). Although the visual and audio components of digital stories have an obvious appeal, especially to a younger generation of students, we must not forget the "deep language acquisition and meaningful practice" (Rance-Roney, 2008, p. 29) that has also been ascribed to the development of digital storytelling. In terms of L2 language, researchers have found that the digital-story genre encourages students to pay attention to grammatical rules (Reyes Torres, Pich Ponce, & García Pastor, 2012) just as much as traditional academic writing (Oskoz & Elola, 2014). The digital story could be considered as a remediation assignment meant to help L2 students develop multiliteracies (New London Group, 1996) and engage with synaesthetic semiosis, or *synaesthesia* (Kress, 2003), in order to push their literacy level beyond the linguistic design of a digital text (New London Group, 1996; Takayoshi & Selfe, 2007).

Blogs

Blogs (short for *weblogs*) are asynchronous tools that allow users to create online journals in which a writer or group of writers post their thoughts and ideas in chronological order. Farmer, Yue, and Brookes (2008) point out that bloggers express their own ideas and views while at the same time engaging in social networks of interaction and exchange. Blogs are therefore transformational in the sense that they allow users to connect with and become part of an active social community while exercising and legitimizing their personal expressive spaces (Melo-Pfeifer, 2015, Papacharissi, 2006).

Although in the blogs students use written, oral, and visual modes, most research to date has focused on content and composition development. Since the early 2000's, L2 educators have seen the possibilities of blogging for intercultural development (Ducate & Lomicka, 2005; Elola & Oskoz, 2008; Lee, 2009); for students to reflect on their own language learning experiences (Hourigan & Murray, 2010; Murray & Hourigan, 2006; Murray, Hourigan, & Jeanneau, 2007) and for practicing reading and writing in the L2 (Chen, Shih, & Liu, 2015; Ducate & Lomicka, 2005, 2008; Leja, 2007; Sollars, 2007; Vurdien, 2013; Ward, 2004). Many blogs have travel or financial themes, and blogs have also been used for online fan fiction writing (Sauro, 2014), a genre which encourages L2 writers to write extensively (Sun & Chang, 2012). While blogging, students engage with a learning topic and also with each other as they develop skills of persuasion and argumentation, while at the same time extending their knowledge and practicing their use of grammar and vocabulary (Vurdien, 2013). It is important to note, however, that blogs foster creativity rather than the attainment of perfect grammar or spelling (Ducate & Lomicka, 2008; Leja, 2007). The journalistic nature of blogs enables students to share their experiences in a personal manner (Ducate & Lomicka, 2008). At the same time, each student's personal content creation, which supplies a strong authorial voice (Li & Storch, 2017), and self-reflection is enhanced by the opinions, advice, and criticism they receive from their audience (Ward, 2004).

Online Forums

Discussion boards or *online forums* are asynchronous tools that provide "a critical common space in which [to] share and verify hypotheses and points of view, to ask for help deciphering meanings of words and concepts, and to constantly negotiate meanings and interpretations" (Bauer, de Benedette, Furstenberg, Levet, & Waryn, 2006, p. 35). The time lag between reading and posting in an online discussion provides time "to recognize connections, understand others' ideas, and develop a detailed response or posting" (Meyers, 2003, p. 60) by giving students the opportunity to contribute external material and experiences (Kol & Schcolnik,

2008), link together ideas, and make relevant points (Arnold & Ducate, 2006; Kol & Schcolnik, 2008; Newman, Johnson, Cochrane, & Webb, 1996) in a way that is less possible in face to face interactions (Sengupta, 2001). In contrast to the other social tools mentioned here, discussion boards and online forums are usually linked to a learning management system, such as Blackboard or Angel, or to open social platforms, such as Google Plus. While they have been used in the FL classroom (Oskoz, 2013), they are more commonly used in telecollaborative environments (Chun, 2011; Liaw & Master, 2010). When participating in discussion boards or online forums users engage in the co-construction of meaning in a collaborative environment, although they write individually.

Research into writing has found that L2 students acknowledge linguistic gains in the areas of reading and writing, and they also report acquiring new vocabulary and noticing the gaps between their target output and the received native-like input (Conley & Gallego, 2012), such as the feedback they receive from teachers or others judged to be skilled language users. However, despite the possibilities they offer for linguistic development, online forums and discussion boards might be best used to help students develop the content knowledge required for writing in more traditional genres, such as argumentative and expository essays, especially when they are used in combination with other writing tools (Elola & Oskoz, 2010a). Online forums have also been associated with online fan fiction because they allow students to develop a story collaboratively (Sauro, 2014) and engage in discussions (Elola & Oskoz, 2010b).

Facebook

Facebook, founded in 2004, is a social networking site whose stated mission is to "give people the power to build community and bring the world closer together" (Facebook, 2019). Although there is no length limit on posts, Facebook users, who create a community of friends, usually write short communications to convey their messages often accompanied by images, emojis or emoticons, and videos. In terms of community engagement, users can share articles and other users' posts, react in a variety of ways to others' posts, and respond to posts with comments. With the use of Facebook, students have reported greater development in multiliteracy and general language skills (Blattner & Fiori, 2011; Kabilan, Ahmad, & Abidin, 2010). Students have reported an improvement in several areas. For example, research has shown benefits regarding L2 reading and writing skills (Aydin, 2014; Terantino, 2013; Wang & Vasquez, 2012; Yen, Hou, and Chang, 2015), as well as in grammar and vocabulary (Blattner & Fiori, 2011; Terantino, 2013). Furthermore, Shih (2011) noted that Facebook-integrated blended learning was an effective way to enhance students' knowledge of the English language through writing activity.

Twitter

Founded in 2006, *Twitter* is another social networking site which potentially lets users know "what's happening in the world and what people are talking about right now" (Twitter, 2019). Users communicate in *microblogs*, or *tweets*, using a maximum of only 280 characters, but can insert images and links; other features include the ability to retweet other people's posts and to use hashtags to connect tweets to a larger community. Despite its prevalence in the social and political spheres, with an average of 330 million monthly active users as of the first quarter of 2019 (Statista, 2019), Twitter is minimally used in L2 classrooms, making it probably the least examined digital tool for language instruction. Both Twitter and Facebook share one common feature: When posting an image, users can accompany it with text in the form of a tag or commentary. The interaction of the text with the image can take various forms, depending on the extent to which the textual and visual messages support, enhance, or conflict with each other (Jones & Hafner, 2012).

Research to date into Twitter's educational uses suggests that the platform can help with the interpretation of hashtags (Blattner et al., 2016a, b), promote collaborative learning (Ullrich, Borau, & Stepanyan, 2010), increase community building (Lomicka & Lord, 2011), and help individuals develop social presence (Lomicka & Lord, 2011). In terms of L2 linguistic development, Twitter has been effective in promoting sociopragmatic skills (Blattner et al., 2016a), increased vocabulary (Perez-Sabater & Montero-Fleta, 2015), and grammar practice (Hattem, 2012, 2014). Twitter has also promoted collaborative writing through corrective feedback (Castrillo de Larreta-Azelain, 2013; Pérez-Sabater & Montero-Fleta, 2015). In its different potentials for linguistic development, it seems therefore that like Facebook, Twitter can enable L2 students to focus on local aspects of the language, such as grammar and vocabulary.

Instagram

Since its first version launched in October 2010, with 25,000 people signing up the very first day, *Instagram* has become, in the characterization of its public website, "the home for visual storytelling for everyone from celebrities, newsrooms and brands, to teens, musicians and anyone with a creative passion" (Instagram, 2018). More popular among youth than other applications such as Facebook, as of June 2018, it had reached over 1 billion monthly active users (Statista, 2019). Although Instagram is mainly a mobile photo-sharing network that conveys meaning primarily through photographs, it also provides users the possibility to write captions to accompany their images and to comment on those of others. However, "textual description and replies to followers are deemphasized in favor of images" (Marwick, 2015, p. 139).

Research on Instagram in the L2 classroom suggests that it can help raise cultural competence (Munday, Delaney, & Bosque, 2016; cited in Fornara, Lomicka, & Hattem, 2018), impact students' level of confidence in participating and communicating

(Manson & Rahim, 2017), build community (Fornara & Lomicka, 2019), promote autonomous learning and motivation (Munday et al., 2016; Al-Ali, 2014; Fornara, 2018), and contribute to creativity and innovation with memes (Purnama, 2017). In terms of language, research has also suggested that using Instagram helps increase informal vocabulary (Zhou, 2016; Fornara, 2018), aids comprehension through images in written posts (Whiddon, 2016), and increases lexical proficiency (Munday et al., 2016). Despite the limited research, it seems that, as with Facebook and Twitter, it might be more relevant to focus on the local aspects of Instagram, such as vocabulary.

Wikis and Google Docs

Wikis and *Google Docs* are perhaps the tools most commonly used for collaborative writing because of their potential to create, transform, and erase students' work with built-in accountability (Arnold et al., 2009; Elola & Oskoz, 2010a, b; Kessler, 2009; Kessler & Bikowski, 2010). The distinction between wikis and Google Docs is that the former is asynchronous while the latter is synchronous. In a wiki, students provide each other with comments using a comment function (also asynchronous), while in Google Docs, users can communicate with one another using the synchronous chat feature. Predominantly used for collaborative writing, it has been found that the collaborative nature of these tools is conducive to content development. This could involve research into the historical background of a novel (Arnold et al., 2009), discussion of cultural topics (Kessler, 2009; Kessler & Bikowski, 2010; Lee, 2010b), the development of informational encyclopedia entries (Sauro, 2014), or elaboration of the objective content of argumentative, expository essays or annotated bibliographies (Elola & Oskoz, 2010a; Li & Zhu, 2017a, b; Oskoz & Elola, 2014).

There are mixed findings regarding the use of wikis for developing linguistic or formal accuracy. Some research has found that wiki-supported collaborative work encourages students to focus more effectively on elements of rhetorical structure and organization (Elola & Oskoz, 2010a). Some student users have also focused on the grammatical accuracy of their own writing (Elola & Oskoz, 2010a) or that of their partners (Arnold et al., 2009). On the other hand, some research illustrates that L2 students are more concerned in using wikis with meaning than with form (Kessler, Bikowski, & Boggs, 2012).

Selecting the Appropriate Tool

The most important aspect to consider about these tools is which one will work the best for a given purpose. Many tools can offer textual, aural, and visual modes flexibly, but it is crucial to understand which tool is most appropriate for which communicative purpose. For example, while one could potentially include images and sound on a discussion board or online forum, these tools are more effective for developing text asynchronously (see Table 2.1). Similarly, wikis and Google Docs are predominantly text-based tools, but they can also include images or voice to support the textual content, either synchronously (Google Docs) or asynchronously (wikis). Facebook and Twitter, on the other hand, only support quite abbreviated written text, but the inclusion of emoticons or images can enhance the text visually. Relevant to Instagram is that since it is was conceived as a mainly visual platform, the written mode of the caption is used to support the image by providing it with context. A powerful characteristic of these tools (Facebook, Instagram, Twitter) is that, although they are asynchronous, they provide for fast and immediate responses from users and followers. Blogs are asynchronous tools that encourage the development of lengthier written texts (textual mode), often accompanied by images to support the message. Finally, the most multimodal tool for writing could be digital story-telling software, in which users combine the visual mode (images), the aural mode (the sound, spoken word, music), and the textual mode (subtitles).

Understanding Digital Genres

Common digital genres (see Table 2.1) produced by L2 students using digital writing tools include the following: blogging, or online journal writing using blogs, usually accompanied by images (Lee, 2009; Herring, Scheidt, Wright, & Bonus, 2005); tweeting, short and succinct messages, often including an image or a link, in which users often comment on a daily news story or personal moment (Blattner et al., 2016a, b; Lomicka & Lord, 2012); and digital storytelling, using multimodal narratives created with digital storytelling software (Nelson, 2006; Oskoz & Elola, 2014, Yang, 2012). While some of these genres are new, others have gone through a process of remediation in moving from print to the digital environment, resulting in genres which "can be aptly described as 'hybrids' that incorporate both old and new aspects" (Heyd, 2016, p. 95). An entry in Wikipedia, for example, has a pre-digital antecedent in the traditional encyclopedia entry. The blog began as a digital diary often used for relating travel and personal experiences. However, once a genre becomes digital, it is transformed in terms of its structure and in terms of the public communicative setting in which it operates. For instance, the blog works by means of counter-chronology posting, in which readers first encounter the latest post written by the author. In a Wikipedia entry, the collaborative writing process, together "with the intricate process and communicative norms associated with it, are a drastic departure from the old genre norms for the production of such texts" (Heyd, 2016, p. 95). Other genres are truly new or emergent genres. This is the case for tweeting, which is possible because new technological advances are fully utilized to set up new communicative environments which do not have an equivalent in face to face communication (Heyd, 2016). It is difficult, as Heyd (2016) continues, "to succinctly trace a pre-digital antecedent for [tweets], either in the spoken or written genre continuum" (p. 95). In fact, we need to be open to the presence of new multimodal digital genres, given that community-specific genres of communication are continually growing "across global networks as new tools, communities, and purposes emerge" (Thorne & Reinhardt, 2008, pp. 561).

These communication changes are expanding the way we think about what a text is and how it is created; they also show us how a genre itself can be constructed and reconstructed. When thinking about digital genres, L2 writing teachers need to remember that "the communicative relevance or necessity of a genre can change over time, both in online and offline contexts" (Heyd, 2016, p. 95). As with traditional genres, users of digital tools/media modify genres to fit their communicative purposes and make rhetorical choices depending on the social situation (Dean, 2008). New digital genres may change, "become fossilized or even irrelevant over time, or they 'recede [...] into the shadows' of the Internet" (Herring, 2004, p. 30).

Tweeting (or microblogging), for example, has changed its communicative purpose over time. In 2006, when it was first developed, Twitter was described on its website as "A global community of friends and strangers answering one simple question: What are you doing?" (McFarland, 2014). As McFarland points out, Twitter has undergone many changes in communicative purpose since its inception, and Twitter today is about "What's happening in the world and what people are talking about right now" (Twitter, 2019). This change illustrates how tweeting has shifted the focus from individual self-expression to a more outward-looking perspective – in a parallel shift to the evolution of blogs, which have expanded from single-authored online personal journals to an extensive collection of content and formats, including multi-author sites (Chun et al., 2016). In terms of the classroom, L2 practitioners must realize that "How genres mediate between language, social context, and medium of expression introduces a certain level of abstraction that is necessary for the development of a critical awareness of language in communication" (Chun et al., 2016, p. 68).

Crucially, this generation of multimodal digital genres has changed our understanding of what constitutes a text, moving from the written text itself to a more complex understanding of what a text might be. Although as Elola and Oskoz (2017) point out, it is not unusual to find on digital platforms the replication of classical writing genres, such as descriptions, narratives, argumentations, expositions, and (cultural) reports or summaries (Arnold et al., 2012; Elola & Oskoz, 2010a; Oskoz & Elola, 2014), the expectation is that new genres will become part of our students' writing repertoires. Digital genres thus "are no longer viewed solely as pathways to more traditional academic genres" (Vandergriff, 2016, p. 71). Learning to use new genres, as Kalantzis, Cope, Chan, and Dalley-Trim (2016) point out, "gives us the power of choice and the linguistic potential to join new realms of social activity and social power" (p. 159). Having the possibility to choose from a broader range of language options and genres expands our capacities and thus our social opportunities (Kalantzis et al., 2016). The inclusion of digital and non-digital genres in the L2 classroom will enable L2 students (whatever their cultural and economic background) to participate fully in the communicative practices linked to success in today's society.

Setting up a Successful Multimodal Writing Environment: Travel Blog Project

Project Background

The Travel Blog Project is a semester-long assignment in which intermediate or advanced L2 students used blogs and Google Maps to complete several short writing assignments in a third-year semester class – for example, in a peninsular Spanish History and Culture class or other class focused on the history and/or culture of a specific region. The project can easily be adapted as well to intermediate or advanced language classes in which students explore the history and culture of any country or region as a way to carry out research and writing in the context of digital media. Although the textbook assigned for the Spanish History and Culture course in which the original project was designed and trialed included literary texts as well as references to major architectural landmarks and artistic artifacts in peninsular Spain, the instructor noticed that, given the volume of material, students found it difficult to connect facts about the history and culture of the country in a meaningful manner. To address this problem, the instructor introduces a class multi-author blog in which students, divided into groups of three, plan a three-week summer trip to Spain with their friends, visiting at least nine cultural landmarks. As a resource, the instructor creates a Google map on which students can mark their cultural points of interest.

The project is composed of two main parts that mirror literacy practices in other travel blogs found on the web: (a) creating posts in the blogs in which the students share their research on current political, cultural, or historical aspects of Spain to acquire background knowledge of the country; and (b) using the Google map resource to highlight and describe historical, cultural, or architectural landmarks (e.g., Cádiz, the home of the development of the first Spanish constitution, the museum Reina Sofía in Madrid, or the Roman aqueduct in Segovia). To ensure a wide coverage across Spanish history and society, students are asked to select three cultural artifacts from three historical periods (specified by the instructor to fit with the course curriculum): the first dating from prehistory up to the 14th century, the second from the 15th century to the 18th century, and the third from the 19th century to the present day. Combining their content knowledge with a writing activity encourages L2 students to become better writers in the FL using the same digital social tools that many of them use in their daily lives. They can practice sharing information in a non-traditional genre while still using formal methods of presentation; they can blend it with semiotic resources and experiment with different media.

Blogs are one of the tools chosen for the project because of their potential to be media-rich as well as to promote classroom interaction and collaboration. A program such as WordPress (free to use), can also be a good choice due to its ease of use for content creation.

A program such as Google Maps can also be useful for enabling students to create routes showing specific cities or landmarks on the map. In terms of linguistic development, students are engaged in a series of activities that allow them to (a) raise awareness of linguistic choices (grammatical and lexical) within a blog text (e.g., use of the present tense to describe current events or to describe landmarks), and (b) consider the relationship between the text of the blog and its broader communicative purpose.

The activity we present follows the bridging activity framework and task-based approach. The bridging activity framework breaks down the writing process into manageable steps that include the integration of vernacular, technology-mediated practices familiar to L2 students from their own languages. By examining practices already familiar to them in their L1, instructors can help their students to foster critical awareness, metalinguistic and analytical skills, and establish personal agency and relevance (Thorne & Reinhardt, 2008). A task-based approach is founded on "the principle that language learning will progress most successfully if teaching aims simply to create contexts in which the learner's natural language learning capacity can be nurtured rather than making a systematic attempt to teach the language bit by bit (as in approaches based on a structural syllabus)" (Ellis, 2009, p. 222). A task-based approach also helps break the process down into manageable steps that guide students in the integration of different media in which diverse semiotic resources interact, while using and remixing digital resources often found on the internet.

Table 2.2 provides an overview of the project phases, which are described in more detail below.

Phase 1: Analyzing Vernacular Texts

Guided by the instructor in class, students view and analyze sample travel blogs and Google Maps in the target language. This activity allows students to focus on the structure of different blogs (e.g., layout, content, presentation) and on the linguistic and rhetorical

Table 2.2. Schedule and Activities for the Writing Assignment: Travel Blog Project

Phase	Schedule	Tasks
Phase 1	Weeks 1–2	Instructor • provides a few examples of blogs and annotated maps in the target language; • addresses copyright issues and plagiarism. Students • view and analyze sample travel blogs and Google Maps in the target language; • choose and bring to class additional blogs that might serve as a reference point for their own class blog.
Phase 2	Week 3	Students • divided into groups of three, introduce themselves, and write about their expectations for the assignment; • comment on two other students' posts and receive at least two comments from other students.
Phase 3	Weeks 4–10	Students • write their monthly posts in the blogs, applying the discourse strategies found in the target language blogs, focusing on one aspect of modern Spain (e.g., nationalist movements, immigration, employment); • include their monthly landmarks in a Google map, adding a picture and a brief description (100–150 words) of the place, applying the discourse strategies found in other Google Maps; • answer and provide comments in the blogs to two other groups; • reflect on the content and use of the language and combination of aural, textual, and visual modes to enhance written communication. Instructor • provides (if needed) additional comments regarding content, structure, and form in the selected blogs; • addresses (in groups) the students' posts in the blogs and in Google Maps in terms of content, structure, and accuracy and combination of modes.
Phase 4	Weeks 11–14	Students • design a three-week trip in Spain, including at least nine of the landmarks described in the project; • reflect on their process of writing and composing their blog and on the implications of the combination of semiotic resources (e.g., text, image, sound), and on remixing and mashing.

structures commonly found in vernacular texts. In groups, students examine the type of content provided (e.g., the different tabs of About us, Destinations, Itineraries) and the language used, with a focus on common grammatical and syntactical structures. Students examine global aspects of the language, such as the structure and organization of the paragraphs. They check the extent to which the use of images (i.e., photographs, graphs, maps) and videos complement and amplify the meaning of the written text. After the in-group discussion, students share their findings with the class. The instructor addresses copyright issues in terms of the media employed and how students should cite appropriately to avoid plagiarism.

Phase 2: Starting off the Blog

Students are invited to join the class blog into which they will post their own entries. After the initial analysis sessions in Phase 1, the students familiarize themselves with the blog by working on the equivalent of the *About me* page ¿Quiénes somos? This is a non-graded writing assignment intended to allow students to get used to participating in a multi-author blog. In addition to writing a brief introduction of its members, using mainly the present tense and adding an image as seen in travel blogs, each team is also to include something on the history and culture of Spain and to indicate which topics they might find appealing. All students have to respond to at least two other groups using the Comments feature of the blog. All groups receive comments from at least two other students.

Phase 3: Deciding on Sources and the Landmarks

In the blog, students write their own posts about a current topic in Spain, applying the discourse strategies that they had previously learned in the first phase. Students also respond to at least two other group members using the strategies and linguistic features of agreeing, disagreeing, complimenting, and other discourse markers (e.g., *then*, *of course*) that they found in the target language blogs. Students also select their cultural, historical, or architectural landmarks and mark them on the class Google map. For each place, each group adds a picture and a brief description, making use of available sources from the internet to obtain information and images or videos (e.g., Flickr) or their own images.

With the permission of the students, the instructor shows a few examples of the students' work (see Figure 2.1) to comment and advise about the content presentation and the structure and organization of the entries. To check that students understand how the integration of digital tools and semiotic resources affect the composing process, students complete bi-weekly journals (see Chapter 4). Students write about issues of mixing and remixing aural, visual,

Figure 2.1. Example of Landmark in Google Maps

and written sources in the blog and in the Google map and they also consider the issues of target audience and collaboration.

Phase 4: Traveling Virtually

Toward the end of the semester, when all of the landmarks have been marked in Google Maps, students are asked to design a realistic three-week tour of Spain, including at least nine of the landmarks described in their project. Each map, together with a rationale for the tour, is included under the Itineraries tab in the blog. In a final reflective essay, students reflect on their process of writing and composing their blog and of using Google Maps, and on the benefits to their digital literacy of working with a blend of semiotic resources (e.g., text, image, sound).

Conclusion

While we do not wish to devalue the traditional academic genres in our L2 writing classes, we recommend that instructors should also explore and embrace the possibilities of the diverse digital genres that are associated with new communication tools and new ways of thinking. As L2 instructors plan instructional methods for these digital tools, they need to be open to the changes that use of different media and multiple semiotic resources might bring to the writing process itself. This new understanding entails innovative and radical approaches to teaching and learning, in which students become aware of the power of multimodality to support written communication, and to form a natural "bridge" linking their classroom assignments and their activities in the outside world. This chapter has aimed to provide instructors with holistic perspectives and views to make the act of writing using digital genres a viable teaching and learning experience. As shown here, the key to success is planning the integration of digital tools in a carefully considered manner.

Ideas for Reflection and Discussion

1. Think of some digital texts that you have created in which you have used different tools and modes. Discuss some examples of work in which you have implemented digital multimodality, in either an academic or non-academic context.
2. Successful integration of digital tools for writing in the classroom depends on the acknowledgment of their value by both instructors and students. Yet there is still some resistance to the integration of those tools in the classroom. What arguments would you use to convince both L2 instructors and students about the benefits of digitally mediated writing?
3. The inclusion of semiotic resources has implications for the creation of meaning within specific genres. Think of a digital genre (e.g., blogging, tweeting) and suggest which semiotic resources could best complement or enhance written texts produced within it.
4. In question 2 of the previous chapter, you thought about how the affordance of the tools affect and modify traditional understandings of the written text. After reading about different tools in this chapter, what new knowledge about their affordances can help you maximize the multimodality of digital genres?
5. This chapter presents an example of a learning task that integrates two different tools and at the same time combines various semiotic resources. Taking into consideration your students' proficiency level, the purpose of your L2 (writing) class, and the tools available for the course, design a writing task in which students make use of more than one tool. Break the task down into different phases, considering different writing processes, and indicate the best tool(s) to be used in each phase.

Chapter 3

Collaborative Writing in the L2 Classroom: Making the Most of Digital Social Tools

Digital Social Writing

The introduction of digital tools into the classroom has changed the nature of reading and writing in both "subtle and not-so-subtle ways" (Blake, 2016, p. 135). Traditionally, reading and writing were considered as private acts that might or might not be publicly shared, and requiring two very different skill sets that could not take place at the same time or in the same physical space. Yet as Blyth (2014) pointed out, the distinction between reading and writing is now becoming blurred because users can comment on each other's written entries in a way that creates "a practice of collaborative reading and writing" (Blake, 2016, p. 135) or *wreading* (Allen, 2003). Although Blyth focused on digital social reading, this concept can also be applied to digital social writing, when students interact synchronously in oral or written chats or asynchronously in discussion boards.

The introduction of interactive digital tools, whether in collaborative or individual writing, expands the social dimension of the writing process. However, this new expression of social writing might seem "to violate teachers' cultural expectations of what it means to [write] based on their shared 'print culture'" (Baron, 2013; cited in Blyth, 2014, pp. 202–203). The familiar but rather narrow vision of what writing is, based on expectations and experience of print, results in instructors' – and often, students' –limited understanding of literacy practices in the academic or school environment. This vision and understanding of writing fails "to acknowledge that digital literacy practices have real cognitive benefits" (Blyth, 2014, p. 203) and that digital media are indispensable tools reflecting "how we think" (p. 203) in the digital age.

Collaborative and publicly shared literacy practices are neither uncontroversial nor new. As Pettitt (2007) pointed out, we have lived through what he termed the "Gutenberg Parenthesis" – the period in Western history in which diverse forms of writing (e.g., letters, poems, plays) were "assumed to be the original products of a single author" (Blyth, 2014, pp. 203–204). In contrast to that era, when writing practices were understood in terms of individual writers and readers, today in the "post-parenthetical period" (Blyth, 2014, p. 204), literacy practices emphasize "collaborative forms of textual composition and interpretation" (p. 204). The shift from print to digital, in which the dividing lines between oral and written expression are becoming blurred, is having far-reaching effects in higher education teaching and learning, especially in the humanities (Hayles, 2012).

Collaborative Writing in the L2 Classroom

Collaborative writing is not a by-product of the digital revolution in the classroom; it is actually part of a long-established approach to L2 education (Storch, 2005; Villamil & de Guerrero, 1996, 1998). However, with the emergence of social media and digital tools, collaborative writing is gaining increasing acceptance in the L2 classroom. From an instructional point of view, collaboration offers a dynamic pedagogical approach to the teaching of writing. The traditional Cartesian view of knowledge transfer focuses the teaching/learning exchange squarely on the individual, and linguistic or cultural content is believed to transfer most effectively from teachers to learners. In contrast, learning within the social learning paradigm – an approach that regards the individual "as person-in-the-world, as member of a sociocultural community" (Lave & Wenger, 1991, p. 52) – is seen not in terms of one individual's efforts but rather as an outcome deeply connected to the physical surroundings, tools, and the overall context in which the learning takes place.

Thus, a collaborative approach to L2 writing fits with the 21st-century view of learning as a social endeavor – expanding experiences and exposing students to social contexts different from their own. Individual writing will always have value, but the relationship between new technologies, social media, and collaborative writing is creating some exciting possibilities in L2 teaching and learning. Not only does this linkage produce an ideal environment for the co-construction of knowledge, it also regards students as agents of their own learning and leads us away from the notion that the instructor must be the sole deliverer of content.

For the purposes of this chapter, we first need to define what we mean by collaborative writing, which is a complex notion. As with individual writing, collaborative writing involves not only the act of writing words down but also the processes that any writer goes through when composing a text: planning, revising, editing, and organizing. The writing process, the nature of the task, its audience, and its purpose will all govern the choice of social tools that will best support each stage of the collaboration. From a pedagogical point of view, of course, the development of linguistic skills and mastery of rhetorical conventions will still remain the overall outcomes of the exercise. To these goals, we also add the use of collaborative practices and awareness of digital tools' affordances that allow users to reach a wider audience, some of whom, in turn, will likely react to and have influence on L2 writers' work. At this point, we need to recognize that while digital tools emphasize the social aspects of writing, not all of them are equally suitable for collaborative writing (i.e., two or more participants producing one single document).

What we Mean by Collaborative Writing

Researchers and educators are still pondering about the essential definition of collaborative writing. Several studies have examined the extent to which students working together, whether online or in face-to-face interactions, engage with one another (collaboration), when they co-construct a written text, or simply work on their own assigned tasks (cooperation) when contributing to a written text (Storch, 2016). Storch (2002) has provided the most concrete explanation of collaboration, based on Damon and Phelps' (1989) concepts of *equality* (i.e., the equal distribution of turns, equal contribution, and equal degree of control over the task direction) and *mutuality* (i.e., the peer engagement with each other's contribution, reflected in such language functions as confirmation, repair, and explanation). She uses these terms – *equality* and *mutuality* – to analyze and explain students' interactions in terms of word/turn and language functions.

Based on the degree of equality and mutuality, Storch (2016) identified four distinctive dyadic relationships:

- Collaborative (high equality and high mutuality): Students both participate in the development of the task and provide each other comments, "often pooling their linguistic resources (collective scaffolding) in resolving deliberations about language" (Storch, 2016, p. 393).
- Expert/Novice (low equality and high mutuality): The expert takes a leading role and guides and motivates the novice to be part of the task.
- Dominant/Dominant (high equality and low mutuality): Students participate in the development of the task but do not engage with each other's contributions, and students limit their production and changes to their own work rather than providing feedback or making changes on others' work.
- Dominant/Passive (low equality and low mutuality): One student takes or is granted control of the task, whereas the

other adopts a less participatory role in terms of advancement of the task and provision of feedback.

According to Storch, students who show a collaborative orientation, whether in a collaborative or an expert/novice pattern of interaction, demonstrate more learning scenarios than the pairs who present dominant/dominant or dominant/passive patterns. The question that instructors should ask themselves is what factors encourage the different types of interactions

Turning our attention to digital collaborative writing, several studies have examined if, when, and how those collaborative patterns emerge in students' wikis or Google Docs interactions. Corroborating Storch (2002), Li and Zhu (2013, 2017a, b) and Abrams (2016) found similar types of dyadic relationships (i.e., dominant/dominant, dominant/passive, passive/passive, or collaborative in nature) in students' digital writing interactions. Task effect and – even more importantly – the role of the leader in charge of monitoring and facilitating the wiki discussion and writing, seem to influence students' interactions (Li & Zhu, 2017a, b).

Previous research into task effect would lead us to expect students to behave differently depending on whether the tasks are meaning-focused or grammar-focused. Yet that would not explain why Li and Zhu (2017a) found that one of their groups presented a collective pattern in the research proposal task and an active/withdrawn pattern in the annotated bibliography, whereas another group presented the opposite behavior, switching from dominant/defensive in the research proposal to collaborative in the annotated bibliography task. Analysis of their data led Li and Zhu (2017a) to suggest that the difference depends on the role of the leader. They proposed the need to encourage a reflective and trained leader who can foster collaborative rather than individualistic behaviors. Li and Zhu also maintained that the role of the leader need not be confined to an individual person. Whether in cooperation or, as preferred, in collaboration, the role of the expert can be assumed by different members of the group at different points, drawing on the resources and mutually scaffolding each other as group members progress through the writing tasks. At the same time, research suggests that other factors can have some bearing on dyadic relationships, including the dyad's L2 proficiency level and task goals which might themselves determine if the dyads would collaborate or not (Storch, 2016).

Why We Write Collaboratively

Collaboration, however defined, makes sense only when it is an integral part of the curriculum and aligned with its objectives. If we view collaboration as complementary to individual practice, the language course can be planned to allow for the seamless integration of writing assignments produced collaboratively and supported by social tools. In terms of FL writing, Elola and Oskoz (2010a) and Strobl (2014) have illustrated the qualitative differences between individual and collaborative writing. Elola and Oskoz (2010a), for example, studied individual versus collaborative writing in an advanced Spanish class. They found that, when working individually, students tended to:

- polish their text (i.e., grammar, editing, vocabulary) toward the end of the writing process, such as in a final draft);
- generate ideas during the various stages of the writing task, including the two revision sessions;
- define their thesis in the wikis; and
- work on the essay structure throughout the entire writing process.

When working collaboratively, however, students preferred to:

- polish their essays during the course of developing multiple drafts – contradicting their own views (as expressed in a student survey) that collaboration on the wikis did not help them to improve their grammar;

- rework, refine, and fine-tune the content already written during the revision sessions; and
- use chats early on to discuss structure and organization, creating useful outlines that later helped them to shape the final essay.

Similarly to Elola and Oskoz (2010a), Strobl (2014) noted that in an advanced German writing class, the collaboratively written texts scored significantly higher on quality of content than individually written texts; however, collaboration did not lead to greater linguistic accuracy than individual work. The same study found that the collaborative texts were more cohesive and coherent than individually produced texts, even though students, when working collaboratively, sometimes had to combine three individually written pieces. Strobl's participants also preferred writing individually because of time constraints, personal style, and work pace differences, even though they also felt they were writing at a higher level when writing collaboratively and learning from each other. In both studies, although all of the students expressed a preference for writing individually – claiming that it allowed them to follow their personal styles and schedules – all of the students agreed that collaboration improved the overall quality of their work.

Theoretical Perspectives for Collaborative Writing

Two theoretical frameworks have underpinned the design of studies into collaborative writing: sociocultural theory (SCT) and, lately, activity theory (AT). According to SCT, tools and artifacts are not neutral (Hampel & Hauck, 2006; Thorne, 2003). The choice of tools and the uses we make of them influence language and writing development and shape mediation in important ways (Werstch, 1991). Therefore, the selection of wikis or chats (all having special characteristics) to support any writing task will influence how students engage with the writing process. Another key construct in

SCT is the use of scaffolding (Wood et al., 1976), which occurs not only in expert–student interactions (Aljaafreh & Lantolf, 1994) but also in student–student interactions (Donato, 1994). In Oskoz and Elola (2014), for example, we observed how students maintained focus on assigned writing tasks and were able to achieve their writing goals and outcomes through chat interactions and the use of scaffolding. We showed that students could control frustration and notice linguistic discrepancies while discussing and developing their essays together.

Students working collaboratively also develop a shared perspective (intersubjectivity) on the nature of a task, which has "a profound effect on how the task is performed" (Ellis, 2003, p. 190). Through a process of metatalk, Ellis' (2003) students oriented themselves as they conferred about task requirements, thus externalizing the goal or end result of the task; they were thus able to reach an intersubjective, shared perspective of the task (Brooks & Donato, 1994). In a complementary study, Oskoz and Elola (2012) noted how students could reach a degree of intersubjectivity when discussing both the goal of the writing assignment and how to complete it, even when from time to time they experienced frustration and disagreements.

Because social tools and their affordances are now at the forefront of pedagogical advances in L2 writing and other disciplines, they have become an integral part of the L2 curriculum and lesson planning. Blin and Appel (2011), taking an AT perspective, studied the essential role of the artifacts used or created by L2 students during collaborative writing practiced in online, asynchronous, moment-by-moment interactions. The integration of a new tool into a writing task influences many aspects of the activity, both tangible and intangible: the object produced, the set of rules conveyed to the students, the shared understanding of the task, and the working relationships among participants. In addition, the object produced provides the student with a defined direction (Leontiev, 1978), and participation in any writing activity implies conscious actions by the student that have an immediate and defined goal (Kuutti, 1996).

Oskoz and Elola (2012) found that, through interactions via social media, students constantly oriented and reoriented their jointly formed actions in relation to the object (i.e., the argumentative essay) and the desired outcome – to become effective writers. Cho (2017) also examined how students' goals triggered them to take specific actions, how these goal-directed actions interacted with their classmates' goals, and how each individual's goals impacted on the group's interactions.

It is clear, then, that established theoretical perspectives underpin the current research into collaborative L2 writing. They tell us about the value of knowledge sharing, meaning negotiation, scaffolding, intersubjectivity, and action completion – all of which are pivotal tenets in collaborative writing as a teaching and learning methodology.

Outcomes of Collaborative Writing

Social tools can give students an opportunity to engage in authentic communication with others as they engage with FL writing. If we could express the affordances of social tools for collaborative writing as a continuum, we could see that emails, online forums, and blogs involve and demonstrate the writing ability of the individual writer; wikis and Google Docs, on the other hand, allow participants to work together on the same document, thus supporting collaborative writing. Common to all tools is that they entail multiple computer-mediated written interactions that allow students to focus on the written discourse while keeping in mind the target audience.

Before deciding which tools to choose to support a collaborative writing activity, the instructor will need to set goals (i.e., form general statements of what the course or activity is attempting to accomplish) and outcomes (i.e., what the student will be able to perform/produce at the end of the course or activity) as an essential precursor to detailed task planning. Having identified goals and outcomes, the instructor can then identify the necessary phases that students will need to progress through to complete the task successfully. The choice of social tool thus depends on the overall goals (e.g., development of linguistic aspects and/or writing conventions); on the specific outcomes of the writing task or course (e.g., sharing ideas, developing content, becoming a better writer, or co-authoring an essay); and on the availability of appropriate technology in terms of platforms or online tools. To ensure successful implementation, the instructor will need a good understanding of the affordances of each tool. The characteristics of the selected tool will also dictate the language elements on which the students will focus. Next, we will describe some situations in which different aspects of L2 writing have been enhanced by the choice and use of particular tools.

Content Development Using Interactive Social Tools

Given that we write to communicate meaning, it is not surprising to find that content development is the most prominent component of any writing task. Linguistic accuracy necessarily takes second place as students interact using social tools with a wider audience beyond the instructor. Awareness of this external audience further motivates students to strongly focus on content. For example, studies of the use of blogs or online personal journals in L2 writing have emphasized the role of these tools as means of self-reflection and free expression (Lee, 2010b; Yang, 2009), promoting creativity rather than just the attainment of perfect grammar and spelling (Ducate & Lomicka, 2008; Leja, 2007). Although blog posts are usually an individual endeavor (i.e., one person writes one post), when used as part of collaborative writing, blogs can help to co-construct knowledge whenever students comment on each other's postings (Lee, 2009). At the same time, the student's experience of personal content creation and self-reflection is enriched by the opinions, advice, and criticism (i.e., feedback) coming from their audience (Ward, 2004).

The benefit of emphasizing content versus the formal aspects of a language when using blogs has been clearly argued in studies by Ducate and Lomicka (2008) and Lee (2009). Ducate and Lomicka (2008) sought to highlight features of the target language; they asked their German and French students to first familiarize themselves with the uses and features of various target language blogs before going on to develop their own blogs. Then, students were asked to maintain their own blogs as responses to pre- and post-readings, while reading and responding to classmates' blogs and applying certain discourse strategies (e.g., agreeing, disagreeing, complimenting) that they had previously learned. Ducate and Lomicka found that despite the suggested analysis of linguistic structures as well as content, and although they had agreed that blogs were an effective way to practice linguistic skills, the students still focused on the content of their posts rather than on linguistic aspects. This study therefore ratifies the notion that despite L2 instructors' intention to focus on form, the blog affordances might encourage learners to focus on content instead.

Although online forums have been less frequently examined in the L2 writing context, these are spaces in which students can reflect on researched information and are ideal venues for content development. Elola and Oskoz (2010b) noted that the slow pace of online forums allowed students to present individually researched content, to discuss collaboratively the different perspectives brought by other group members, and, ultimately, to bring to their own essays a much deeper understanding of the topics. Like online forums, wikis and Google Docs also provide an environment in which "students can take their time to produce more extensive and reasoned content" (Pellet, 2012, p. 227). Given that wikis and Google Docs are the ultimate collaborative writing tools, they are perfect arenas for students to engage in content development, even in situations of less than total collaboration (Arnold et al., 2009, 2012; Kessler, 2009; Elola & Oskoz, 2010a; Pellet, 2012). For example, Arnold et al. (2012) explored the development of wikis by German students in three different universities; the results indicated that students do cooperate when working on content development. Elola and Oskoz (2010a) corroborated this result, but also found that although most students contributed content, not all participants shared the workload equally.

Linguistic Development

Linguistic development as a feature of L2 writing has attracted numerous studies; these studies have examined accuracy, syntactic complexity, and discourse development, and have compared the use of various social tools (e.g., email, wikis, online forums, blogs) to support linguistic development.

Email was perhaps the first social tool used in L2 writing classes. González-Bueno's (1998) study explored how linguistic skills could be developed through the use of email. Because her Spanish language students had ample time to spend on their writing, consult references, and edit their messages before sending, they produced long messages covering varied topics and with complex linguistic characteristics. However, González-Bueno also found that although at the beginning of the semester, students demonstrated a high level of grammatical accuracy – perhaps due to a preference for short sentences with simple grammar – by the end of the second semester, when longer and more complex topics had been selected, their grammatical accuracy had decreased. Echoing St. John and Cash (1995), González-Bueno (1998) suggested that with growing linguistic confidence, students might reduce their self-monitoring, leading to a decline in accuracy. This trend did level out by the end of the study period in a U-shaped learning curve, showing that students could eventually compose more complex sentences for the longest exchanges with a commensurate rise in accuracy.

Although email might have fallen out of favor with most researchers, the omnipresence of this tool still makes it a relevant tool for L2 writers. Nearly a decade later, Shang (2007) examined (a) the syntactic complexity, grammatical accuracy, and lexical density of 40 non-traditional English as a foreign language (EFL) students, and (b) the differences between the number of email exchanges and the students' writing performance. Students were asked to summarize and email each other two paragraphs with their summaries, opinions, and comments regarding the reading assignments. Then the students exchanged views with each other on content and grammar and composed a new text about the article topic. Finally, they submitted their written texts, including copies of all of their correspondence, to the instructor electronically. Shang then assessed the potential learning benefits of the interactive approach. In terms of grammatical accuracy, although there were no significant differences between the original and final texts, students made fewer grammatical errors in the final text than in the original text. Shang suggested that students tended to improve their writing (syntactic complexity and grammar) the more emails they wrote.

Studies that have examined the inclusion of online forums in the L2 classroom have highlighted the benefits of those interactions for genre and discourse development rather than for linguistic gains in terms of accuracy and syntactic complexity. With the purpose of teaching their students written argumentative skills within the intercultural objectives of their year-long French course, Hanna and de Nooy (2003, 2009) set objectives for their students to (a) learn the use of appropriate connectors to express logical progression, cause, and consequence, and (b) familiarize themselves with the argumentation style and vocabulary of debates to discuss French current affairs. The students first analyzed French written forum conventions, the length of messages, digressions, and the formality and correctness of the language, and then they participated in forums of their choice. Regarding linguistic development, Hanna and de Nooy found that when their students listened to the form of language used by native speakers (e.g., use of different registers and genres), they began to imitate those features in their writing. The results indicated the relevance of genre and suggested that adopting a culturally appropriate manner of communicating was more likely to lead to successful interactions in online forums than would attention to politeness or linguistic accuracy.

Following in Hanna and de Nooy's (2003, 2009) footsteps, Ritchie and Black (2012) asked their 20 third-year French students to participate in blogs and discussion forums. The students were asked to write once a week for 10 weeks in a French discussion forum or blog of their choosing. Focusing on the first and last posts by each student, on writing improvement in general, and on the use of connector words such as *quoique* (whereas) and *Il est vrai que* (it is true that), the authors did not find any significant difference in the number of words, lexical density, or number of syllables per word or per sentence; this outcome suggests that a semester might not be long enough for students to show a significant improvement in linguistic production. The authors did find that, judged by the use of expressions of concession and opposition, one-third of the students had improved their argumentative skills and used a greater variety of connectors. The question remains as to whether these were learned through in-class analysis of text or whether they were acquired from interactions with native speakers, as suggested by Hanna and de Nooy (2003, 2009) and Savignon and Roithmeier (2004).

Participation in online forums can also take place in tandem intercultural environments (Edasawa & Kabata, 2007; Savignon & Roithmeier, 2004; Sengupta, 2001; Vinagre, 2005) or in FL classrooms (Elola & Oskoz, 2010b; Kol & Schcolnik, 2008). Although not always focused on language development, these studies provide insights into the value of online forums for writing development. In one of the first studies of online forums in the FL context, Sengupta (2001) found that her Japanese students of English, when using language to build a classroom community, tended to use agreement and praise expressions, based either on their own cultural norms or on learned discourse protocols. Similarly, Edasawa and Kabata (2007) found that the discussion boards helped L2 students improve their discursive skills and syntactic complexity. Overall, the students focused on conveying clear messages, and so long as their partners' messages were understandable, they did not feel the need to address any grammatical errors.

The development of a *coherent text* (i.e., the relation of all sentences or utterances in a text to a single global proposition) is an important objective of students' online forum interactions. Local connections or structural links provide the desired cohesiveness to a written text. As Savignon and Roithmeier (2004) pointed out, elements that offer cohesion to a text are pronouns, conjunctions, ellipses, comparisons, or parallel structures. In their study with English as FL students at a German gymnasium (i.e., secondary school) and third-year German as FL students in a Midwestern U.S. high school, Savignon and Roithmeier examined the extent to which online forum postings on four topics led to the production of coherent, cohesive texts. Despite unequal participation rates (the American groups participated more frequently than the German groups), the authors found that all students occasionally picked up words or terminology used in prior postings and reused them in their own postings. Although the authors cautioned that the subsequent appearance of a word cannot always be considered a sign of uptake, they did find that – when discussing ideas – the repetition of expressions could represent conscious lexical choices; the students did not just repeat a word but often restated or rephrased ideas in later postings, bringing in one or two new ideas or sometimes mentioning personal experiences. Therefore, the improved quality of postings on a single topic supported the creation of a text in collaboration. In sum, the collaboration of all of the participants created a "network of intertwined postings that makes sense after reading prior contributions" (p. 284).

In terms of wikis, several studies suggest that the collaborative nature of this tool allows students to focus on local issues, although with mixed results (Elola & Oskoz, 2010a; Kessler, 2009; Lee, 2010a; Li & Zhu, 2013, 2017a, b). For example, Kessler's (2009) study with preservice teachers from Mexico focused on EFL linguistic development in the context of a course about cultural aspects of life in the United States. Kessler found that when grammatical errors did not hinder meaning, the students tended to ignore linguistic accuracy. This finding was partially confirmed by Elola and Oskoz's (2010a) study, which showed that although students working on multiple drafts promoted accuracy, the students tended to adjust grammar more often in passages they had written themselves. On the other hand, Lee (2010a) found that her 35 undergraduates in a low-level Spanish course worked well collaboratively on language errors at the sentence or word level in meaning-focused writing tasks. These mixed results may be due to several factors, including:

- reluctance to address their own errors or provide feedback about those of their partners;
- lack of accuracy as a task criterion in the rubric;
- an excellent command of the L2;
- a tendency to overlook problems in their partners' writing;
- reluctance to correct their partners' errors in the early stages of establishing a working relationship;
- task design effects, such as group size, language level, assessment issues, or the problem-solving nature of the task.

More recently, Oskoz and Elola (2014) investigated how the nature of a particular task affected the accuracy and complexity of eight students' texts by comparing collaboratively written wiki-produced argumentative and expository essays. The results indicated more sentence complexity in the former, but greater accuracy in the latter.

Rhetorical Aspects

Understanding genre is an essential step toward mastering the conventions of academic writing, and this includes recognizing typical structures, identifying how information is organized and presented, and observing what effect genre might have on linguistic choices. Genres have perhaps been less examined when addressing the impact of digital social tools. When they have been, research has focused mainly on academic writing. Oskoz and Elola (2014), for instance, noted that genre influenced complexity at the sentence level and also affected accuracy. When comparing a collaboratively written argumentative essay versus an expository essay, several differences were observed in students' practices. For example, less attention was paid to source selection in the expository essay than in the argumentative piece. This is probably because argument calls for the careful evaluation of evidence (Newell, Beach, Smith, & VanDerHeide, 2011), and in academic contexts the evaluation of evidence is related to the choice of sources to cite. In contrast, exposition requires more attention to organizing the information and presenting it (de Oliveira, 2011). In addition, more time overall was spent on genre-specific structure as well as on paragraph-level organization for the expository essay than for the argumentative essay, perhaps because the genre-specific structure of the expository essay was more challenging.

Combinations of Tools in Collaborative Writing

Although most research has considered the use of only one social tool at a time (Kost, 2011), there are also other studies that have explored the educational value of integrating two or more e-communication tools (McLoughlin & Lee, 2007). In fact, attention to the effects of combining two or more tools has increased in recent educational/linguistic research, such as chats and wikis (Oskoz & Elola, 2010a) or videos and wikis (deHaan, Johnson, Yosimura, & Kondo, 2012). Combining different tools "lends itself to catering for individual learning styles" (Hampel, 2010, p. 149), and therefore, it can be "more conducive to students' learning to combine online tools with specific curricular aspects" (Stickler & Hampel, 2011, p. 70). The educational value of communication tools in the classroom stems from exploiting their affordances to enable sharing, communicating, and information discovery (McLoughlin & Lee, 2007). The key educational value of multimodal curricular design is that it stimulates dialogic interaction, possibly leading to a higher level of critical thinking (Hampel, 2006).

It is vital that a multimodal approach to writing be offered as part of a structured environment, which should offer a clear sequence of interconnected writing tasks and allow students to build on previous interactive use of social tools (Ware & O'Dowd, 2008). For example, Elola and Oskoz's (2010a) study found that students tended to use chats to address general issues related to genre, structure, and organization, and they used wikis to elaborate in more detail on structure and organization. In a later study, the same authors provided a snapshot of how students collaborated when using discussion boards, chats, and wikis to complete an expository essay in an advanced Spanish writing class (Oskoz & Elola, 2013). Analysis of students' synchronous and asynchronous interactions in that task indicated that they were able to exploit the affordability of each tool judiciously.

In spite of the familiarity of today's young students – from K–12 through college – with social media, their expertise with social tools does not guarantee that they have the required knowledge to use them in the classroom appropriately. For social tools to add a valuable dimension to the L2 writing class, they must be integrated and implemented in a planned manner. They also have to be used as a regular, complementary classroom activity. Their use, whether in the classroom or outside class, needs to be carefully coordinated and planned. The in-class environment is the perfect setting for pedagogic instruction regarding: (a) research and topic development, through students' analysis of readings, reflections on those, and selective use of sourced information in their own writing; (b) characteristic elements of genre; (c) linguistic features related to genre or topic; (d) use of feedback, including how to receive and act on it; and (e) sharing models of good writing or bad models to be avoided. To be successful, students "need to receive adequate and substantial tuition in exploiting [social tools] for learning purposes" (Hourigan & Murray, 2010, p. 212). Without accompanying in-class instruction, the use of social tools in any collaborative exercise will lack direction and ultimately fail. Early orientation sessions need to convey to students that social tools can help their language development.

Instructors need to choose social tools and platforms that can meet the task goals, are supported technically by the institution, and are easily accessible to students at home or in class. Students need to understand the purposes of different tools and how they are related to the writing task. For example, when brainstorming a topic, *discussion boards* are tools that provide students with an asynchronous space where they can post their informed opinions about the essay topics before starting the composing process. Other tools, such as *online chats*, can be a vehicle for meaningful interactions in real time during work on the composition. Social tools, such as wikis or Google Drive, are good media to choose for paired writing tasks, largely because these tools allow students continuous access to a document in collaborative production. Once students understand the principles of selecting tools that will help them to develop a collaborative writing assignment effectively, it is essential to allocate training time in the use of these tools before they start the first writing assignment. This is a period of familiarization, when students complete practice exercises on ungraded writing assignments, using the same social tools with which they will complete a subsequent graded writing task.

Are Students on Board with Collaborative Writing?

Because students are the agents of their own learning when working collaboratively, an increasing number of studies over the last two decades have canvassed students' perceptions of the benefits and drawbacks of implementing collaborative writing in the FL classroom. Students have acknowledged the benefits of using email for writing development (Leh, 1999; Mahfouz, 2010; Shang, 2007). While some research highlighted minor problems with writing collaboration, such as differences in pen-pal interests or unreliable writing partners (Leh, 1999), all studies revealed generally positive attitudes toward the use of email. In terms of perceived linguistic gains, Mahfouz (2010) found that although his Jordanian EFL students tended to ignore the style and mechanics of writing (e.g., proper paragraph structure, spelling, linking words, punctuation marks, and capitalization), students acknowledged that email helped them to form well-structured sentences and improved their vocabulary and use of idiomatic expressions. Most of Shang's (2007) students also indicated that email interactions let them practice writing and social interactions with peers and allowed them to self-monitor. Those who did not like the email experience cited the length of time it took to complete the activity and also mentioned their poor keyboard skills, unfamiliarity with the computer, or the unavailability of computers. These perceptions support other findings regarding the use of email to enhance syntactic complexity and accuracy (Kendall, 1995; Shang, 2007; Wu & Lee, 2008), to improve grammar and discrete language functions (Greenfield, 2003), and to incorporate new vocabulary and idiomatic expressions learned from native speaker pen-pals (Ishida, 1995; St. John & Cash, 1995; Van Handle & Corl, 1998). Those who engaged in regular email exchanges believed that they had improved their writing skills significantly more than those who had exchanged email less regularly. Students wrote longer, more elaborate messages when working independently from home rather than on the school computers, supporting González-Bueno's (1998) findings.

Collaboration, of course, also means students writing together to create one document, and this brings with it a special set of challenges. When working in wikis, several of Elola and Oskoz's (2010a) L2 students at the advanced level felt that, due to mismatched proficiency levels between partners, issues of grammar could not always be properly addressed. Because it was difficult to address language mistakes to a partner diplomatically, these sometimes remained unexplored. Even though the students sometimes lacked the time to revise and proofread together in the wikis or chats, they realized that their partners were surprisingly able to identify their own mistakes and correct them when revising the text on their own. Elola and Oskoz's students found that writing collaboratively using tools like wikis was best for content development. Through collaboration, students (a) generated more ideas and created a more complete text than when working alone, and (b) challenged their co-authors' ideas and were also pressed to explain their own ideas. Listening to each other led to the generation of additional content and stronger arguments in their essays. Similarly, students appreciated a more structured way of working. For example, they had to create an outline together before starting to write; creating an outline collaboratively in turn facilitated the joint planning of the task and division of the work, helping the partners move toward successful completion of the assignment.

Students also saw the benefits of a multimodal approach to the writing task. For example, Elola and Oskoz's (2010a) students found that, despite encountering certain technical problems, the use of voice chats was very useful for the exchange of ideas. As with wikis, chats were not always regarded as the ideal vehicle for discussing and improving grammar, but they were thought very useful for discussing matters of content and structure. By communicating via voice or written chats, students discussed the overall direction of the essay, combined their thoughts, and came up with better ideas. Students also remarked on how chats could offer a useful way to allocate ideas when building the structure of an argument. Similarly, students found that generating and sharing ideas with the group on the discussion boards offered a useful opportunity to discuss multiple possible ideas and arguments for the essay.

Setting up a Successful Collaborative Writing Environment: Collaborating with Different Tools

Project Background

This project, in which learners work together with different tools, is a semester-long assignment in a fourth-year semester L2 class but could be adapted to lower-level courses. Most institutions offer advanced courses to L2 students in which the main goal is to develop academic writing skills in their L2 and build cultural knowledge. Genres explored in these courses include descriptive, narrative, argumentative, and expository texts, many of which will be of interest to students pursuing graduate studies. The instructor's purpose for including collaborative writing rests on her interest in creating meaning-oriented situations in which students engage in a dialog with each other about three interrelated aspects of the assignment: the topic itself, the writing conventions or genre, and the linguistic features.

The project is made up of three main parts, which take place in three consecutive weeks. During the first week, students brainstorm and discuss ideas about the topic of the essay. This includes asking students to share their own opinions and also to search for additional information that can support and advance their ideas and those of the group. During the second week, students write their collaborative essays following a process-oriented approach, in which students work on different drafts of the same essay using the wikis or Google Docs and the chats. When working on these assignments, students can access the wikis from different locations. During the third week, after receiving the instructor's feedback, students make the necessary changes in content, structure, organization, vocabulary, grammar, and editing to their final essay.

The instructor uses discussion boards, wikis, and chats as a way to develop the content of the writing as well as to highlight the linguistic and discursive features appropriate for the genre. The discussion board gives students an arena to discuss the topic in small groups. The wiki or Google Docs gives students an ideal space to write the essay collaboratively. The online chats, which can be the written chats in Google Docs or voice chats from another platform, such as Skype or Zoom, allow students to discuss issues regarding the essay's content, structure, or the organization of ideas. It might not be either realistic or useful to ask students to communicate a specific number of times. However, at least one chat interaction should take place when students generate further ideas about the topic, discuss global issues – such as structure and organization – and plan the group's internal logistics (i.e., make sure that each member knows what she/he will be doing while working separately).

Following a task-based approach to process writing, essay composition can be broken into phases that follow each other sequentially. These phases can be expressed as interrelated but distinct pedagogic tasks that combine to form a full schedule – that is, a teaching module (see Table 3.1).

Table 3.1. Schedule and Activities for the Writing Assignment: Collaborating with Different Tools

Phase	Schedule	Tasks
Phase 1	Week 1	Students and Instructor • discuss the topic of the upcoming writing activity in class. Students • discuss the topic of the upcoming writing activity in the online forum.
Phase 2	Week 2	Students and Instructor • discuss the topic, organization, and structure in class. Students • work on writing out assignments collaboratively using wikis and chats; • turn in Draft 1 in the wikis. Instructor • provides comments regarding content, structure, and form in the wikis (within two days); • using selected, anonymized student essays, discusses teacher feedback and practice how to revise for improvement of content, structure, and accuracy.
Phase 3	Week 3	Students • continue working on their writing assignments collaboratively using both wikis and chats to revise and edit their first draft; • finalize their final draft in the wikis.

Phase 1: Thinking about the Topic

The instructor and students begin with a preliminary discussion of the topic (e.g., effects of globalization on French traditions) in the class. The essay topic is introduced in class, and the students and instructor briefly discuss either the content of a reading assignment or their personal ideas about the topic. Although the instructor may initially want to select topics based on textbook content or the syllabus, it is advisable to select topics based on students' expressed interests (Canagarajah, 2002). After in-class discussion, students will be asked to continue their conversations on the discussion boards, where – divided into groups of three or four – students will research and discuss the topic, looking for ideas that support their arguments and opinions.

Example 3.1. Discussion Board Prompt (translated)

> **The person as symbol:** There are people who acquire a symbolic or mythical stature in the consciousness of a people or in the consciousness of humanity. Think of a person who has played a significant role, preferably in the Francophone world in general or in a specific Francophone country.
> **Group leader:** Think of a person who has or may have had a great impact in society due to political, social, environmental, or artistic work. As a group leader, describe the person that you chose and analyze why and how that person became a symbolic figure.
> **Group members:** Respond to the group leader and to another group member by supporting the group leader's suggestion, explaining your reasons, and adding more information. If you do not agree with the person proposed by the group leader, propose another person whose social, political, or environmental work you consider to be more important. Describe the person, the work the person has done, and its value in society.

Following Arnold and Ducate's (2006) suggestions, each discussion board group should have a leader (rotated for each topic). Shin (2008) and Wu (2003) suggested the instructor should adopt a "restrained presence" during this phase and refrain from commenting during discussions, thus encouraging students to find and voice their own opinions. The instructor can facilitate collaboration and interactivity by designing structured interactions and by assigning roles in the group discussions (Wu, 2003). The leader oversees starting, maintaining, and wrapping up the content of the discussion, while the other members are responsible for answering postings. As Wanner (2008) also observed, the thematic organization of the discussion boards encourages an information-based style of communication in which students provide snippets of information as well as learning how to debate.

Phase 2: Genre Structure and Topic Development

If our language students are to perform adequately in graduate programs or professional settings, we need to teach genre-related knowledge as part of their academic writing programs. It is often difficult, however, to analyze the various cognitive and linguistic demands inherent in each of the genres, let alone to estimate the relative difficulty each brings to a linked writing task. For example, Hamp-Lyons and Mathias (1994) considered argumentation to be cognitively more difficult but to demand less accurate language than exposition. However, Kuiken and Vedder (2008) found that a cognitively more complex writing task yielded more accurate, although not syntactically more complex language, supporting Robinson's (2001) cognition hypothesis for task performance. Despite the conflicting results, instructors may need to acknowledge the way the varying cognitive demands of genres may influence how successfully students can complete a writing task. Instructors considering genre may need to predict what obstacles students might meet and tailor in-class instruction to address them. During the collaborative process, instructors can highlight those potential problems by modeling them with examples and by giving the kind of precise feedback the students are to attempt and revise.

After the students have discussed the topic for a week online (Phase 1), in a final in-class discussion, the instructor and students reflect on and elaborate on ideas for the content of the essay. Then, the instructor outlines the structure of the argumentative essay and asks the students to work on their essays in pairs. Students will discuss the content and structure of the essay using the chats and develop the content in the wikis. The instructor will begin this with a suitable prompt or introductory wording:

Example 3.2. Prompt for Writing Task

> There are people who acquire a symbolic or mythical stature in the consciousness of a people or in the consciousness of humanity. As with any important figure in history, some see these symbolic or mythical figures as heroes who have changed history in valuable ways; others, however, see them merely as individuals whose actions did not leave a positive legacy on their country's history, politics, or society. Please, describe the two different perspectives for the figure of your choosing to present a clear picture of who this figure is and what she/he represents. Describe both the positive and negative aspects of this person, but then make it clear which position describes the real person according to you.

Students will have five days to complete the first draft, leaving the instructor two days to provide feedback on content, structure, organization, and lexical and grammatical accuracy (see Chapter 5 for more on feedback). Then, in class, using selected, anonymized essays, the students and the instructor discuss the teacher feedback and practice how to revise to improve content, structure, and accuracy.

Phase 3: Editing the Final Essay

Students continue working on their writing assignments collaboratively using both wikis and chats to revise and polish their final draft. As in Phase 2, there is no need to ask the students to communicate a specific number of times. However, the students should be encouraged to engage in at least one chat interaction in which they revise the content, structure, and organization of their essay in response to the instructor's feedback. This will help them to focus on and remediate any specific weaknesses in their writing.

Conclusion

Collaboration has the potential for developing knowledge, linguistic skills, and composition in a co-constructive manner not always easily achieved through individual writing. The proliferation and increasing sophistication of social tools is leading to their inclusion in the L2 classroom as an adjunct to collaborative writing. In this chapter, we have discussed the potential of social tools to foster and support contemporary learning approaches, such as collaboration, that meet L2 students' literacy needs in the digital age. There is a growing body of research in this field; we are now beginning to understand more about the tools' affordances and what they are best suited for (e.g., topic exploration, linguistic skill development, argumentation), while facilitating "ways of doing, relating, thinking, and being" (Hafner, Chik, & Jones, 2015, p. 2).

Instructors can employ more than one tool or bring in different tools at each phase of the writing process. For example, online forums can be used for content development, while online chats can support planning of the writing task and organizing the composition. Students need to be aware of each tool's purpose, why it should be used, and how it relates to the writing process. A task-based approach that matches social tools with different phases of the writing process is an ideal pedagogical model that encourages students toward optimal use of the social tools and towards becoming digitally literate. Finally, collaboration will be an increasingly important feature of students' professional and personal lives in the future; so, as teachers, we need to develop pedagogical methods that will match the demands of the outside world.

Ideas for Reflection and Discussion

1. This chapter has presented studies that explore the efficacy of different social tools, such as discussion boards, wikis, or blogs, for fostering digital literacy in collaborative assignments. Think of your writing goals (e.g., accuracy, content development, genre development, or a combination of several elements), and suggest why you would use these social tools (or other tools such as Facebook or Twitter) to achieve your goals.
2. Collaborative writing can be defined as students participating in a writing task, either for developing their individual texts or for the division of labor to complete a text (coordination) or for co-constructing a single document by two or more writers (collaboration). Considering these definitions and your students' proficiency level, outline a possible technology-based collaborative task that could be implemented in your classroom.
3. The chapter presented the difference between collaborative and individual writing in terms of focus on content, organization, structure, and/or linguistic development. Based on the results of the studies mentioned and the tools employed, design an outline of a syllabus (curriculum) in which both collaborative and individual writing are included to support writing development. How would you integrate these two approaches into your syllabus? What tasks (and sequence of tasks) would you choose to address both collaborative and individual writing? What tools would you include to promote collaboration among participants?
4. Technology-based collaborative writing can be fostered by using one or several tools for one task (e.g., Google Docs with chats). Taking into consideration your students' proficiency level, learning goals for your FL (writing) class, and the tools available, design a writing task in which students make use of more than one tool. Break the task down into different phases,

considering different writing processes, and indicate which tool(s) could be used in the different phases.

5. Research that has compared collaborative to individual writing has focused on advanced language courses. Think of a study which compares individual to collaborative writing in lower-level language courses. Which tool(s) would you use? Which language components would you choose to focus on?

Chapter 4

Developing L2 and Multilingual Students' Identities as Writers: Acquiring a Voice

Expanding Instructors' Views of L2 Students

In the last decade, researchers and educators have been trying to reduce the tension that the impact of globalization has generated between what is taught in the L2 classroom and what students will need in the real world (Kramsch, 2014). While we avoid entering the debate of whether globalization has had a positive or negative impact on education and, more particularly, on L2 education, we think it is clear that today's society has placed some stress on educators to expand and modify the teaching of "language rules and conventions at the microlevel of age, gender, social class, and ethnicity and to teach what the diverse forms mean" (Kramsch, 2014, p. 301). Although there are increasing variations and non-standard versions of language used in everyday life, much of language teaching continues to be harnessed to "the pure linguistic standard established by the national gatekeeping academies monitored by [native speakers]" (Kramsch, 2014, p. 299). Such teaching conforms to a monolinguistic view of language education that is becoming obsolete in the multilingual, multicultural, and multimodal world in which our students function as digital users who are also language learners.

There have been numerous attempts – led, for example, by those promoting the initiatives of the Learning by Design and bridging activities frameworks – toward developing comprehensive pedagogies that can bridge these two worlds: the classroom and the outside world. Multiliteracy-based pedagogy has lately tried to harmonize these two contexts with the idea of bringing "multimodal texts, and particularly those of the new, digital media, into the curriculum and classroom" (Cope & Kalantzis, 2015, p. 3). The intention is to renegotiate students' ethnic and cultural identities and give them a voice through exposure to the various literacies that emphasize "the multiplicities of languages, genres, and modalities [...] while also honing learners' agency, all with the goal of generating active and dynamic transformation" (Kumagai & López-Sánchez, 2016, p. 3). It is no longer appropriate "for schools to focus on a 'a singular canonical' language form" (Rowsell, Kosnick, & Beck, 2008, p. 110): all modes of communication should be equally recognized, respected, and championed in schools.

Thus, the pertinent question is how can we language professionals address these changes, triggered by globalization and enabled by technology, as we seek to promote L2 digital literacies and L2 writing in particular? More importantly, how can we develop our often multilingual students' literacies in a way that reflects the linguistic richness that exists in multicultural communities? How can we foster our students' evolving identities, construed by how they position themselves with respect to others, and how they operate in wider political and social situations? That is, we need to decide how best to leverage digital written literacies to provide a platform and a forum for our students' authentic voices.

As researchers and educators, we need to expose multilingual students to the heteroglossic real world of linguistic hybridity, known as "truncated multilingualism," made up of "linguistic competencies which are organized topically, on the basis of domains or specific activities" (Blommaert, Collins, & Slembrouck, 2005, p. 199). We also need to expose multingual students to phatic interactions (e.g., *yes*, *right*, *uhm*, *hmm*, *lol*, emoticons, and other visual and written expressions displaying online presence), which do not replicate the traditional communicative goals that L2 pedagogical approaches have long proposed. That is, students are faced with needing to express, negotiate, and interpret intended meanings in communication forms not often considered or seen before in the L2 classroom, in order to interact with other digital community members.

Digital tools have introduced fundamental changes into socially allocated genre and register conventions and challenged standard communication, pragmatics, and grammar taught in the L2 classroom; they have also, crucially, dissolved the strict separation between languages and minimized the importance of linguistic accuracy in favor of comprehensibility of the message and the ability to socialize in the online community (Kern, 2014). This expanded and modified vision of communication supports the idea of literacy learning as a social process, in which language students actively participate and enact social roles and negotiate their situated identities (Lam, 2000). Identity therefore cannot be presented as a fixed construct, but rather must be seen as evolving and plural constructs that are shaped and reshaped through projecting new identities in the way language and discourse operates in virtual spaces (Kilmanova & Dembovskaya, 2013). In the case of L2 students utilizing social tools, identities are not only transformed through their ongoing connection to the target language and to the social world, but are also mediated by textual and multimodal tools while embracing new literacies and communicative genres (Thorne & Black, 2011). As Norton (2000) explains, examining how students socially construct and transform identities over time and space allows researchers and educators to discover and map the student's language learning journey.

This chapter recognizes the relevance of bridging the gap between classroom and real-world practices in L2 teaching that values multilingualism and identity construction; it embraces the implications of technological change for L2 education. The connection between classroom and real-life practices will also help us understand how linguistic variation (e.g., dialects or different languages) could have a place in the L2 classroom; how we could see students' identities change and grow as we allow them to develop voices true to their linguistic backgrounds. First, we address how the prevalence of some languages over others and variations within languages have traditionally governed our L2 teaching practices. Then we explore how multicultural and multilingual learners have made use of and even capitalized on their knowledge of languages to establish themselves not only as L2 learners but as active members of their selected communities. Third, focusing more specifically on identity, we illustrate how, with the use of digital tools, L2 learners have found a forum to express their evolving identity in ways that traditional classroom methods did not. Fourth, we discuss the degrees and types of identity that digital tools encourage, according to their distinct affordances and the perceived or real audience for their texts. The chapter concludes with an activity illustrating how L2 learners can explore their multilingual and multicultural identity in the language classroom.

Linguistic Variation in Digital Texts

This world is truly multilingual, yet it is inequitably multilingual – a fact which is particularly apparent in the worlds of research and learning (Ortega, 2017). First, research has illustrated how in some ideologically monolingual societies many live with their bi/multilingualism as a liability, just because it does not conform to the rigid monolingual attitudes of mainstream society (De Houwer, 2015). In this context, it is important to understand the reality of our (often bilingual) L2 students' lives. The more students experience linguistic continuity across family, school, and outside world, "the less incentive they may have to pursue multilingualism" (Ortega, 2017, p. 288). On the other hand, as linguistic continuity decreases, the more multilingual people will become. In terms of L2 language settings this dichotomy suggests that while more privileged groups may see the learning of another language as a positive way to enhance their linguistic repertoire, for those who belong to less privileged groups, language learning can easily become a stigmatizing experience. They may live with their multilingualism as a liability and even be vulnerable to ridicule (De Houwer, 2015).

Second, in terms of language learning, there has been a double standard that reflects the symbolic value of different world languages and their variations (e.g., English as a *lingua franca* or dialects of the Spanish language compared with standard, official versions of Spanish). Certainly, there is a growing issue of status regarding world languages. Due to increasing globalization, command of English has "become an important symbolic good to many people, either through compulsory school study, or later during their working adult life, and often both" (Ortega, 2017, p. 287), perhaps to the detriment of other languages, which could seem less desirable or useful. In fact, when reviewing research into computer-assisted L2 language learning, Sauro (2016) noted the strong tradition that has emphasized standardized English over other languages. She further pointed out that computer-assisted language learning is globally referred to as computer-assisted *English* language learning. The perceived prevalence of some languages, in particular English, versus others implies that we are in a society that privileges certain types of bilingualism or multilingualism and some languages, and even some varieties of language, over others.

Third, as previously pointed out by Canagarajah (2007), the languages of a multilingual speaker and writer are interconnected (García & Li Wei, 2014). That is, even though we have labeled and separated languages at the conscious level, languages cannot be separated in authentic communication, since they create single communicative repertoires (Ortega, 2017), in what is called *holistic multilingualism* (Cenoz, 2013). In fact, Canagarajah (2013b) prefers to talk about translingualism (others prefer the term *translanguaging*), an individual's repertoire of semiotic resources used to cross linguacultural boundaries, given that "the term 'multilingual' typically conceives of the relationship between languages in an additive manner" (p. 7) and usually refers to language groups that occupy different areas in separation from others. According to Canagarajah's (2013b) notion of translingualism, dynamic exchanges between languages and communities need to take place in open environments where translingual practices already exist organically. In fact, we ourselves are quite familiar with the use of Spanish and English together to construct a text or chat message, either at the lexical or syntactic level. Therefore, since translanguaging is a widely used practice by many of us, perhaps, as Ortega (2017) suggests, we should "purposefully use translanguaging in language pedagogy" (p. 291). This is, no doubt, a thorny issue among L2 educators, who have been trained to be concerned with the correct use of the target language during instruction and students' production. However, as research in neurolinguistics tells us, multilinguals never employ one language only. Rather, as Ortega (2017) reminds us, multilinguals cannot engage in one-language-at-a-time processing, because all of their languages are co-activated for comprehension and production "regardless of a bilingual's intention to use one language only" (Kroll, Bobb, & Hoshino, 2014, p. 160). If that is the case, we should be asking why do we continually make such hard distinctions between the languages used in our L2 classrooms?

Language Choice

It is clearly a defective notion that students are predominantly monolingual speakers learning other languages as separate mental representations (Dooly, 2011). Speakers often display a multilingual competence in environments where the linguistic system is hybrid and flexible, and where communication is multimodal. For instance, language choice in globalized platforms such as Flickr is directly related to how writers seek to position themselves as either global or local participants (Lee, 2016).

The implications of multilingualism and translingualism have perhaps been more widely explored in the context of English as an additional language or L2 in online fandoms (Lam, 2000, 2006;

Black, 2006, 2009) or in the context of the digital wilds – that is, the "informal language learning that takes places in digital spaces, communities, and networks that are independent of formal instructional contexts" (Sauro & Zourou, 2017, p. 186) – rather than in the context of structured L2 learning (Blyth & Dalola, 2016; Kanno, 2003) or HL learning (Darvin & Norton, 2014). Within the first group of studies, research has shown that the co-deployment of English and local languages, for example, in fan fiction practices, produced by young people around the world, helped L2 learners "to project a cosmopolitan identity" (Lee, 2016, p. 125). The integration of different languages is very relevant to our instructional practices because in the traditional academic context, in a dominant language scenario, the bilingual speaker is often viewed from a deficit perspective, in which her/his first language is seen as something detrimental that will only interfere with acquisition of English.

That is, online fandom practices put L2 learners into a position usually barred from them in most English-speaking contexts, including schools (Black, 2006). For instance, Lam (2006) found that her Cantonese participant, Lee, exhibited and used his trilingualism – that is, English, the language of his school; Japanese, the language he was learning; and Cantonese, the language he used at home – to create his multilingual persona. His knowledge of Japanese provided him with standing as an integral member of the anime community as well as access to original anime videos in Japanese which he translated into English and Cantonese. In addition, his use of the different languages, as well as his technical skills and content knowledge, positioned him not in the lowly place of the language learner, but as an English speaker and as a user affiliated to an anime youth culture that is global and borderless (Lam, 2006). Similarly, Nanako, Black's (2006) native Mandarin Chinese speaker, who also developed a web page for anime, used the anime Chinese characters for bringing Mandarin, her first language, into her writing. That is, Nanako's extensive use of romanized Chinese, and even her minimal use of Japanese, positioned her both as an insider in the Asian realm of anime and as an effective user of several languages, including but not limited to English. In her writing, Nanako became an expert who made Mandarin accessible to speakers of other languages, by juxtaposing the English and Mandarin languages when providing translations of Chinese text. In contrast to her traditional school-based context, in this online context Nanako was admired by other English language users, whether learners or native speakers, because of the language mastery that enabled her to use multiple languages effectively in her texts (Black, 2006). Leppänen's (2007) L2 writers also displayed their knowledge of languages with a very distinctive linguistic purpose: they used their native language (Finnish) to perform a narrative function and their second language (English) to engage with fan fiction characters and in this way presented themselves as legitimate members of the English-speaking world.

That is, rather than regarding English as the only valid print-based medium and rather than following Western writing conventions and values, members of these anime fan fiction sites appear to display a positively multicultural attitude: they appreciate the use of multiple languages, diverse cultural views, and multimodal texts, illustrating the fans' solid adherence to global popular culture and underscoring the significance of communication, social exchange, and diversity in digital spaces (Black, 2006). Chen (2013) found that, using Facebook, her L2 learners began to act as multilingual writers: navigating across multiple languages and cultures, they constructed multiple identities – social, cultural, and professional – expressed through their various literacy practices, language choices, and selection of content.

The inclusion of multilingual and translingual practices such as these has been much less studied in the realm of L2 education. It does not come as a surprise that the FL classroom has been dominated by a "monolingual orientation" that rejects or discourages the use of any language in the classroom other than the target one. However, studies have shown that the first language can be put to good use as a cognitive tool to aid in the development of the

L2 in the classroom (Levine, 2011; Swain & Lapkin, 1995). The interchange of different languages also replicates our L2 learners' behaviors when using social media. Blyth and Dalola (2016), in an interesting study, sought to break away from these monolingual behaviors, typical in the L2 classroom, and to bring in translingual routines common in our learners' everyday literacy practices. Their study provides a rare example of translingualism in the classroom, making use of social media to escape the rigid prescriptivist views and monolingual bias typically found in FL classrooms.

Despite some resistance to change in this area, Blyth and Dalola (2016) overcame difficulties and experimented with providing a Facebook page to L2 learners, intended to serve as an enrichment space and tool for learning. In this Facebook page, instructors and students engaged in conversations with both Francophones and Francophiles, and participants were granted the freedom to play with the French language in novel and imaginative ways that are usually not encouraged in the traditional classroom. As time went on, the moderator of the page, who exhibited a high degree of translingual playfulness, served as a model of translingual practices, including code switching and lexical borrowing, to create a kind of "translingual disposition" among the participants. In this environment, learners played with and practiced their different linguistic repertoires, and they integrated various semiotic resources into the conversations to add meaning when presenting their multicultural and multilingual identities. That is, the inclusion of the moderated social network (Facebook) became an open space where translingual and non-traditional classroom practices were welcomed and even celebrated. As in the online fandoms, utilizing other languages and semiotic sources turned Facebook into a significant resource for digital users, even for those who are considered monolinguals and who have yet to learn to cope with situations of translanguaging (Lee, 2016). This pedagogical shift from prescriptive monolingual practices to multilingual/translingual approaches is in tune with our continuing quest to support and encourage our students' evolving identities and our exploration of digital practices in tune with multilingualism.

Evolving Identities: Acquiring a Voice

Although voice and identity could each merit their own section, considered together they allow us to explore their intertwined relationship (Tardy, 2016). Matsuda (2001) defines voice as "the amalgamative effect of the use of discursive and non-discursive features that language users choose, deliberately or otherwise, from socially available yet every-changing repertoires" (p. 40); Matsuda and Jeffery (2012) consider that individual and social voices are mutually constitutive and inevitable. That is, L2 writers can negotiate their viable positioning using the discourse resources available to them (Ivanič, 1998). Identity, or "how a person understands his or her relationship to the world, how the relationship is constructed across time and space, and how the person understands possibilities for the future" (Norton, 2000, p. 5), has also been understood as "the different subjectivities and subject positions they inhabit or have ascribed to them within particular social, historical, and cultural contexts" (Block, 2013, pp. 129–130). From this point of view, learning to speak a second language is a social rather than a cognitive phenomenon, motivated by the desire and the ability to increase the range of our existing identity as we explore other worlds (Kanno & Norton, 2003). It is within this social paradigm that identity and voice are linked to L2 students' discursive contexts and are built within and through discourses, highlighting the relationships between constructs of identity and voice and those of genre and discourse (Tardy, 2009). Although current studies have generally examined identity and voice within a single language, much can be learned from those studies that have explored the same topics in the multiple languages in which writers today compose (Tardy, 2009), design text, or move into digital genres where multimodality is key (Darvin & Norton, 2014).

From a social view of learning, language learning and identity construction are mutually constituted (Gee, 2003; Norton, 2000) given that L2 learning is seen as a way of positioning oneself within a larger context, since actual learning entails a process of becoming (Atkinson, 2001). Identity therefore has to be understood through the L2 learner's relationship to the world, to the culture of the language she/he is studying, and to the learner's assumed affiliation with that culture and its natives (Norton, 2000). This definition of identity implies that, rather than being static, identity is constantly renegotiated: "identity construction is a dynamic and discursive process in that individuals continuously engage in presenting, representing, and performing who they are in relation to others and in revising their sense of self while interacting and observing how others position themselves" (Yang & Yi, 2017, p. 100).This way of looking at identity implies that people are continuously co-constructing and negotiating their identity (although with individual and social restrictions) and will present themselves differently in different settings (Tagg & Seargeant, 2016). That is, identity development is not something which is done alone but is done in relation to the self and others in social situations (Bucholtz & Hall, 2005), a progression that is executed and mutually negotiated with the recognition, acceptance, or dismissal of other individuals (Butler, 1990). Identity is not the product of the individual mind or socially determined, but is rather socially and culturally formed and situated (Ivanič, 1998; Pavlenko & Blackledge, 2004). After all, either offline or online, identities are enacted to a certain extent through the alignments individuals make with varied groups, views, and cultural matters, and they are connected to "the communities with which they align themselves" (Tagg & Seargeant, 2016, p. 344). However, we need to understand that the shape and development of these alignments might take different forms in the L2 classroom, according to the affordances of the digital tools that writers choose to express them.

L2 Identity in the Digitally Mediated World

The burgeoning amount of current research on student identity, showing that it is negotiated and constructed in the process of interacting with others in online contexts, highlights the relevance of this topic for L2 learning. Whether they are examining HL learners, immigrant populations, or traditional L2 learners, multiple studies have found that language learners negotiate and renegotiate their identities through literacy practices in digital contexts, using their L1 and/or L2 and/or L3 (Black, 2006; Klimanova & Dembovskaya, 2013; Lam, 2000; 2004; Pasfield-Neofitou, 2011; Sauro, 2017; Thorne & Black, 2011; Yang & Yi, 2017; Yi, 2009). For instance, digital storytelling has often been used in the language classroom for heritage speakers, immigrants, L2 or multilingual learners to explore the construction of identity (Elola, Padial, & Guerrero-Rodriguez, in press; García Pastor, 2017; Vinogradova, 2014).

In this context, digital stories have allowed learners to explore their HL identity and to continuously reconstruct and perform their social identities in relation to the people they interact with (Hornberger & Wang, 2008). As Vinogradova (2014) points out, HL learners can negotiate their identities through the selection of topics, characters, and events in their narratives within or between groups based on language use. Hull and Katz (2006) found that through the construction of digital stories their heritage learner signaled an awareness and exercise of social power. Darvin and Norton (2014) also pointed to the digital story as a way for migrant communities to create bilingual narratives that allow for the creation of transnational identities that reflect multiple ideologies, communicative practices, and multi-stranded relations, in that way helping the marginalized to become active agents in their own learning (Chen, 2013). Focusing on English L2 university learners, García Pastor's (2017) learners presented the multiple, split, fluid, and clashing nature of their identities, as each moved from being a learner to becoming an intercultural speaker – a transition that allowed them to acquire an identity of competence that placed them on an equal footing to that of the native speaker. Overall, digital story creation allows both HL speakers and L2 learners to develop themselves as able writers, valued member of their communities, and even as social critics.

What is relevant from the studies on identity is the general understanding and acknowledgment that the digital medium brings new factors (e.g., extended audience, multimodality, multimedia) that influence the ways we form our identities in virtual settings (Graham, 2016). Just as we do not compose in the same manner or engage with genres using the same tools (Kern, 2015), the interactional patterns – how we relate with one another in the online community, and how we develop our identity – is not necessarily the same for every online platform (Graham, 2016). In fact, Graham cautions about the inclination to group all digital forms of communication together and that we should rather pay attention to the potential to unite people of all nationalities and backgrounds. To understand the extent to which users develop relationships and identities in online environments, Graham examined the perceptions of the audience, the limitations and capabilities of different media, and the goals of interaction – how people establish ties online when creating virtual communities. To those factors we would also like to add that the possibility of engaging with an eclectic range of semiotic resources will have a positive influence on how L2 learners present themselves as individuals.

Audience

In this context, *audience* refers to a group of socialized members of a collective—that is, an aggregate of people who are in some way connected or share ideas or opinions. This group of people become the intended audience in L2 online environments, even when they are not always known to the writer. For example, when posting in an online forum or in a blog, writers rarely know exactly who will receive their messages. This lack of knowledge governs the strategies used to establish the identity of writers or to gauge their alignments with interlocutors (Graham, 2016). King (2015), for instance, who examined how her Chinese students developed their own identity as writers while writing for Wikipedia found that because her students were writing for a community that lay outside the educational institutions, they found themselves writing as writers and not as learners. When developing their Wikipedia entries, students pitched their work to an unknown audience who were reading their work for the content of their messages and not for a grade. That is, there was a recognized authenticity in writing for Wikipedia that prompted a change in their perceived selves. Being aware of a potential audience, either the general public or a community, led students to make more advanced use of their knowledge and communication skills.

Although in a different medium, Chen (2013) also found that her multilingual writers negotiated their own identities in Facebook through the use of English and Mandarin, depending on their audience. Jane, for instance, who wrote for an international audience, composed in English, her L2, to build new global, local, cultural, and social identities and to reflect about her multilayered social (e.g., student, teacher, friend, researcher) and cultural repertoires (e.g., Chinese native, American participant, global citizen, local Tucsonian). Cindy, on the other hand, who wrote mainly for a Chinese audience, often shifted between Mandarin and English, negotiating language choices and cultural identities tentatively because she felt herself to be on the periphery of the host nation discourse and navigating uncertainly between her identities as a Chinese person and a struggling student. The identity constructions of Jane and Cindy illustrate how students negotiate their identities through the linguistic codes and symbolic resources familiar to multilingual learners, to position themselves personally and in relation to the world.

Therefore, the presence of a real or perceived audience will have an impact on how L2 writers' position themselves and how they construct and reconstruct their identities. As such, using a tool such as Facebook, which provides an environment where friends are invited or suggested, Facebook users write for a known audience, while in other tools such as in blogs, the blogger may be aware of both a close audience, those whom the blogger has in mind to understand her/his message, and a potentially infinite audience – those who, either accidentally or purposefully, come across a blog posting (Warschauer & Grimes, 2007). Whatever digital tools we use, they bring with them the opportunity that students may be heard and valued in an online environment: this will foster their sense of achievement and nurture their awareness of identity (Pasfield-Neofitou, 2011).

Digital Tools

In the same way that particular digital tools ought not to be associated with specific genres, "some digital environments lend themselves more readily to the interactive co-construction of identity and relationality than others" (Graham, 2016, p. 310). Graham distinguishes between those tools that allow users to project an identity in the virtual space, focusing on the individual rather than on the formation of group identities, and those tools that are more conducive to creating and establishing relationships among groups of people. For instance, Twitter allows users to tweet personal statements or retweet comments that they find noteworthy, which a follower can subsequently comment on or retweet. Identity in that case is constructed by the comments the user decides to make or retweet. Thus, we can claim that this platform allows for the construction of an identity but does not facilitate in-depth conversation and the negotiation of relationships. In contrast, when we interact in an online forum, messages are posted with the expectation that the ensuing interactions will connect people by sharing their thoughts and feelings as an expression of their constructed identities, generating exchanges that can foster alignment – or conversely, create distance.

The various digital tools are also associated with different contexts and language use. As such, Pasfield-Neofitou (2011) found that her participants in an Australian–Japanese encounter, who made use of a broad range of digital writing tools to communicate and create alignments among themselves, differed in their language selection and identity performance according to the tools they used. For instance, her Australian learners of Japanese used two social networks sites very differently to speak to their Japanese counterparts: they used mainly English on Facebook (which is based in the United States and operates as an English domain), and mainly Japanese on Mixi, which is based in Japan and therefore identifies as a Japanese domain. Thus, in the context of the L2 classroom, it is clear that the identities which are performed in online communication will likely vary, largely based on the tool employed (e.g., online forum, Twitter, blog) and will be shaped by the affordances of a particular tool and the social conventions that occur in specific forms of communication (Merchant, 2006). As we have pointed out, the digital tools we use are not neutral, and this factor influences the ways L2 writers will express their identity and assume roles – sometimes as experts (Black, 2009; Lam, 2004), sometimes as foreigners (and to be treated as such) in these virtual worlds (Pasfield-Neofitou, 2011). The tools themselves offer users built-in flexibility or, conversely, limitations to interactive communication.

Interaction

Writing about the goals of interaction, Schwämmlein and Wodzicki (2012) identified two types of identity relating to groups, *common-bond communities* and *common-identity communities*, and described how these are associated with different computer media (Graham, 2016). Common-bond communities are those in which individuals are connected because they are interested in one another. For example, in Facebook users tend to focus on the individual posts and friends' responses to an individual identity. In this case, users create and reinforce bonds between individuals, while the topic under discussion is less relevant. In common-identity communities, in contrast, individuals share a unifying interest, "which results in a more cohesive and unified group identity" (Graham, 2016, p. 311). Online forums, for example, in which users discuss a particular topic, are more likely to create common-identity spaces. However, this distinction between the two identity communities is by no means clearly drawn and is only regulated by the medium (Graham, 2016). In fact, what started as a common-identity medium can morph into a common-bond community. Further, a Facebook page or group can be created with the specific purpose of engaging users who are connected not by physical proximity and common background, but by individuals' affiliations based on mutual interests (Tagg & Seargeant, 2016) in what has been called "affinity spaces," which are defined as "a place or set of places where people affiliate with others based primarily on shared activities, interests, and goals, not shared race, class culture, ethnicity, or gender" (Gee, 2003, p. 67). In these contexts, users do not create deep social relations with unknown members in terms of topics, interests, or practices (Tagg & Seargeant, 2016). As Byth and Dalola (2016) remind us, although participation in an affinity space allows users to present an identity, this does not necessarily lead to a sense of shared identity.

For our purposes, we need to know more about how these types of communities are enacted in the L2 classroom. Regarding common-bond communities, social networking sites, such as Facebook or Mixi, are sites in which L2 students investigate who they are in relation to the world; in that process they adopt virtual "subject positions" (Kramsch, 2009, p. 20) for themselves through choosing and appropriating an eclectic mix of resources in the form of words, photos, videos, and other modalities. The idea is that the social nature of social media tools allows you to "write yourself into being" (Mills, 2011, p. 344) through the interchange of postings, feedback from the community, and continual reflection and self-appraisal. Students project themselves in relation to others in the networked space and define how they expect others to perceive them. In doing so, L2 learners exert their agency through the selection and adoption of language, discourse, social role, and negotiation of cultural values and beliefs.

On the other hand, online forums, which are often preferred by users engaged in fandoms, could be considered common-identity spaces. Lam (2006), for example, found that her student, Lee, worked with a group of peers having similar goals and interests on a project that was relevant and challenging. In fact, he referred to his fellow anime fans as "friends" who shared resources and helped each other with projects on the internet; Lee came to see himself "as part of a grassroots movement to democratize the enjoyment of anime music and movies" (Lam, 2006, p. 19). Black (2006) wrote about Nanako, who did not speak any English on arrival to Canada and who had difficulties in school and struggled to make friends. Yet she assumed the identity of a popular author in the online fandom community, which valued her for her specialized knowledge. Through her fandom interactions, Nanako progressed from being a novice in the world of fan fiction writing to achieving group recognition as an expert and knowledgeable fandom user. The important aspect in terms of identity development is that as Nanako became a more experienced fandom writer, well-known to all her readers, she began to disclose more about herself. In time, Nanako included her knowledge of different languages into her narrative and started to introduce themes and topics that were more closely related to aspects of her identity as an Asian female (Black, 2006). In this way, she was also creating a common-bound identity space.

Despite examples like those of Lee and Nanako, it would not be realistic to say that just because these types of platforms are offered in the classroom, L2 learners will inevitably develop and share their identities. Although it is true that each individual's identity is constructed through her/his interactions with others using social digital tools, early L2 research has also indicated that students are more interested in the academic uses of digital tools than activities they see as just socializing (Reinhardt & Zander, 2011). This finding suggests the need to explain to our students the importance of finding a balance between traditional academic ways of composing texts and new digital forms of communicating that allow them to present themselves not as L2 learners, but as L2 writers. We are fortunate to live in today's multilingual and multimodal communication world that more often than not offers the chance for all students to have a voice.

Multimodality

Multimodal texts are formed from a variety of cultural materials, such as images, video, sound, and games, demonstrating a range of literacies and cultural understandings that young users bring to the creation of these texts. Multimodality through "languaging" is also a meaning and identity construction phenomenon, since the student has to assemble linguistic signs and merge all of their language knowledge (including dialects) with their own semiotic repertoires, providing a glimpse of the unique identity of the user. With texts like online fan fiction there is the potential to construct fluid identities that can be negotiated and transformed over time (Thorne & Black, 2011). For instance, when working on his anime project, Lee became the curator of the anime works and resources submitted on the website, to the point that his fellow anime fans considered him an expert and began to ask him questions as a multimodal master. Through his activity in the anime world, he positioned himself as a "part of the global economy of semiotic workers" (Lam, 2006, p. 185), a prestigious identity that the school environment did not allow him.

When developing a digital story with the application of transformation and transduction, Nelson's (2006) students expressed their bicultural and tricultural identities by playing with images, sizes and text colors, and juxtaposing items from visual, written, and oral modes. In another example, Tardy's (2005) L2 graduate students demonstrated and projected their identities through careful arrangement of multimodal semiotic resources expressed in multimodal PowerPoint presentations. They purposefully selected visuals and color themes from scientific discourse to make a statement about their disciplinary affiliation, demonstrating their membership of their chosen professional group. Blyth and Dalola (2016) demonstrated how in their Facebook page participants used a variety of semiotic resources, including orthographic creative elements and the mixed modalities to present themselves as language learners and also proficient users. For the L2 practitioner, these studies show that the introduction of multimodal digital tools to the classroom should be seen as an extension of the range of written communication tools at students' disposal for developing and expressing their identity rather than as a distracting initiative that undermines the development of L2 writing skills.

Exploring Students' Identity through Fan Fiction Practices: Identity Awareness through Fan Fiction

Project Background

To provide learners with a space to develop or expand their linguistic and cultural identities, this semester-long project is carried out in a third-year Spanish heritage class. As part of the class, students are asked to reflect about their cultural heritage in terms of the larger community in which they live and of their immediate and extended family. In this process, they often read novels which they discuss in class; they also conduct interviews with family members and write accounts of their personal experiences. By adopting fan fiction practices, the instructor introduces an ongoing writing activity in which students develop the side stories for several of the characters from the English-written novel, *I am not your perfect Mexican daughter*, by Erika L. Sánchez (Sánchez, 2017).

Although critics of including fan fiction in the curriculum caution about bringing literacies practices outside the educational context into the learning context – because it might hinder learners' agency in their own creativity (Lin, 2015; cited in Sauro, 2017) – it was thought to be a good way for HL students to develop their writing skills, to explore social issues they face in their local environment, and to illustrate HL multilingual and transnational identities for their audience. The benefit of fan fiction practice is that it gives students access to a type of writing that re-imagines or improvises on stories and characters that other fan fiction authors have already written about (Jamison, 2013). Research has also suggested that fan fiction incorporates a variety of genres and styles of stories written in response to particular texts or media, focusing on literary and linguistic conventions of the source material (e.g., plot, theme, character, characters' dialects, speech style, word choice, etc.) with the intent to transform stories and characters into something that is new but recognizable at the same time (Sauro & Sundmark, 2016).

The project is made up of two main parts. First, students analyze the characters, including their own interpretations of them, and they identify the genre conventions and linguistic repertoires used in the novel. Because the novel is published in English, the students decide on the language or languages (e.g., Spanish or Spanish/English) in which they will re-imagine the stories. As they peruse fan fiction pages, students also consider the relationship between the textual, visual, and aural components of the wiki page and their communicative purposes. Second, in self-organized groups of three, students either collaboratively compose alternative storylines or they individually expand on storylines that were not developed in the original version. To consolidate students' understanding about the relationships between digital tools, semiotic resources, and the composing process, they complete individual bi-weekly journals on the development of their stories, using a combination of modes and resources. This project emphasizes sequenced activities that foster reflection, analysis, and responses to a literary text and that encourage language and identity awareness through literary analysis.

The instructor uses a free-use wiki platform, such as Wikia, for the project because of its ease of use for creating content. Using a wiki-based project modeled upon fandom also allows for the interpretation of the novel across course sections and institutions, either in one particular semester or across different semesters and years. Therefore, rather than being considered a one-semester assignment for a specific class, this project has the potential to be revisited – allowing students in subsequent years to revise and expand previous content based on their own understandings and experiences. While participating in this wiki, students are writing for a real audience (the current students and writers participating in the project) and also for a potential audience (the future readers and writers from subsequent courses). They are also creating and establishing relationships with other students while participating in a common-identity community.

Drawing on a Learning by Design instructional approach (i.e., experiencing, conceptualizing, analyzing, and applying pedagogical goals), this project allows HL students to engage in close reading and analysis of the themes and language of the novel, which, in turn, allows them to produce an original creative work that re-imagines or re-interprets the original text. Students also engage in a series of activities that allow them to analyze the novel, explore fan fiction sites, and heighten their awareness of the linguistic choices (language, dialect, grammar and vocabulary) that comprise a text on a fan page. Following this approach, students will create a multimodal text which is easily recognized as fan fiction and in which the topic of identity can be freely explored.

Phase 1: Connecting Experiences

The students read the novel by the fifth week of the semester. Following the Learning by Design model, the instructor focuses on experiencing the known – making connections between the theme of the novel and their own experiences – by preparing a series of activities in which students can brainstorm in groups to share their opinions on themes and characters, and also to reflect on how the story brings new understandings to situations they might have already known or heard about from their families and friends.

Students adjust the new information into their own experiences by working in groups and trying to pinpoint ideas that are new or not previously thought about. In class, they discuss issues of identity based first on their own experience, and then they are encouraged to look for new perspectives that result from the reading of the novel. The instructor helps students to develop an idea map in which their new experiences are incorporated into their analysis of the book. Students are then asked to reflect about these two types of experiences in class (known and new) in order to gain a deeper understanding of the novel.

Phase 2: Conceptualizing

There are two parts in this phase. First, guided by the instructor, students view and observe different online fandom sites in class like the ones in Archive of our Own in which users engage with different fandom characters' development. The act of classifying the different elements of a fan fiction genre moves students from the stage of experiencing to the stage of conceptualization that requires analysis of the genre structure and adoption of corresponding terminology. Second, both instructor and students focus on the analysis of the novel itself, discussing the notion of identity, how the main protagonist feels about not being the "perfect Mexican daughter," or to be what her mother would like her to be. Students concentrate on the main storyline as well as on the characters, including both less developed storylines and characters, with a special focus on their lexical choices, speech style, or grammatical idiosyncrasies of the characters to capture their voices (conceptualizing by theory). Instructors also emphasize the multimodality of the fandom by asking students to pay attention to textual and visual resources.

Phase 3: Analyzing the Texts

In this phase, students focus on two areas: (a) they concentrate on the linguistic aspects (e.g., syntax, grammar, lexicon of language(s)

Table 4.1. Schedule and Activities for the Writing Assignment: Identity Awareness through Fan Fiction

Phase	Schedule	Tasks
Phase 1	Weeks 4–5	Instructor • discusses with students the topic of identity based on their own experiences and new perceptions that came out of their reading of the novel. Students • share their perceptions about the novel regarding the identity issues of the different characters.
Phase 2	Week 6	Instructor • provides a few examples of online fandoms in their own L1 and in the target language; • discusses the novel with the students, focusing on identity. Students • view and analyze sample online fandoms examining the arrangement of textual and visual resources; • discuss the different storylines and characters they will develop; • converse about issues of identity.
Phase 3	Week 7–9	Students • divide themselves into self-selected groups of three and select the storyline that they would like either to develop or change; • introduce a description of their selected characters, providing the characters with their own personal spin if appropriate; • start to write in the wikis their own storyline analyzing the discourse strategies they will use to reflect their understanding of the novel; • include images, videos, or other media that support their stories; • focus on the content and use of the language(s) and combination of aural, textual, and visual modes to enhance written communication; • bring in stories from their families and their own personal experience or create their own fictional story. Instructor • provides (if needed) additional comments regarding content, structure, and form in the wiki pages.

Phase	Schedule	Tasks
Phase 4	Weeks 10–11	Instructor • with students' permission, showcases a few stories and provides guidance in the creative elements of the fan fiction piece. Students • finish developing their stories; • make sure that the story incorporates issues of identity and polish the integration of diverse modes (e.g., text, images, sounds).
Phase 5	Week 12	Students • create hyperlinks between the different storylines; • present their stories to the class; • compose an individual final reflection on what they have learned about the theme of the novel, identity and stereotypes regarding immigrants, as well as the genre of fan fiction.

choice) that, in conjunction with other semiotic resources, they will need for the stories they will create in their collaborative groups; and (b) they concentrate on analyzing the untold stories or storylines of less developed characters, or on the dismantling of stereotypes. Language choice and the ways students want to express their story are important, especially if we want our students to tap into their multilingual selves (as the main character also does). Once students select the storyline that they would like to change or develop, they write descriptions of their selected characters from their own personal perspectives, in the open wiki community prepared for study of the novel. These descriptions, however, are not final and, as they read and find out more about the novel and understand the characters in more depth, students will need to revise their entries. In this phase, students focus on linguistic issues, since capturing the voice and perspective of an already existing character asks students to pay attention to and mimic the lexical choices, speech style, or grammatical idiosyncrasies of their character. Students also reflect on other resources that can bring the multimodal text to life. This phase characterizes the way in which students put all of the modes of the text together, making sure they construct a multimodal text which considers the linguistic and non-linguistic repertoires that give voice to these stories and their characters.

Phase 4: Creating Their Own Stories

At this point, students create their own stories, ensuring that they are introducing fan fiction features appropriately – in other words, that they are creating a text that is easily recognized as fan fiction. Self-divided into groups of three, students work creatively, composing a multimodal text that illustrates the topic of identity in the fan fiction genre. At this point of the story development, students are granted autonomy in terms of plot, theme, character selection, literary devices, and point of view. As in Phase 2, students focus on linguistic aspects and also introduce stylistic devices, since the development of the argument requires them to apply narrative conventions, such as time or space. For this phase, to create inspiration for their storylines, students are encouraged to bring back into focus their personal stories and to interview family members and friends – in particular cases, some could mine their family stories about migration. Each group will also add images, videos, or other media to support their own stories.

With the permission of the students, in this stage the instructor shares a few examples of the students' work with the class to offer advice regarding the presentation of the content and discuss the structure and organization of the storylines and the character development. Students are asked to discuss issues of developing, mixing, and remixing aural, visual, and written sources in the wiki community and also to consider the impact of audience response.

Phase 5: Showcasing Their Stories

In the last phase, students will present their stories to the class so that they can discuss what they have learned from the novel and from creating a new story for one of the characters. To validate the nature of the fandom, students will create hyperlinks among the different stories so other readers can also participate as authors. Finally, the students will reflect on a number of issues: the process of working on fan fiction in relation to genre, working collaboratively, and developing linguistic skill as they provide voices to characters and share identities in the context of multimodal text creation.

Conclusion

This chapter has functioned as a space within which to reflect on how to be a multilingual, translingual, multicultural, and multimodal designer with the use of social tools. Although the main goal of L2 writing is to help students to become better writers, an aspect of instructional practices that should not be forgotten is the importance of nurturing the identity of our students and their unique voices. Globalization has directly or indirectly shifted pedagogical goals by alienating the monolingual perspective in educational curricula. By incorporating multilingual (and translingual) practices in the setting of class assignments, instructors may hear students' voices more clearly through alternative modes of communication as they guide students through their linguistic journeys. Through new approaches to pedagogy, L2 students can be empowered to decide for themselves how to communicate, how to position themselves in regard to their own values and those of others. They will gain the freedom to express themselves by choosing their preferred language, to explore the translanguaging phenomenon, and to choose digital tools that best express their own voices. The fact that the construction of identity evolves through a community with an audience inside and outside the classroom allows for more critical pedagogies that think outside the in-class education box. Our mission as L2 educators has always been to build a bridge between the classroom and the real world, so this is the right time to start the remodeling of our curricula, to review our sometimes obsolete approaches, and to be as creative as we want our students to be.

Ideas for Reflection and Discussion

1. Reflect on and discuss the challenges for instructors seeking to introduce multilingualism/translanguaging in the L2 writing curriculum. Explore in which areas of the writing curriculum you could support this phenomenon in order to validate your L2 students' identity and possibly their multilingual practices outside the classroom.
2. Translanguaging is a phenomenon that our L2 students often practice and play with in their daily lives. Explore the benefits that translanguaging could bring to L2 learners' writing practices. Suggest how L2 instructors could begin to include translanguaging opportunities in the L2 classroom.
3. The chapter has suggested that identity evolves through students' positioning regarding issues of multilingualism and multiliteracies. Explain how you would advocate to colleagues and administrators for curricular changes that would allow you to develop digital multilingual tasks that encourage students to express their identities and give voice to issues that concern them.
4. Think of three different digital tools (e.g., blogs, Twitter, Google Docs) and discuss their potential benefits for L2 students to express identity and to develop their writing skills. Explain the nature of identity that students could develop by reflecting on the role of a real or perceived audience and consider whether certain digital tools encourage a common-bond

community, a common-identity community, or an affinity space.

5. Considering the affordances of various digital social tools and drawing from Learning by Design pedagogy, develop an activity, broken down into phases, that encourages students' personal narratives connected to issues of identity, multilingualism, or student voice, and that questions the rigid monolingual perspective existing in educational settings or in another environment. Think of the extent to which your selected digital social tool encourages students to create ties with the surrounding online community and audiences.

Chapter 5

Becoming Digitally Literate: Rethinking Feedback and Revision

Creating Learning Moments

Feedback and revision have always been closely allied in L2 learning. The idea of signaling a problem and then asking students to reflect on it and attempt to solve it is conducive to scaffolding practices that have been shown to foster both linguistic and non-linguistic development. Provision of feedback is thus well-established in L2 learning environments as a practice familiar to both students and instructors. Until recently, feedback has usually focused on correction (local issues such as grammar) and writing conventions (global issues such as organization). The introduction of digital social tools has led to several changes: a redefinition of the role of feedback as applied to multimodal texts (covering both linguistic and non-linguistic features), new types of feedback, and new ways of providing it to suit digital genres and tools.

If emerging digital tools have been associated with multimodal genres, often unfamiliar territory to instructors, their advent has also brought the potential for novel and sometimes complementary modes of feedback not experienced before. Feedback has usually been delivered orally or in written form and sometimes in a combination of both. However, oral feedback was not usually recorded (e.g., a tutoring session) – it was ephemeral and thus regarded as less helpful than written feedback, which could be read and re-read. The reputation of oral feedback therefore suffered from its very impermanence. The introduction of digital tools, such as screencasting software now allows for oral feedback to be saved in a form that allows students to refer back to it. Further, screencasting now allows instructors to provide multimodal (written and spoken) feedback to students' written work (Ducate & Arnold, 2012; Elola & Oskoz, 2016). These tools allow for individualized feedback through digital formats which "can provide students with the most salient and actionable opportunities" (Kessler, 2016, p. 63). Also, digital tools such as blogs and Twitter offer a novel approach to written communication that suggests the need to modify our conceptions about types of feedback. The development of a blog entry, which potentially anyone can read, requires an understanding of the rhetorical and linguistic characteristics of the digital genre; and the composition of a tweet assumes knowledge of particular linguistic conventions and semantic connections, including the value of the hashtag feature. In these cases, keeping a balance between developing students' writing proficiency, and also addressing changing writing conventions through provision of effective feedback, could be challenging for the instructor.

In this context, (digital) feedback "not only takes into account the student but, ideally, also the tool, the interactions as well as the outcomes" (Caws & Heift, 2016, p. 131). Therefore, the roles of instructors and peers as feedback providers are "radically changing while, at the same time, becoming more critical," with the idea of helping students become "progressively digital literate[s]" (p. 133). Despite Caws and Heift's call, the increasing incidence of multimodal learning tasks has not yet greatly modified the way in which feedback is provided. Instructors still focus on language development rather than on all of the components of multimodal texts – except perhaps in the case of the digital story, a genre in which instructors have started to expand their focus to provide feedback on both linguistic and non-linguistic elements of the task. In fact, the study of feedback in the L2 research context has focused on its relation to students' revision success or lack thereof, on traditional views of feedback types and modes, and on the impact of digital texts and genres.

The aim of this chapter, therefore, is to provide a better understanding of the role and efficacy of feedback in L2 digital texts. We begin by alluding to some theoretical approaches that relate to digital feedback and then provide a rationale for expanding the use of feedback to cover both linguistic components and also other modes encountered in a multimodal text. The chapter also examines the affordances of various digital tools to create suitable environments for scaffolding, while challenging traditional pratices of revision within the digital context, and then offers guidelines for feedback in the L2 classroom.

Triggering Learning in the Digitally Enhanced L2 Classroom

Some researchers (Truscott, 1996; Truscott & Hsu, 2008) have questioned the value of feedback for L2 students (finding that they may improve from draft to draft but continue to make the same errors in new pieces of writing). However, recent SLA studies have confirmed that linguistic learning takes place not only from draft to draft (Ferris, 1999, 2006), but also when new pieces of writing are completed (Ellis, Sheen, Murakami, & Takashima, 2008; Sheen, 2010). Based on interactionist and sociocultural theories, writing improvement is regarded as evidence of language acquisition (Manchón, 2011) and of learning (Bitchener, 2012). Both theoretical approaches see feedback as an important element in teacher–student and peer-to-peer interactions, emphasizing the relationship between expert and novice and also as a useful way to increase linguistic knowledge (Lantolf & Thorne, 2007).

The *interactionist theory* sees the provision of feedback as an essential instructional practice for providing negative evidence, which highlights learning gaps and encourages the reorganization of students' linguistic cognition. Corrective feedback is used to draw students' attention to mismatches between the students' production and the target-like realization of the intended form (Sauro, 2009). By doing so, corrective feedback can stimulate the occurrence of noticing gaps, "the first step in language building" (Schmidt, 2001). According to the noticing hypothesis (Schmidt, 1990), for learning to occur, L2 students must attend and notice details and differences between their representation of their interlanguage in their produced output and the target language. When applying the interactionist approach to writing, Polio (2012) notes that input (re-reading a corrected or reformulated version), output (rewriting a corrected essay), and feedback (written correction) all have the potential to improve learning. Corrective feedback is therefore accepted as a technique that provides L2 students with the opportunity to notice differences between their interlanguage and the target language and thus foster learning. The action of "noticing" an error directs students to an awareness of their linguistic gaps (Swain, 2001) and its effect can be increased when L2 writers engage with problem-solving activities as they seek to express their ideas. In situations that require decision making, L2 writers generally come to recognize their limitations or gaps as they try to match their linguistic knowledge to the demands of formal academic writing (Swain, 1985).

Perhaps because of the emphasis on written chat and email communication in the initial uptake of widespread classroom technology, the first generation of human–computer-mediated (as opposed to automated) feedback studies analyzed types of feedback, types of errors, and students' responses (Sauro, 2009; Vinagre & Muñoz, 2011; Ware & O'Dowd, 2008). In the digital written environment, students can see their interactants' contributions, which might trigger the provision of alternative linguistic models and promote the noticing of linguistic gaps. The interactional adjustments that can take place "are seen as tools for facilitating comprehension and for triggering cognitive processes (e.g., noticing the gaps and uptake) deemed essential for L2 development" (Sauro, 2011, p. 380). Furthermore, the slower pace of asynchronous and even synchronous computer-mediated communication gives students more opportunity to focus on form (Vinagre & Lera, 2008).

For instance, in a series of studies into students' attention to form through the use of corrective feedback, Vinagre and Lera (2008), Vinagre and Maíllo (2007), and Vinagre and Muñoz (2011) noted that students working with email exchanges tended to focus on lexical and orthographical aspects for correction, while most syntactic structures and linguistic gains were treated by remediation, providing information that allowed students to revise or reject the wrong rule with which they were operating. Similarly, referring to blogs, Lee (2012) found that focus on form was very evident in expert–student interactions. The clarifications requested by the students showed students noticing gaps in their own writing and engaging in metalinguistic discussion. However, in one of the few feedback studies with digital tools that focused exclusively on writing – a study using screencasting software, which combines audio and video with the comment function of MS Word – Ducate and Arnold (2012) concluded that although the use of screencasting had a positive affective effect, there was only a small cognitive effect on how accurately students corrected their essays.

Sociocultural theory (SCT) also sees feedback as essential; however, given that feedback is regarded as a dialogic process between teachers and students or between expert and novice (Lantolf, 2006), its main strength rests on its potential to scaffold the student to a higher level, if pitched at the student's current proficiency level or *zone of proximal development* (ZPD). Storch and Wigglesworth (2010), who examined the efficacy of reformulations and coding symbols, noted that uptake and retention appeared to be affected not only by a linguistic factor (type of error), but also by affective factors (students' attitudes, beliefs, and goals). Regarding the use of feedback with the help of social tools, Oskoz (2009) confirmed that student-provided feedback in written online synchronous (chats) interactions helped fellow students to advance if the feedback was at the students' ZPD. Yet there is still a relatively small number of studies on technology-mediated feedback. This is surprising given that, as already suggested by SCT, higher forms of mental activity, such as planning and monitoring, are mental processes mediated by psychological or semiotic tools, such as language, or by physical tools and artifacts (Vygotsky, 1978). Lee (2010a), following a socio-constructivist framework, noted that in wiki interactions students were able to provide feedback and correction on sentence-level errors, rather than just on global issues.

Following an activity theory (AT) framework, Blin and Appel (2011) noted that students revised (with one exception) all of the peer feedback received through Group Forum or Google Docs that was linguistic or related to writing conventions. In fact, it is only recently that research has examined the effect of different feedback tools on L2 students' performance through this overarching sociocultural lens. Elola and Oskoz (2016), using screencasting and MS Word reviewing features, noticed that instructor feedback through MS Word was better accepted for grammatical and vocabulary issues, whereas screencasting was preferred for global issues, such as organization and genre-related structure. Also applying AT, Oskoz and Elola (2016b) examined how both instructor and peers provided feedback on linguistic and non-linguistic components of digital stories, which improved the digital story as a whole, making the multimodal storytelling text more cohesive and coherent.

Tailoring Feedback to the Digital Context

Before delving further into the provision of feedback via digital tools, we should examine what research and pedagogical approaches have told us regarding how feedback should be provided. The question of how to provide feedback remains a "subject of heated debate" (Cotos, 2011, p. 422). This discussion reverts to the earliest days of computer-assisted language learning (Godwin-Jones, 2018), when attempts were made to regulate the nature and volume of feedback on user interactions with tutorials (Otto, 2017).

Determining how to use feedback is difficult because of the complexity of factors that affect choice and use of the feedback, such as: (a) what linguistic aspect to focus on, especially, when students write in multilingual or translingual ways; (b) amount of feedback to be given; (c) students' proficiency level; (d) individual learning style; and (e) curricular context (Godwin-Jones, 2018). Additionally, although feedback might be digitally mediated and often L2 writing activities have been conceived with a communicative purpose and audience in mind, more often than not, the end reader has been the language instructor, who typically delivers feedback on both global (content, structure, organization) and local (grammar, vocabulary, editing) aspects of the writing process, generally replicating the feedback behaviors modeled by non-digital writing assignments. Further, digital corrective feedback has added complexity to the multifaceted issue of linguistic correction because the electronic options (e.g., using screencast) have expanded previous feedback possibilities substantially (Goodwin-Jones, 2018). The inclusion of social digital tools, which allow for a more easy integration of multimodality and expands the notion of audience (who can also provide feedback), questions previous practices. The emergence of digital genres and the use of new technologies for providing feedback as well as offering options for language choices and expression of writers' identity and voice force us to redefine our approaches to feedback.

To instructors considering the implications of feedback in the digital environment, we recommend careful examination of each of the areas shown in Figure 5.1. Posing several questions impels us to reflect not only on the nature of feedback and how we understand it, but also on how feedback should be used and what instructors and students should expect from it.

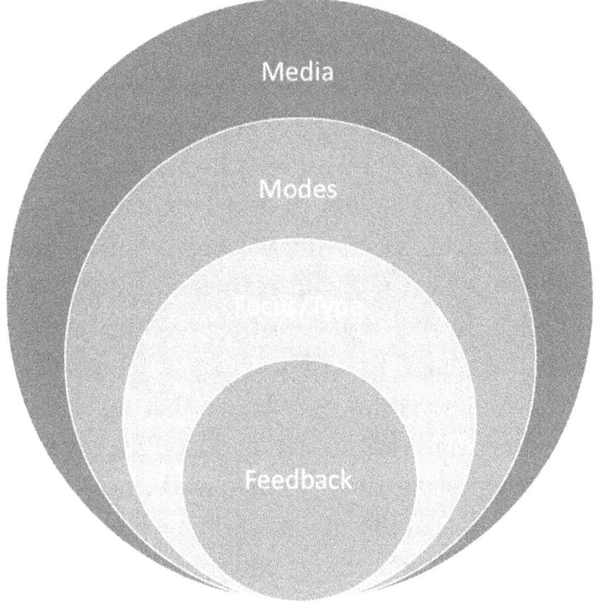

Figure 5.1. Feedback Considerations

Focus of Feedback

The focus of feedback refers to the type of linguistic issue such as grammar, vocabulary of the L2;[1] rhetorical aspects of L2 writing (e.g., content, structure, and organization); and non-linguistic issues, such as the integration of images and sound, as in the case of digital storytelling or blogging. Before providing linguistic or non-linguistic feedback, instructors need to match the focus of the feedback with the L2 curricular goals. It is essential for them to consider the students' proficiency level, as well as the objectives of the tasks, so that the feedback focuses on one, a select few, or all of the following features: grammar; vocabulary; orthography; writing conventions such as genre, structure, and organization; register; and/or selection and integration of two or more multimodal elements, such as sound, image, and text. For instance, a fourth-semester language course may place emphasis on improved use of the past tense. This curricular goal can also be achieved if the choice of genre supports the same linguistic use, such as using the storytelling genre to compose personal narrations in the past tense.

Another issue that is less frequently considered because of the linguistic standardization in language courses is the idea of linguistic variation and the use of translanguaging, as in the case of heritage language and multilingual learners. Instructors are not normally prepared to work with learner languages that are not consistent with a formal register or a prestige variety. Yet they find themselves wondering how to provide feedback in a useful and respectful manner for a population that may have minimal familiarity with metalinguistic terms describing parts of speech or error codes (Mikulski, Elola, Padial, & Berry, 2019). Students' linguistic variation and translanguaging behaviors support a heteroglossic approach (i.e., addressing multiple varieties of language). These linguistic practices push instructors to provide feedback that is accepting of variation when they are teaching features of the prestige variety. It is important for L2 teachers to give feedback on students' writing without stigmatizing other varieties, especially when students have the greatest communicative competence in a local or contact variety (Valdés, 1997). A heteroglossic approach becomes even more complex when it involves digital genres that do not include only written text and that reflect the HL learners' translanguaging and multimodal reality outside of the classroom (Mikulski et al., 2019).

Additionally, an important aspect of feedback provision is the instructor's decision about whether the feedback is targeting one or a few pre-established errors or whether all errors in the text need to be targeted. This decision leads consequently to two types of feedback: corrective feedback that is *focused* (i.e., pre-selecting linguistic errors to help students with specific language constructions), as shown in Ducate and Arnold's (2012) study, or *unfocused* (i.e., provision of feedback provided on all types of errors observed in the text), as in Elola and Oskoz's (2016) study. Yet, the importance of feedback choices does not lie in the dichotomy of the choices. For instance, the issue may not rely on deciding between a focused (error categories predetermined)/unfocused (error categories not predetermined) type of feedback, but rather in the complementary use of the different types of feedback that instructors can provide to scaffold students during the process of correction or revision. For example, instructors might use both direct and indirect feedback because they deliver different but complementary results (Ferris, 2010). It is then safe to say that the type of corrective feedback is significant because of its impact on students' ultimate revision success or lack thereof. Clearly, understanding the diverse types of feedback with varying degrees of explicitness can help the instructor to map how feedback is delivered to suit different purposes.

Corrective feedback, however, is not, or should not be, the only feedback instructors provide for students' digital writing. Apart from linguistic development, instructors usually need to provide feedback on content and genre structures. When the student task replicates traditional genres, such as argumentative or expository essays, instructors' digital feedback has generally followed traditional feedback behaviors. For instance, in the first studies examining wikis in the L2 classroom, Arnold et al. (2009), Lee (2010a), and Elola and Oskoz (2010a) provided feedback on content and/or genre structure and organization.

As instructors are becoming more at ease with newer digital tools and understand the impact that both linguistic and non-linguistic elements have on the L2 composing process, they are moving away from feedback comments targeted to more traditional genres, such as an argumentation or narration in the wiki; they now are beginning to use feedback aligned to semiotic resources or multimedia to comment, for example, on the development of a digital story. They may decide to provide feedback on whether chosen images correspond to the topic of the story, whether there are too many explicit rather than implicit images, whether the sound/music enhances the story or obstructs it, whether the music volume overpowers the voice of the narrator, or other types of feedback tailored to a digital multimodal text (Oskoz & Elola, 2014, 2016b; Yang, 2012).

Also, very relevant and topical is the idea of how instructors can provide feedback to students who disclose in their writing personal details of their backgrounds as heritage, multilingual, or translingual speakers. The question about the focus of feedback would then expand normative views based on the languages used, and instructors would have to recognize the linguistic features that are acceptable within wider linguistic parameters in which use of multiple languages should take precedence over "correct" use of the languages. The focus of the feedback in that case moves beyond the formal academic expectations we have in place. Arguably, altering the type of feedback instructors provide can change the way students see themselves and will make them more likely to view their texts as valued contributions in the classroom. If students' agency in the provision of feedback is consistent with the academic writing goals of the course, instructors will ensure rich and varied practices and experiences.

Some questions about focus of feedback that instructors might consider are:

- Are the goals of the curriculum to emphasize academic writing or to develop a range of digital genres that match L2 students' out-of-school life?
- Should I provide feedback on content and genre structure first so they can revise a first draft, just the linguistic aspects, or both at the same time?
- Should I provide feedback on translingual writing, or is the purpose of the task to master the target language only?
- How can I provide feedback on multilingual text features to empower and strengthen students' voices and identities?
- How do I provide feedback that addresses the creation of meaning with both linguistic and non-linguistic resources?

Provision of Feedback

Provision of feedback refers to the manner in which the feedback is given, for instance, direct feedback, such as explicit reformulations, or indirect feedback, such as posing questions or underlining the text. Most L2 instructors, concerned with linguistic development, will want to choose between types of corrective feedback, such as explicit or direct, and implicit or indirect. As seen in Figure 5.2, instructors can provide feedback with different degrees of explicitness. They can choose from providing very explicit and direct feedback, such as reformulation and metalinguistic information, to less explicit feedback, such as indicating in the margins the number of errors per line or circling the errors without explanation.

The advantage of *direct feedback* (reformulation with or without metalinguistic explanations), is that it may (a) reduce confusion that students might feel when they do not understand why they have made an error, which often happens with lower-level students (Ferris & Roberts, 2001); and (b) facilitate the revision process when students feel they do not have sufficient information to resolve complex errors (Roberts, 1999). *Indirect feedback* – coding, underlining, or noting the number of errors per line – on the other hand, requires students to engage in problem solving, and so may cause reflection, thus promoting long-term acquisition. For learning to happen, though, students first need to notice their error themselves. Once the error has been noticed, feedback may encourage students to participate in hypothesis testing (Bitchener, 2008), which according to Ferris (2002) will promote internal processing and ultimately the internalization of correct forms and structures.

Direct or Explicit

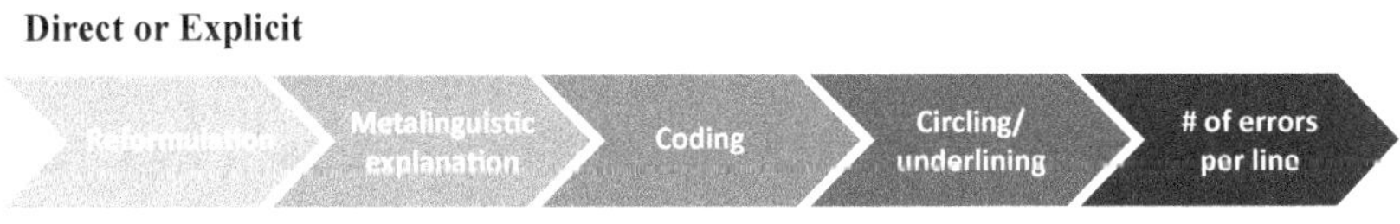

Indirect or Implicit

Figure 5.2. Types of Feedback

Instructors might have to consider carefully other issues the student may encounter with feedback. As Chandler (2003) pointed out, the greater cognitive effort required of students when provided with indirect feedback (although conducive to long-term acquisition) might be offset by the delay in knowing whether their hypothesis is indeed correct. Although the distinction between implicit vs. explicit written feedback has been questioned because, after all, all written feedback is explicit (Ellis, 2009; Sheen, 2007) in the sense that it is written down, Li (2010) insists on the importance of the implicit/explicit continuum. This continuum describes reformulation (correctly rewriting what the student had written) and metalinguistic feedback (explanations about the error) as the most direct (i.e., most explicit) types of feedback, whereas coding, circling, and underlining are indirect (i.e., least explicit, or most implicit) because the recipients of the feedback need to correct the errors themselves. Studies in digital tools have also examined approaches to feedback provision in the online environment. For example, Sauro (2009) used recast (less explicit) and metalinguistic (more explicit) feedback in written chats with EFL students to explore the efficacy of the different degrees of explicitness in feedback. Regarding online tutor practices, Samburskiy and Quah (2014) found that recast and text enhancement were the most frequently used feedback types.

Independent of what what type of digital feedback has traditionally been provided, some questions that can guide instructors are:

- Should I continue using indirect feedback with lower-proficiency students if they do not understand what I want them to change?
- What feedback should I use with higher-proficiency students about linguistic aspects we cannot cover in class?
- What corrective feedback should I use in cases in which the students' "errors" cannot be explained by the standard rules (e.g., this is the way it is spoken rather than written)?

- What feedback should I use if I am teaching a class of mixed-proficiency learners?
- How can I combine explicit and implicit feedback in areas not related to linguistic issues?
- How can I provide feedback on non-linguistic issues such as sounds and images? Is it better to indirectly suggest that something is not working and let them think of solutions, or should I tell them why it is not working and help them with modifications?

Mode and Tools for Giving Feedback

Feedback mode and tools refers to whether the feedback is provided in oral, written, visual (images, icons) mode or mixed modes, and what tool (e.g., use of track changes or recording software) we can utilize. Although research has been performed into feedback by mode (written vs. oral), or by means of different technology media (e.g., screencast video vs. MS Word), instructors need to have a good grasp of the tools' affordances when targeting different types of errors. That is, instructors need to plan how to address the different linguistic and non-linguistic issues, considering the scaffolding potential of each tool. New digital tools offer important benefits for feedback: they range from sophisticated programs developed by testing services (Lavolette, Polio, & Kahng, 2015), to screencasting software (Ducate & Arnold, 2012; Elola & Oskoz, 2016), chat and comment function of Google Docs for direct and indirect feedback (Shintani & Aubrey, 2016), and MS Word, of course, with its powerful track changes in-built tool for giving feedback in an asynchronous way (Ducate & Arnold, 2012; Ene & Upton, 2014; Elola & Oskoz, 2016; Ferris, 2012; Ho & Savignon, 2007) and in synchronous way (Ene & Upton, 2018).

Clearly, the mode and the tools are intrinsically linked when providing feedback. The use of screencast (visual and oral) for giving feedback on errors can be more beneficial than MS Word (written) because the oral explanation resembles a conversation and shows care on the instructors' part (at least, this is what students perceive): students can also play it over and over until the information is fully understood (Ducate & Arnold, 2012). Other venues less explored, such as online written corpora, used to provide students with a number of linguistic repertoires from which to select a correct answer, can also be used to provide feedback. Siyanova-Chanturia (2015) and Strobl (2017), for example, indicated that students were able to improve the use of collocations and cohesion devices. However, in terms of feedback, the value of digital tools is not limited to their own special affordances – it lies in the ability to use two or more tools.

By such combination of tools we can provide multimodal feedback that can help students to attend to both global and local issues. For example, instructors can use chats or screencast for feedback directed to global language issues, such as content, structure, organization, sources and the style of communication that suits the chosen genre. Another example relates to the different features of wikis and chats – differences which demonstrate that each tool has its place and offers different affordances to incorporate instructor feedback to students. Yet studies that have examined bimodal digital feedback (e.g., written feedback in MS Word vs. oral feedback in screencast mode) are still scarce (Ducate & Arnold, 2012; Elola & Oskoz, 2016). Elola and Oskoz's (2016) study, which used the same type of feedback as Ducate and Arnold's study, also showed that better revisions of content, structure, organization, and accuracy were made when students received oral e-feedback via screencast videos. Students themselves, however, suggested that they generally preferred oral screencast feedback for content, structure, and organization, but MS Word feedback for linguistic issues.

There are as yet few studies in this area, but those mentioned above suggest the potential benefits of providing computer-mediated feedback. Common to all of these digital tools is their capability of handling instructor–student feedback more flexibly than traditional feedback techniques. Thefore, when thinking about the tool and the mode of feedback provision, some questions instructors might ask are:

- How does student proficiency level, translanguaging behavior, or use of nonprestige language varieties influence the tool I might choose to provide feedback?
- Which tools can benefit my students' understanding of the linguistic and non-linguistic feedback I am proposing?
- How can I use screencast both effectively and efficiently? What do I focus on, the multimodality of the text, the images, the voice in the text, the genre structure, or some combination of these features?
- Which tool can better guide my students to concentrate on the 'text' as a whole rather than on local issues?

Peer Feedback in the L2 Classroom

Peer feedback is a technique that many instructors commonly use in L2 classes and that is generally modeled by the instructor's feedback practices. It provides students with opportunities to construct and polish their knowledge and skills through social interactions in virtual environments. These are principles that relate to social constructivism in the sense that meaningful interactions in a learning environment have the potential to enhance sharing perspectives and experiences in communities of practice (Birch & Volkov, 2007; Vygotsky, 1978; Wilson & Stacey, 2004; Woo & Reeves, 2007). Furthermore, the degree of interaction that digital social tools bring to the L2 classroom, where the students often interact with one another and with the wider community, provides a deeper understanding of the use of feedback. In fact, one particularly useful affordance of the interactive tools is their potential for collaborative dialog between experts and novices. The advantages of peer feedback include its potential for providing better social or affective support than face-to-face interactions (Lee, 2015); being less threatening than face-to-face interactions (Chen, 2016); developing a sense of audience and text ownership that validates the task (Lee, 2015); augmenting range of vocabulary (Chen, 2016); and fostering successful revisions (Arnold et al., 2012).

Although the benefits are clear, the potential for peers to provide inaccurate or unhelpful comments to co-authors or peers might exist (Cho, 2017; Liao, 2016; Tai, Lin, & Yang, 2015). Some instructors and students have expressed concerns about working with peer feedback for several reasons: (a) the extent to which, when working collaboratively, students provide comments to one another (collaboration) or rather focus on their own errors (cooperation); (b) the extent to which students feel comfortable giving feedback on form, and to certain extent on meaning; and (c) how successful students are at providing feedback to one another. However, looking at peer feedback in the digitally mediated world, we can see how L2 learners are learning new ways to provide formal and informal feedback to each other's writing in digital genres using digital social tools.

The central pedagogical question to ask is how digital tools might facilitate L2 writing development. Regarding electronic feedback in writing, Tuzi (2004) found that electronic feedback from instructors, students, or external audience, submitted via a purposefully created for the class website, was suitable for adding information or drawing attention to a particular section of text. In the case of MS Word, AbuSeileek and Abualsha'r (2014) found that the track changes function in MS Word was an effective tool for peer-to-peer feedback due to its efficiency in flagging and highlighting errors, and it performed better than traditional ways of marking error by providing recasts or metalinguistic information. Perhaps Yeh (2014) is the author who has studied the most inclusive integration of writing tools. She used EtherPad (a web-based collaborative real-time editor) in conjunction with a reflective essay in which students were able to co-author and edit a text document simultaneously. All of the participants' contributions could be viewed in real time, and students could display each text in their own color while simultaneously using the written chat to discuss the writing process, allowing for provision of feedback and subsequent revision. In this study therefore Yeh showed how the integration of selected tools during the writing process helped students to provide peer-to-peer feedback. Shih's (2011) study also confirmed that peer-led practices, such as peer comment and feedback, had the potential to enhance students' learning.

Although these studies showed how peer feedback is useful, the peer feedback given still resembles the feedback given on more traditional academic texts. When looking at texts that include multimodal features, the type of feedback given can change accordingly. For example, the use of the Facebook platform allows learners to work peer-to-peer; they can add written or multimodal comments using features such as emoticons (Shih, 2011) or could be asked to improve the quality of an original text (Tseng & Tsai, 2007) by reviewing each other's texts. The beauty of bringing in social tools is that they allow users to provide feedback in a more informal, perhaps more organic, manner. In Facebook, for instance, feedback can be provided simply by the use of the "Like" button with its variations (e.g., smiley or sad faces) or other alternatives, such as one-click rating and voting. This one-click feedback feature is of interest because it enables a social communicative action in the form of a minimal reply in a specific rhetorical situation – thus creating what is called genre chains (Swales, 2004) that can be unary (like), binary (thumbs up/thumbs down), ternary (yes, no, maybe), or take the form of schemas based on settings, such as rating a product from zero to five stars (Müller, 2011).

Feedback can also derive from a larger external audience. Such responses may differ from classmates' feedback but can also be multimodal, including video or audio clip commentary or other forms of digitally mediated responses. That is, in dynamic online environments the interaction with the audience might become both multilayered and multimodal because writers and readers have the agency to choose a variety of modes, forms, and modalities, and to use an open-ended multi-user communication channel (Andrews & Smith, 2011) where meaning can be negotiated by all parties.

When helping learners to provide effective feedback to one another, questions that instructors might use with their students in a pre-feedback training session include the following:

- How do the linguistic and non-linguistic elements employed reflect the characteristics of the genre you and your classmates are following for this task?
- What type of content and linguistic and non-linguistic elements do you expect to see in the task?
- Are the vocabulary, syntactic choices, and modes of the chosen language(s) working in the text?
- Can you see that this text expresses your classmate's voice by the choice of language (e.g., vocabulary), images, sounds, or tone (in a digital story)?
- Can you understand the multimodal text as an entity or is there a mismatch between the words, the images, the movement, and the sounds?
- How can you praise your classmates' work without using written words?
- To what extent does this multimodal text mirror the types of texts that you will use outside the classroom?

Although digital tools are bringing many interesting possibilities to the peer feedback process, we should not ignore the usefulness of face-to-face feedback when used in conjunction with multimodal texts. For instance, in the world of digital storytelling, the use of story circles – small groups that discuss a digital story at different stages of its development (Lambert, 2012) – can serve to highlight the different stages of the digital story creation: Is the purported story worth telling? Should it be told differently? Which visuals and audio could complement it? How do selected semiotic resources affect the pace of the story? What tone or spoken accent should the oral narration aim for? Students should try out different modes in feedback sessions, and even though technology may be helpful, face-to-face interaction should also be considered a useful and often suitable technique. The guidance of the instructor is essential to enable students to mine the full potential of a multimodal narrative piece.

Below are some possible questions for students to think about and to pose to their classmates in the story circles:

- What is the story about? Why is this particular story being told? Can you elaborate on these points (if this is possible without making your classmate uncomfortable – remember always to start your feedback with "If this were my digital story, I would….")?
- Who is the audience of this story (i.e., family, friends, classmates, local or global community)?
- What images did you choose and why? How are your images arranged? In what order do they appear? Is there any logic to them?
- What rhetorical, linguistic, and multilingual conventions do you use? If you are using more than one language, why are you meshing those languages in the script? (This could be a good moment to ask if it works well or if some changes need to be made.)
- What audio components did you choose? Music, silence, sounds? Why did you arrange them in the way you did?
- What do you think of your voice and the way it sounds? (This could be a good moment to discuss whether the pace is too fast or the voice too low, or whether the voice and music clash.)
- What do you like about this digital story that other students might try to emulate in their own work?

(adapted from Adsanatham, 2012)

After the circle session, students consider peer and instructor feedback and then complete their digital story scripts; they re-assess their selected images and music, searching for additional visual, audio, or musical sources, and discarding others. These sessions are scaffolding moments that can benefit everyone in the story circle at both linguistic and non-linguistic levels as well as at the performance level. Students might feel less reluctant providing feedback because they are working with genres they are familiar with in their daily lives. As Yu and Lee (2016) noted, the benefits of peer feedback in a story circle can be increased by pre-training students in group interaction strategies – for example, asking them to share positive peer feedback experiences and to identify different approaches to giving peer feedback, even involving the use of their L1.

It is safe to say at this point in the chapter that we have found that adding peer feedback to teacher feedback seems to be the most successful method, either because such feedback is enriched by additional peer activities (Tai et al., 2015) or because peer feedback can benefit from additional instructor feedback (Cho, 2017). Also, each type of feedback can target different issues: for example, peer feedback can be used during the development phase of the texts, or instructor feedback can be given at the end of the writing project.

Revising with Diverse Digital Tools

In addition to the feedback provided either by the instructor or the peer, there is also need to examine what L2 learners do when revising their own work based on their comments. There are three aspects that need to be considered when looking at revision practices:

How do students approach revision?
What types of revision are needed?
How do students perceive the feedback they receive?

Students' Approach to Revision

The social and collaborative nature of many of the new social tools have promoted collaborative practices in which feedback and revision can add significant value. A closer look at these practices reveals that students' engagement behavior is more cooperative than collaborative. For example, Kessler (2009) found that when his students worked with wikis on traditional essays, they were more focused on self-editing than on peer-editing. Arnold et al. (2009) found that, overall, students preferred to self-edit their individual sections rather than editing their classmates' work: that is, when content has been created by others, students are hesitant to make meaning or even form changes. The type of task, however, might also affect students' collaborative or cooperative behaviors. Arnold et al. (2012), who specifically examined the extent to which students worked in collaboration vs. in cooperation, found that students behave differently according to the nature of the task: the class that read a novel and then wrote about it worked more cooperatively than the participants who created entries on the topic before reading the novel, in an attempt to provide opportunities for instructor and peer-led feedback. These interactions, whether instructor–student or between students, allow students to immerse themselves in a topic and help to establish a feedback practice that ultimately increases more collaborative revisions. Thus, it is likely that it is the way we ask students to engage in feedback and revision that affects the quality of their revisions.

The Types of Revision Needed

A major focus in much classroom-based research has been on students attending to form or meaning revisions. This emphasis on form and meaning was a by-product of the usual type of traditional essay set in L2 classrooms. The emphasis on form and meaning revisions is understandable, since multimodality had yet to come to the fore in the L2 classroom; however, such a dichotomous view (form vs. meaning) does not provide the full picture of students' revision behaviors. As we try to optimize the benefits of students' own revisions, it is clear that the tools and the genres themselves play a significant role in our students' revision practices.

If we look at Google Doc and wiki studies, for instance, we see that students all show the greatest interest in the development of content. After all, the very purpose of writing is to communicate an idea to an audience, so it should not be surprising that students tend to pay more attention to meaning than to form. Kessler (2009), for example, found that the overall tendency among his students was to focus on meaning, and often even in terms of design and style aspects, rather than form. Even in those cases in which form was made central to a revision, the revision was often accompanied by changes to content. It is evident that in this case the task itself influenced how the students perceived the relative importance of content and form. That is, if students are required to talk about a concept, such as culture, it is quite likely that they will put their effort on the development of the content rather than on the accuracy of their writing (Kessler, 2009).

It appears, therefore, that that as long as form errors do not impede communication, students would rather focus on the elaboration of meaning. Similar results were reported in Aydin and Yildiz's (2014) EFL wiki study, in which students made more peer corrections in the argumentative task than in the informative and decision-making tasks, yet still concentrated more in meaning than on form. Abrams' (2016) Google Docs study with first-year German students revealed that although students were able to attend to both, they tended to prioritize meaning over form despite their low level of proficiency. Perceived reluctance on the part of the students to edit their partners' texts (Aydin & Yildiz, 2014; Kessler & Bikowski, 2010; Lee, 2010a) might also be due to students feeling more comfortable expanding, elaborating, or asking for clarification of the existing text rather than on correcting errors or commenting on ideas.

Moreover, focusing on content and meaning does not necessarily mean that students do not pay attention to solving linguistic problems. For example, when examining the overall performance of students in the wiki, Arnold et al. (2009) found that although the most common types of revisions were meaning-making changes, these were followed closely by formal revisions and then by stylistic revisions. Lee (2010a) found that her students attended to both content and formal errors at the sentence and word levels in the wiki. Similarly, Oskoz and Elola (2014) noted that students paid attention to both form and meaning; however, the type of genre chosen affected the linguistic area of focus (i.e., different types of complexity issues between an argumentative or expository essay). Therefore, thinking about the type of task can help the instructor to anticipate the type of revision students may tend to follow. There is a great opportunity for the instructor to prescribe sound guidelines for the type of correction, revision, and editing they expect from the students, because those choices are more important than whether the revision is about form or meaning.

The studies referred to above provide a more complex view of students' attitudes to revision than we might initially expect. Finally, to complicate matters even further, students will be bound to encounter the issue of how to revise non-linguistic or multimodal resources that may need to be adjusted or better integrated to fully develop meaning. Most studies at this juncture have noted an improvement in students' management of multimodal resources; unfortunately, we have not found empirical evidence of such improvement. Nevertheless, we can say that students show a tendency to respect their peers' feedback on non-linguistic as well as linguistic text components.

Students' Perceptions

Given that students' beliefs and attitudes are "a significant contributory factor in the learning process and ultimate success" (Bernat & Gvozdenko, 2005, introduction, para. 2), students' own perceptions cannot be overlooked when addressing the role of feedback in the FL classroom (Arnold & Ducate, 2012; Cho, 2017). Yet students' perceptions on the use of computer-mediated feedback are still largely unexplored. In terms of medium, Tuzi (2004) compared oral face-to-face feedback to written electronic feedback provided on a course website he created. Although students tended to prefer oral feedback, they made more revisions after receiving the written electronic feedback. Similarly, when comparing oral vs. written computer-mediated feedback, both Ducate and Arnold (2012) and Elola and Oskoz (2016) found that students preferred the oral screencast method. Although there were no statistical differences in the success rate of error correction between both types of feedback, students felt the instructor cared more about their writing and could understand the feedback provided better when using the screencast option. Ducate and Arnold concluded that despite not having any marked cognitive effect, use of the screencast software had a positive influence and could be a motivational force in the L2 classroom. However, it is important to realize that, as Strobl (2017) noted, the form of feedback students prefer might not actually be the most effective. This clash suggests the crucial role of training in feedback modes so that students can become knowledgeable about new ways of L2 learning.

Feedback in a Multimodal Writing World: Peer and Instructor Comments in Digital Storytelling

Project Background

The project involving provision of peer and instructor feedback in digital storytelling is a semester-long endeavor in a third-year semester class, for example, in a HL class, in which students complete a digital story to present an intercultural experience. Following previous research on feedback, the instructor wants to combine the digital story circles for students to discuss and receive feedback about their stories in class (Lambert, 2012) with other tools that allow him to provide feedback focusing on global (content, structure, organization) and local aspects (grammar, vocabulary) of the language (Ducate & Arnold, 2012). Guided by instructor and peer feedback, students work with different degrees of multimodality to create a digital story and offer bimodal feedback (oral and written) on a multimodal text (digital storytelling) as they develop and improve their stories.

Screencasting software and Google Docs are the tools chosen for the project because of their potential to be media-rich as well as to promote classroom interaction and collaboration. A program like Screencast-O-Matic (free for use up to 15 minutes) is a good choice because of its ease of use. In addition to recording voice, it also marks with a circle those parts of the text on which the instructor hovers the mouse when providing feedback. Using Google Docs allows the instructor to provide unfocused indirect feedback using the symbol system. Google Drive is a platform that allows students to upload their documents as well as allows the instructor to upload the large screencast recordings. In terms of linguistic development, using a genre-based approach framework, students are engaged in a series of activities that allows them to (a) extend content knowledge of the topic and (b) develop an understanding of genre by analyzing digital stories. Students learn how to identify key structural features of the genre of storytelling and how to make linguistic choices for storytelling (such as use of the present tense to describe current events or to use the past for personal narratives), which prompt students to see the relationship between the written text (Google Docs) and the multimodal text in the digital story in the context of their broader communicative purpose.

Phase 1: Analyzing and Providing Peer Feedback

Students analyze digital stories to identify the specific characteristics of the digital storytelling genre, the integration of different semiotic resources, and any copyright issues. This exercise helps student identify which areas they might be able to provide feedback

Table 5.1. Schedule and Activities for Instructor and Peer Feedback on a Digital Story

Phase	Schedule	Tasks
Phase 1	Weeks 4–5	Students • analyze digital stories to learn about the characteristics of the digital storytelling genre, the integration of different semiotic resources, and matters of copyright; • bring to class the digital story idea that they would like to develop; • provide feedback in the story circles on the content of the potential story; • write an elaborated outline based on peer discussion. Instructor • checks each script outline in Google Drive for its potential as a story.
Phase 2	Weeks 6–8	Students • write the digital story script based on peer and instructor feedback in Google Docs (first draft). Instructor • uses screencasting software to provide feedback on global issues, specifically genre-related issues, and content (screencast is uploaded to Google Drive and link sent to students); • provides feedback on local issues in the Google Doc.
Phase 3	Weeks 9–10	Students • provide feedback in the story circle on images, sound, and oral narratives of the second draft; • revise digital story based on story circle feedback. Instructor • makes sure that students receive and implement the peer feedback.
Phase 4	Weeks 11–12	Students • provide feedback in the story circles on the pace of oral narratives in conjunction with the integration of sound and images; • polish the digital story and upload the new version (third draft). Instructor • uses screencast to provide feedback on the integration of text, sound and images (screencast is uploaded to Google Drive); • provides feedback on grammar, vocabulary and polishing the written text in Google Docs.

Phase	Schedule	Tasks
Phase 5	Week 14	Students • upload the first version of the digital story to Google Drive and show their digital story to the classmates during class time; • provide in-class feedback on the execution of the digital story (storyline, transduction, and transformation); • revise the final digital story which will be presented in class the following day; • upload their final version of their completed digital story to the YouTube channel. Instructor • provides in-class comments (storyline, transduction, and transformation).

on and how best to deliver it. During the first story circle, students will bring a story idea and share it to ascertain whether it is worth telling and to discuss how best to tell it. After the provision of peer feedback, students make the necessary adjustments to the story. The instructor then accesses the story in Google Drive to assess whether it conforms to the storytelling genre. He provides content feedback for the elaborated outline when necessary in Google Docs.

Phase 2: Developing the Script

After students write a first draft of the script based on peer and instructor feedback from Phase 1, the instructor then supplies feedback in two modes: using screencast for the content, and genre-related issues of the digital story, and Google Docs for the linguistic issues. Although previous research has illustrated that there is not a large difference in the number of errors corrected when using either MS Word or screencast (Ducate & Arnold, 2012; Elola & Oskoz, 2016), this same research suggest that students seem to prefer the use of MS Word for feedback on local errors (grammar, vocabulary, and editing) and screencast for global errors (content, structure, and organization). The instructor can therefore use abbreviations

Soy la influencia

No tengo herencia hispana y nadie en mi familia habla español. Además, crecí en un pueblo primordialmente blanco y por lo tanto hasta que (tiem) llegara a la universidad, no (asp) tenía ninguna conexión con la cultura española. De mis cursos solo conocía la cultura estereotípica de España que tenía que ver con el flamenco, la corrida de toros y las tapas. Por eso, cuando decidí estudiar en Granada por cinco meses durante mi tercer año en la universidad, no sabía verdaderamente lo que esperar, porque ¿qué es la cultura granadina?

Al llegar y a través de los cinco meses allí, (asp) notaba que Granada era (art) el recipiente de muchas culturas y que yo era un testigo de la globalización de la ciudad. La influencia más obvia era la de los árabes. La Alhambra, la última fortaleza de los árabes antes de su expulsión de España, ahora es una atracción turística, y también por el resto de la ciudad hay tiendas árabes dispersadas por las calles donde se puede comprar un llavero o un collar de la hamsa (un símbolo de protección, común en islam y judaísmo) o (refl) se puede relajarse en los baños árabes que están llenos de azulejos de cerámica mora. Además de los árabes hay muchos gitanos que viven en las colinas alrededor del centro y que bailan (art) el flamenco en las calles y dentro de sus propios bares. Es común verlos vendiendo romero

Figure 5.3. Example of Local Feedback in Google Doc

in parenthesis (see Figure 5.3) to address the local aspects, and screencast to offer oral comments on issues of content, structure and organization (see Figure 5.4).

When using Google Docs, the instructor can label errors of form using error codes – e.g., (agr) agreement (for incorrect subject–verb, article–noun, or noun–adjective agreement), (prep) prepositions, (art) articles, (conj) conjunctions, (ort) spelling and punctuation, (rel) relatives, (asp) verb aspect, (mod) verb mood, (per) periphrasis, (refl) reflexive verb, (T) tense, (eng) English translation, (voc) vocabulary, and (???) not understandable. When using screencasts, the instructor first provides comments on content, structure, and organization of the digital story, then enumerates the number and type of errors in each sentence, addressing, for example, erroneous use of a verb (tense, aspect, mood) or subject–verb agreement. The instructor often hovers with the cursor in the area where the error is or to indicate whether the error has occurred at the beginning, middle, or end of a sentence.

Regardless of the mode of delivery (oral, visual or written), all students receive indirect, unfocused feedback based on their individual needs as observed in their essays, rather than focused

La mejor decisión que tomé en mi vida hasta ahora fue estudiar en Granada, España. Vivía allí durante cinco meses con una familia española, y espero que le haya influido tanto como me ha influido. Vivía con mi madre, Carmen, mi padre, Jesús, y mis hermanas, Carmen y Blanca, y hacia el final del semestre quería agradecerles por todo lo que habían hecho para mí. Decidí que quería demonstrar la apreciación por compartir la cultura estadounidense con ellos, y como me gusta hornear mucho, decidí hornear galletas con trozos de chocolate, un postre muy estadounidense. Me parecía una buena idea porque Carmen tenía cinco años y Blanco tenía dos, y por lo tanto pensaba que ellas disfrutarían de ayudarme mezclar la masa y ponerla en la bandeja de galletas. También, sabía que en España el postre típico contiene frutas, y pensaba que horneando galletas sería una experiencia cultural.

El plan parecía sencillo. Envié un correo electrónico a mi madre en los EEUU y le pregunté si ella podía mandarme la receta que habíamos usado durante tanto tiempo como

Screencast-O-Matic.com

Figure 5.4. Example of Screen-O-Matic Software

feedback designed to address a predetermined problem flagged for all students.This could be, for example, the selection of the imperfect or preterit tense, a topic that might have been recently studied in class and with which students might have ongoing issues. At this advanced writing level, indirect feedback might be the preferred form of feedback because it (a) engages students in problem solving and reflection that may be more likely to foster linguistic improvement and writing accuracy (Bitchener & Knoch, 2010), and (b) is a viable practice for students who are advanced enough to self-correct (Chandler, 2003).

Phase 3: Developing the Digital Story

After students have written the second draft, they provide peer feedback to each other in the story circle regarding the integration of text, images (or video), sound (or music, voices, etc.), and oral narratives. This peer feedback allows students to focus on global issues (content as well as the structure, and organization of the digital story) or local aspects of the language (grammar, vocabulary, editing) or other semiotic resources (images and sound). Following the story circle, students revise their story. Then, the instructor checks that all students implement revisions based on the peer feedback.

Phase 4: Polishing the Digital Story

Students get together in the story circle, where they present their oral narrative in conjunction with the images and sounds they want to use. When reading the script form of the digital story, peer feedback focuses comments on ensuring that the narrator's voice is clear, well-paced, and aligns with the story's visual and/or sound components. Once the students rewrite the third draft in Google Docs, the instructor provides the final oral and written feedback to complete last-minute additions. This is a good opportunity to think of the story as whole because they now see it as a single digital text.

Phase 5: Presenting the Digital Story

Students upload the first version of the completed digital story to Google Drive. In a class session, both students and instructor provide feedback (e.g., storyline, transduction, and transformation) on the digital story. The students use this feedback to improve the final version and upload it to the YouTube channel. Students will present the digital story in the following class.

Conclusion

This chapter has suggested some ways to think about the complexity of providing feedback with digital tools and how instructors can approach that task. We believe it is necessary to move beyond the use of feedback to signal a linguistic problem or unsuccessful use of grammar or vocabulary. We can now use feedback in new ways to help L2 writers notice problems themselves – often with the help of additional clues from the instructor – and think of potential solutions. It is clear that the introduction of digital social media has altered our understanding of not only the elements on which feedback should focus, but also how feedback should be provided. This reconceptualization of feedback due to the advent of digital tools and digital texts has raised new communicative issues in the L2 writing classroom.

Moving to newer ways of writing, we have seen that tools such as wikis, for example, have often been used to develop more traditional classroom genres, such as cultural topics (Arnold et al., 2009, 2012), argumentative and expository essays (Elola & Oskoz, 2010a), and cultural discussions (Kessler, 2009). Consequently, feedback in those cases will look more traditional. In contrast, the development of a blog or a digital story, which potentially anyone can have access to, can include both linguistic and non-linguistic resources. Consequently, feedback may need to address the text's multimodality as well as the usual linguistic issues. In other words, digital feedback cannot be confined to linguistic concerns or repertoires because of its typical integration of images and sound. Such feedback and the modality in which it is provided may also be multimodal. In fact, decisions about how instructor feedback or peer feedback is provided appear to influence the quality and efficacy of the feedback. Indirectly, digital tools have actually shed light on the potential of feedback: we can now recognize different degrees of explicitness, and we can present oral feedback (via screencast) in a way that gives writers time to reflect on it. Finally, feedback also has an important role in our students' choice of language(s) to express their opinions, voice, and identity. Feedback will have to address the linguistic varieties that our students' practice and experience since their linguistic repertoires are valid, albeit different from notions of standard language or prestige varieties chosen by the speakers of those varieties. Feedback needs to nurture expanded pedagogical views if we intend to make those changes in L2 curricula.

Note

1. Recall that we are using the general term L2 for less dominant languages – FL, ESL, HL, L3, etc.

Ideas for Reflection and Discussion

1. The chapter has presented different studies that have explored feedback from diverse perspectives, such as type of feedback or medium in which it is provided. Think of the feedback you generally provide: type (direct vs. indirect), mode (written and/or oral), medium (MS Word), and suggest why you would use social tools to provide more effective feedback.
2. Multimodal feedback can be used with written texts or other texts such as digital stories or blogs. How does the text itself and the task guide you in deciding the mode in which you will provide feedback?
3. Peer review, either in collaboration or cooperation, can occur while students are working collaboratively on a text or on their individual essays. After reading the results of studies mentioned in this chapter, devise a process approach to a task and indicate how you might provide feedback at the different phases of its completion. First, think of a task; next, write a prompt; and finally, provide specific recommendations to guide instructor and peer feedback. Indicate how the feedback will be given (e.g., through wikis, Google Docs, chats, MS Word).
4. As you have seen, feedback provision is a complex task whose goal is the improvement of students as digitally literate citizens. How would you focus provision of feedback to reflect a more inclusive classroom?

Chapter 6

Assessing Digital L2 Writing: Challenges with New Tools and New Genres

Reconsidering Our Notions about Assessment

Just as digital multimodality has questioned our assumptions about writing in the L2 classroom, it has also challenged traditional assessment practices that have primarily related to writers' linguistic development in the areas of accuracy, complexity, fluency, and vocabulary selection – followed by mastery of writing conventions, such as structure and organization. The advent of digital tools and digital genres in the classroom requires the instructor to rethink what type of assessment practices might be most appropriate – not only in terms of L2 students' linguistic abilities, but also by recognizing and allocating marks to non-linguistic aspects, such as creative and integrative use of images and sounds. We need to address both linguistic and non-linguistic aspects in order to assist L2 students to become successful communicators as they become increasingly digitally literate in the 21st century (Caws & Heift, 2016). Further, as McGrail and Behizadeh (2017) point out, overlooking multimodal components of a writing task in formal assessment not only devalues creativity, but also "raises issues of social justice and equitability" (p. 30). Can we afford to ignore our students' evident preoccupation with use of "social media to create digital multimodal content, to share, collaborate and connect with peers and other audiences" (p. 30) or should this now be a validated factor in assessment practices?

To be clear, we are not advocating for the abolishment of established writing assessment practices, such as those traditionally used for argumentative or expository essays. On the contrary, such assessment has a place in our students' professional and academic lives. However, we need to consider how best to assess multimodal texts as well as traditional written texts for at least two reasons. First, the multimodal task provides a more complete picture of what students are able to do and already do with the L2; in other words, it reflects a new dimension in our understanding of literacy, which in today's world must incorporate digital knowledge and skills. Second, in terms of language, multimodal texts provide tangible evidence of L2 students' linguistic development, evidence which is tailored by the affordances of digital tools and their associated genres. Assessing multimodal texts therefore requires us to move beyond the focus on linguistic features, practiced within traditional genres, toward consideration of other qualities just as essential. For instance, assessment could include effective collaborative writing in wikis, the audience impact of blogs, the use of hashtags in Twitter, and the integration of sound and images in digital stories. Such criteria require a revised model for assessment that "moves toward multimodal, multiplatform, collaborative and socially authentic forms of assessment" (Lotherington & Sinitskaya Ronda, 2012, p. 122). This new assessment model should highlight how students maximize the affordances of a digital tool when developing a text (the process) as well as judging the success of the student's final multimodal product. Finally, we share the idea that assessment can be integrated with classroom instruction; that is, that an ongoing evaluative approach could aim to guide students through performative practice rather than merely test knowledge gained at the end of the process (Adsanatham, 2012; Borton & Huot, 2007; Huot, 2002). As concluded by the Conference on College Composition and Communication (2009): "Writing assessment is useful primarily as a means for improving teaching and learning" (para. 4). In the L2 writing classroom, therefore, the vital role of assessment should be to improve teaching, learning, writing, and rhetorical understanding.

Assessing the New Digital Tasks

As educators bring multimodal practices, such as blogging, fan fiction, or Wikipedia entries to the L2 classroom, it is a natural decision to also adopt multimodal, multiplatform, collaborative and socially authentic forms of assessment (Lotherington & Sinitskaya Ronda, 2012). Educators accepting that premise face at least two obstacles, however. First, writing instructors often feel they have "little help in conceptualizing multimodal assignments" (Anderson, Atkins, Ball, Homicz Millar, Selfe, & Selfe, 2006, p. 79), and many have "struggled to find exemplary materials that clearly and concisely illustrat[e] multimodal assessment strategies and techniques" (Murray, Sheets, & Williams, 2009, Preface, para. 1). Second, even though L2 classroom activities often represent a wide range of current and often multimodal communicative practices, instructors still rely on traditional tasks based on achievement that stress grammatical accuracy out of context (Adair-Hauck, Glisan, Koda, Swender, & Sandrock, 2006; Adair-Hauck, Glisan, & Troyan, 2013; Adair-Hauck & Troyan, 2013). That is, the methods that many L2 instructors use to assess their students have been much slower to evolve than, or are not parallel to, their classroom practices (Adair-Hauck et al., 2006; Glisan, Uribe, & Adair-Hauck, 2007).

It is still the case that despite engaging L2 students in multimodal assignments, there is a tendency to assess tasks on quality of the printed text, a process with which instructors are more familiar (Yancey, 2004). In fact, as Sorapure (2006) mentions, and we ourselves have witnessed and practiced, we tend to ask students to accompany a media project with the familiar option of a written essay or report, or we may require a new media response in addition to the written essay. Although pairing an essay with a new media response is a useful strategy and provides the instructor with insights into how well students understand the connection between media-based and writing-based processes, relying exclusively on this practice "can also allow us to avoid assessing how the new media work on its own" (Sorapure, 2006, p. 3) and reflects the instructor's "uneasiness when assessing something other than the written text" (p. 3). It is therefore time to recognize the inherent value of the multimodal text for successful L2 and literacy learning and to update our assessment practices accordingly. That is, multimodal practices should not be considered as activities that only contribute "towards [traditional] examinable skills" (Lotherington & Sinitskaya Ronda 2012, p. 110), but rather as practices that develop several literacies, and for which it is essential to create tailored assessment tools that dovetail with students' multimodal composing processes. Thus, when adding multimodal texts into the curriculum (Reiss & Young, 2013), we also need to adopt the *four Rs* of the digital era (see Chapter 2) for assessment purposes – *Reuse* (backup), *Revise* (adapt), *Remix* (combine), and *Redistribute* (share). This new understanding acknowledges that today knowledge is fluid, dynamic and constructed in collaborative ways.

What We Might Want to Assess in Multimodal L2 Texts

Kalantzis and Cope (2008) proposed a new model for assessment that includes identity and social cognition, triggers metacognition, is ubiquitous, provides formative assessment, fosters authentic learning, and encompasses multimodal texts. The model is designed on six principles – multimodality, multimedia, connectivity, collaboration, dynamism, and hybridity – which together challenge traditional assessment by shifting the focus away from traditional linguistic- and information-based and often summative practices to formative, dynamic, social, and multimodal ones. The question that now arises is how and with what criteria we assess tasks according to these new principles in the L2 writing classroom.

In this chapter, we suggest a set of criteria that can be used in conjunction with assessment of multimodal texts. We should caution that not all genres will need all of the elements described in these criteria, nor are we setting out to provide a complete and exhaustive list for every single task. We hope, however, that our suggestions and associated questions will help L2 instructors and students to develop the assessment standards that best fit their particular needs. Developing assessment criteria for a multimodal composition requires establishment of its rhetorical, linguistic, and non-linguistic elements and providing them to students at the very beginning of the set task. In this way, assessment can be integrated with ongoing instruction (Adsanatham, 2012), while also reinforcing related rhetorical concepts in multimodal composing, such as audience, context, purpose, and strategy.

Audience

A critical difference between writing today and in the recent past is that the nature and role of the audience for student content creators has been extended and amplified (Lunsford & Ede, 2009). Because today's interactive digital tools and interfaces enable increased communication with the reader through the commenting feature (and other built-in functions such as the like-button) (Andrews & Smith, 2011; Lunsford & Ede, 2009; Wolff, 2013), writers expect and hope that their multimodal contributions will be widely distributed and will instigate a comment or response. Therefore, for today's generation of multimodal composers, the audience and the interactivity with that audience are integral features in online multimodal composition and distribution because at each part of the process, audience interaction nurtures and motivates the writer toward the completion of their task. That is, users create and recreate knowledge in blogs, wikis, and social networking sites such as Instagram for either an authentic or an imaginary and invented audience, with the aim of developing texts that will invite a response. Given that the idea of audience is essential to digital text creation, multimodal assessment frameworks have to "incorporate interaction with the intended audience about their response and experience of the multimodal compositions they review during the composing and assessment processes" (McGrail & Behizadeh, 2017, p. 35).

Some questions we can ask when considering the role of the audience in a multimodal composition context are:

- What audience did the author have in mind?
- What did the author expect from their audience(s)?
- How did the audience's responses affect the author's multimodal composing?
- What did the author do in response to constructive audience feedback? Or to feedback the author did not find useful?
- How were multimodal resources used to attract the audience?

Multilingualism and Translingualism

L2 considerations in digital texts have generally followed the standard version of the digital literacies of the classroom target language. However, recent language ideologies, shifts in pedagogies, and the fact that the majority of people frequently experience languages in contact with others (due to historical circumstances, migrant status, and media access), have provoked a change in the way in which multilingual and translingual practices are seen, and in some pedagogical contexts, accepted, in the L2 curricula. Canagarajah's (2013a) course study stands as an example. As Canagarajah explains, multilingual and translingual positioning sees literacy not as a product but as a combination of processes and practices of cross-language relationships. Specifically, translingualism concentrates on the communication that goes beyond the notion of separate languages and understands language as a vehicle that includes other semiotic resources, such as color, images, sounds, and symbols (Canagarajah, 2013a). In this communicative, process- and practice-oriented view, the concept of genre shifts from the *grammar* of genre to consideration of the *performance* of genre (Lu & Horner, 2016).

The questions that many instructors may ask are: How do students code-mesh digital texts, and how should we be guiding them on these kinds of practices? How do we assess the communicative success and rhetorical efficacy in divergent forms that do not conform to dominant language norms (target language) and writing conventions? Canagarajah (2013a) believes the use of multilingualism and translingualism is only problematic if instructors do not negotiate text and assessment with the multilingual writers and their texts. Therefore, he advocates for negotiated literacies in pedagogical environments that are conducive to students' use of outside-the-classroom strategies that are frequently used in language contact areas. Instructors need to work on developing language awareness, rhetorical sensibility, and writing practices that students can build on for translingual literacy.

Following Canagarajah's (2013a) study of his composition course, assessment tools can take the form of reflections about the writers' awareness of writing and language (as applied to all students whether or not they code-mesh in their writing), and the writers' learning trajectories and realizations. Thus, instructors could measure the quality of awareness, degree of reflexivity, and trajectories of the learning presented, and not solely focus on the written product. The instructor can also conduct interviews in the middle and at the end of the course to determine how students process their writing.

For this type of multimodal/translingual approach, clear participation between students and instructors is needed to ensure an effective and comprehensive assessment; that is why an instructor needs to establish clear guidelines, expectations, objectives, and outcomes for the course; only then can this conversation about assessment occur. There is no need to see features such as code-switching, code-meshing, borrowing, and blending of languages as instances of language interference or incomplete acquisition of specific languages; instead, they need to be accepted as the norm (Horner, Necamp, & Donahue, 2011).

The following questions can help instructors think about multilingualism or translingualism:

- What are the guidelines, goals, and outcomes of the course so I can create assessment criteria that can include multilingualism/translingualism?
- What kind of assessment tools can I use to evaluate students' multilingual and translingual texts?
- What kind of assignments can I create to give students the opportunity to think about their awareness of their language(s) and writing conventions and their learning trajectory during a course?

Multimodal Composition

The multimodal character of digital texts requires students knowing what to include and exclude from their written narrative accounts. As Jewitt (2003) points out "[T]he student is involved in the complex work of processing information, starting with the multimodal resources available in the classroom and moving to a more restricted modal response in the form of writing" (p. 84). Today's digital tools bring together a range of representational modes to accompany the written text. There is a need, therefore, to help L2 students understand "the unique conventions for creating such divergent multimodal compositions" (McGrail & Behizadeh, 2017, p. 34) and to teach them what elements are pertinent to the various multimodal genres, with the aim of applying these particular elements and procedures in their own multimodal designs. The conventions found in the multimodality displayed in our students' work makes traditional forms of writing assessment less relevant. Traditional assessment emphasizes local and global aspects of the language and falls short when required to acknowledge the impact and role of additional semiotic resources in multimodal composition.

To address this failure, following Adsanatham (2012) and reflecting our own work with digital storytelling, we propose the following questions to guide multimodal assessment:

Visuals

- Do the images correlate with the story being told and are they integrated meaningfully throughout the story?
- To what extent does the quality of the image interfere with or support the message conveyed?
- Do images support the theme of the story and help the audience see story's main points?
- To what extent do images enhance and enrich the story rather than being merely a replication of the written or oral text?

Aural (Music, Sounds)

- To what extent does the music tie in with the theme or the emotional atmosphere of the story?
- Does the volume of the music (e.g., soft, strong) or interludes of silence help to express meaning in the story?
- Do the sound effects, if any, complement the narrative flow of pictures and words throughout the story?
- How do music and sounds reflect and augment the purpose of the story?

Textual

- What is the purpose of including written text?
- To what extent does the text support or clarify the author's meaning? Does the text suit the still or moving pictorial elements that came before, after, or during it?
- How does the positioning, font, style, color, and content of text support the message the author want to convey?
- If the text is necessary, is it shown on screens long enough for the viewer to read it?

Gestural (Movement)

- Are multimedia transitions used (e.g., music or pictorial) to enhance the story, without distracting the audience from the text?
- Do the chosen transitions reflect a change of emotion or signal a change in direction in the storyline?
- What is the role of special effects (e.g., increasing or reducing the size of text or image, fadeout, etc.) in moving the story along?

Oral

- Does clear articulation and pronunciation of the narrator help the audience follow the story?
- Does the author use repetition or pauses meaningfully in telling the story?
- Does the oral narration help to tell an engaging story?
- Does the oral narration have an emotional effect on the audience?

Language

- Is the story told with an appropriate amount of detail; that is, not too long or too short?
- Is there a range of (multi)linguistic structures (e.g., verb tenses, subordination, or lack of subordination) evident in the narration of the story?
- To what extent does the author use varied vocabulary to enhance and enrich the story?
- Are pauses, sounds, or special effects used judiciously to enrich the story?

Genre Characteristics

Just as instructors do not assess a narrative account in the same manner as an argumentative essay, new assessment practices need to consider how the characteristics of digital genres differ from those of traditional written composition. Multimodal composing is very different from traditional writing; for instance, composing a digital story has its own idiosyncrasies and best practice criteria, which often do not correspond to those of the printed text. When assessing digital genres, therefore, we need to determine what characteristics we expect to see in a good Wikipedia entry, what a traveling blog should look like, or what might be the rhetorical characteristics of a tweet. If we define these characteristics, we can work out how to evaluate the success (or otherwise) of composing in a multimodal genre.

McGrail and Behizadeh (2017) posed a set of questions for creating and evaluating multimodal composition which show the need to understand what elements constitute a genre before developing assessment criteria:

- How does the author compose for the ear (composing an audio essay) as opposed to composing for the ear and eye when sound and images/videos are part of the story?
- To what extent are the different narrative elements of the genre present (e.g., the dramatic question to be answered and its resolution in a digital story)?
- How does the author determine what constitutes a good audio essay or video essay?
- How does the author effectively integrate different sources to develop a storytelling genre?

Authorship

Multimodal digital projects are likely (but not always) to be collaborative endeavors. Importantly, in such collaborative projects, as Lotherington and Ronda (2014) point out, we must realize that "With shared authorship comes collective authority, which calls into question the dimension of content production" (p. 22). In terms of assessment, the expanded concept of authorship implies that we need to reconsider our evaluation practices. If traditional forms of assessment were based on individual performance, the inclusion of digital tools that allow for collaborative compositions require assessment practices that value the achievement and contributions of a collective authorship. Therefore, when evaluating our L2 students' performance in collaborative work, we must consider both individual and joint contributions. This is perhaps best achieved by combining peer and self-assessment with traditional instructor evaluation.

Questions that can help develop this amalgam are:

- To what extent does the final project reflect the author's intellectual contribution equally with that of their collaborators?
- How does the collective group integrate all its members' voices?
- How does communication among authors result in a respectful discussion of different ideas and lead to a democratically produced product?
- To what extent do the collaborators play to their own strengths (e.g., linguistic, visual, or aural knowledge) to enhance the quality of the final product?

Ownership

Given the reuse and remix of semiotic resources that takes place in digital writing, another element to take into account is ownership, not to be confused with authorship. Ownership refers to the fair use of external sources by acknowledging and crediting ideas, images, and the eclectic range of semiotic resources that might be included in L2 students' multimodal projects. The question of ownership is of relevance given that "Many young people today consider what exists on the Internet as freely available raw material to be used however they see fit" (Chun et al., 2016, p. 69). This appropriation is further encouraged by the abundance of easy to use tools for copying and modifying raw material and for the understanding that remixing and repurposing is largely anonymous and seemingly authorless. The problem is not, as Chun et al. (2016) point out, that users borrow content from others, but "rather the sense that borrowing does not require any acknowledgment" (p. 69). There is therefore a need for students to learn about intellectual property, copyright, and fair use, as well as about changing conventions for attribution of online materials (Bloch, 2012).

Questions that we might ask regarding ownership are:

- Does the author credit and cite those whose ideas they have included in their work?
- Does the author invite you to visit websites to confirm that the source material is publicly available?
- What steps does the author take to obtain permissions for copyrighted material?

Developing Collaborative Grading Criteria

In most cases, assessment criteria have been instructor-generated and designed to suit essay prompts rather than multimodal texts. However, there have been calls – in particular, for multimodal texts – for the inclusion of the student's perspective to help instructors improve the quality of their assessment criteria and rubrics. Hessler and Lambert (2017) speak of co-constructing a successful and effective rubric by including students in the process and considering their design perspectives as well as those of the instructors. Van Kooten (2013) and Adsanatham (2012) offer an assessment model with equal emphasis on process and product, and with student involvement in the assessment at every stage, including the student production of a reflection video.

To help L2 students grow in their knowledge and become active creators of and contributors to knowledge in our teaching and evaluation, there is a need to "begin a discourse of assessment with our students about their writing" (Huot, 2002, p. 170), by inviting them to offer input in the grading process and encouraging negotiation and consensus between students and instructor. By involving students in the grading process, we make them aware that their voices matter and that they can make a difference in their classroom, as well as in society at large. This leads "to more engaged learning and deeper understanding of writing" (Inoue, 2005, p. 222). Further, by inviting the class to co-construct the grading criteria, we can use their insights to enrich our understanding about effective assessment practices.

Rather than perpetuating teacher-centered pedagogical and evaluative approaches that posit the instructor as the sole source of knowledge and authority in the classroom, instructors and students can benefit from meaningful dialog with one another through the process of co-constructing grading standards. In this collaborative process, it is possible to turn evaluation into a mutual learning process based on principles of respect, collaboration, openness, and listening (Shiffman, 1997) that arrives at democratically agreed grading standards (Adsanatham, 2012). In the case of digital writing, students come to learn the features of an effective multimodal text by developing, testing, and using the grading criteria they themselves designed; that is, they "learn to compose by learning to assess" (Borton & Huot, 2007, p. 3). By following these processes, the assessment of L2 writing becomes a dynamic means to enhance learning, teaching, and composing.

Current Trends in Assessment: Peer and Self-Assessment

Given the participatory nature of digital written texts, the importanace of peer assessment has been brought to the forefront (Lotherington & Sinitskaya Ronda, 2012). We believe that for L2 students to engage with multimodal writing processes, instruction should include a reflective component that emphasizes and encourages their awareness of all of the elements to be considered in the writing processes as well as the final product. Further, assessment should be a mixture of formative and summative tasks performed at different stages of the writing activity. Formative assessments will foster students' engagement with the task and suit a process approach that is appropriate for dealing with the complexity of multimodal texts. Summative assessment collects information about the final product and judges its quality.

Peer Assessment

Due to the collaborative nature of the multimodal digital text, and given that digital content is liked, shared, retweeted, remixed, and distributed within a community of users, it makes sense that peer assessment should be a prominent method of assessment (Lotherington & Sinitskaya Ronda, 2012; McGrail & Behizadeh, 2017). While it is only one of several assessment models used in the L2 classroom, peer assessment can be a valuable inclusion given that it is a "component that mirrors the feedback commonly built into social media platforms" (Lotherington & Ronda, 2014, p. 23). Peer assessment can be both informal and formal. For example, features such as the Like icon, the thumbs up emoticon in Facebook, or the heart in Twitter can be conveniently used by L2 students to indicate the extent to which they like a comment or post. Students are, in such informal ways, assessing the quality of their classmates' contributions. By leaving their own comments and reactions, L2 students (i.e., the audience) are reacting to the message and to some extent influencing their classmates' future contributions.

Students and instructors might use such informal responses as advisory comments while they revise and self-evaluate, or use them to evaluate graded student-generated multimodal compositions. However, acknowledging classmates' comments does not signify that we should assess the suggestions of the respondent(s), but rather it is the writer's reactions in response to audience comments that is most important. In preparation for such collaborative assessment, instructors could provide specific guidelines for external reviewers (including student reviewers) regarding assessment criteria and the roles of reviewers in terms of assessment (Kalantzis, Cope, & Harvey, 2003). In a more formal manner, L2 students can assess each other in terms of contribution (authorship) when working collaboratively, and on the product (when working individually), following a rubric that reflects all of the elements of the multimodal composition.

Self-assessment

Learners' evaluation of their own work could take the form of self-evaluation of their performance following an established rubric, or be a post-reflection on a writing task (Reiss & Young, 2013). The criteria and rubric which, as we mentioned, can be elaborated in collaboration between instructor and students, will allow the latter to assess their own performance in different aspects of the composing process, including audience, multimodality, ownership, and authorship. In addition to giving a numerical assessment or grade, L2 students might examine their own learning and think about "how their multimodal compositions [help them] achieve their goals" (Reiss & Young, 2013, p. 179) in a written piece. This reflection, which can be formative and/or summative, can consider all aspects and phases of the composing process, including interactions with an either real or perceived audience, what they learn from the audience, and how it influenced their developing piece (McGrail & Behizadeh, 2017). They can also bring in other aspects, such as the multimodality process (the combination of aural, gestural, textual, oral, and visual modes), and issues of genre, authorship, collaboration, and ownership, and how these had influenced their writing. The written reflection is an excellent opportunity to expand on areas that often receive only a specific grade in a traditional rubric (e.g., a mark for language use). By reflecting on how they designed their multimodal digital text, students can also address what they would do differently and what features they would use again in a future assignment.

In our L2 writing classes we have included written self-assessment as students engaged in their multimodal digital text in both formative and summative evaluation, during or at the end of the composing process. In our reflective formative assessment, we asked students to answer in the online discussion board some reflective questions about their writing process. We reproduce below two examples of prompts relating to a digital story assignment that served as formative assessment

Reflection 1 (Formative Asessment)
Digital story: On November 6th we reviewed the first draft of your digital story in class. What content (topic) of your essay helped you write your digital story? How did your digital story change as the semester progressed? You received comments about content and organization from your classmates in the story circles. What aspects of the structure and the Spanish language do you realize now you had not considered before starting working on the digital story? What benefits and challenges came from listening to other people's suggestions? How do you think your comments might have helped others to improve their digital story?

Reflection 2 (Formative Asessment)
Digital story: (a) What decisions about tone and pace did you make as narrator of your story? (b) How did you select images for your digital story? How did those images help you write the narrative of your story? (c) How did you use the transitions (from one image to the other) to express the emotional content of your story? (d) How do the images and the music help you to become immersed in the topic of your story? (e) What "layers" of information do the images and music reveal that cannot be expressed solely with words?

L2 students reflected on their composing process as they were composing the digital story (e.g., drafting, editing, searching for images, selecting music, combining the semiotic resources). When at the end of the semester writers had completed the digital story, we asked them to reflect on the creative process they had gone through (see Phase 3: "Setting up a Successful Multimodal Assessment Practice"), according to the instructions below.

Final Digital Story Reflection (Summative Assessment)
In this advanced writing course, you have created a digital story to develop, in a more personal manner, one of the topics that you have worked on in class (i.e., expository or argumentative essay). The creation of the digital story has been completed in several stages, some of which have been quite new to you in this writing class.

The purpose of this paper, **Reflection on my digital story**, is to examine, in an introspective manner, the creative process of your digital story from the beginning steps to the final product. In the **narrative** of this reflection of about 4 pages (minimum), make sure that you respond at some point to each of the following questions.

Script/Narrative
Developing a digital story means creating a personal account within the current political-economic context and then transforming it from the written word to the spoken word.

- What content of your written essay was easiest to transform into a digital story?
- What was the "aha!" moment that triggered your ideas on what you wanted to write? Describe how you arrived at that moment?
- How did your ideas about what you were going to do change or grow while you were working on your digital story?
- How did your expectations about the composing of this digital story change from the beginning to the end of the semester?
- How does the final product of the digital story differ from the other, more traditional, writing assignments, such as expository and argumentative writing?
- How did the knowledge that this digital story will have an audience outside the classroom influence your writing process? How did this knowledge challenge your previous ideas about the act of writing?

Images, Music, Tone, and Rhythm of the Digital Story

Working on this digital story has involved looking for images, deciding on the rhythm of the narration, choosing the music, and, at the end, combining all of those elements.

- How did you select the images for your digital story? How did these images help you to enhance the narrative of your story?
- How have you used transitions (from one image to the next) to convey the emotional content of your story?
- How do the images and the music help you engage with the topic of the story? What layers of information do the images and the music provide that words alone cannot?
- How would you describe the tone and rhythm you selected for the narration of your story?
- Creating a digital story implies the acquisition of a set of skills that differ from those used in more traditional writing genres. What have been your challenges to learn, to understand, and to adapt yourself to this new form of written/oral expression?

Audience Impact

Digital story is a genre with which you have less experience compared with more traditional writing assignments, and it often means that you depend on other people (especially if you are working in a partnership with other students).

- How did the audience affect your writing and the digital story creation process?
- How did taking part in story circles help you with the creation process and/or revision of your story (narrative)? Did this help you focus on the story as a whole (including narrative, images, sound)?
- What were the advantages and disadvantages of exchanging comments with your classmates?
- What was your role in the creation of your own story and the creation of your classmates' stories? What were the roles of your classmates and instructor in the creation of your own digital story?

Assessing a Multimodal L2 Writing Task

Digital tools, as we have explained, organically support various digital genres and consequently the evolving linguistic repertoires that L2 students need to acquire. At the same time, not all genres feature the same rhetorical structures and organization. If we are using Twitter, for example, we would not expect tweets to be in long complex sentences (although, of course, we need to take into consideration who the author and the intended audience of the tweet are); instead, we might focus on the accuracy of grammar and vocabulary, the use of hashtags, and the interplay of comments. If we are using wikis, however, for the collaborative writing of an academic report, we would expect longer sentences, sophisticated academic vocabulary developed during participants' interactions, and continuous revisions based on feedback.

If only for practical reasons, assessment practices for multimodal genres need to be different from other traditional forms of assessment, such as a written composition in an exam or a dedicated classroom writing day. In such a situation, students are asked to compose linguistically accurate content according to a rubric that reflects static assessment practices that may only measure one skill. On the other hand, when we assess our L2 students' performance using digital tools, we look for assessment tasks that mirror as closely as possible the kinds of writing tasks that students will encounter outside classroom testing situations. That means we need to create authentic tasks that reduce the gap between typical classroom linguistic instructional practices (sometimes learned in a vacuum) and skills that students will need in real-life situations. Also, we need all-inclusive assessment practices, such as integrated performance assessments that reflect the cyclical relationship between examining and analyzing vernacular texts and linguistic development in the target language(s).

By nature, working in a digital genre (e.g., digital story) is a process-oriented, often collaborative activity in which L2 students create and use and reuse content from other sources and semiotic resources, provide feedback and communicate with each other, and perform and present the final product to their classmates and instructor, or to a wider audience. Therefore, if authentic assessment in the L2 classroom "replicates or simulates the contexts in which adults are "tested" in the workplace, in civil life, and in personal life [...with] particular constraints, purposes, and audiences" (Adair-Hauck et al., 2006, p. 361), it makes sense to develop assessment practices that evaluate "the students' knowledge and abilities in real-world situations, or those that occur outside of the classroom context" (Adair-Hauck et al., 2006, p. 361). Only then can we develop assessment tools that match the authentic scenarios of these tasks. In other words, if in real life the purpose of the blog is to inform its readers about a current event or situation, why should we ask our students to create a blog that only talks about their daily routines?

In relation to this question, Shrum and Glisan (2015) have highlighted several salient characteristics of the authentic task and its subsequent assessment. According to Shrum and Glisan, authentic tasks:

- need to be contextualized;
- engage students in meaning making and meaningful communication with others;
- elicit a performance of some type;
- encourage divergent responses and creativity;
- can be adapted to serve as either formative and summative assessments;
- address at least one mode of communication.

Given that authentic tasks should teach learners "what the 'doing' of a subject looks like and what kind of performance challenges are actually considered most important in a field or profession" (Wiggins & McTighe, 2005, p. 337), a digital writing task should support L2 learners to use the target language to perform tasks that they are likely to encounter outside of the classroom. Such tasks will require multi-staged research and interaction with other students and the instructor. The result should be meaningful use of language for real audiences (Shrum & Glisan, 2015), not just for the instructor. When developing a Wikipedia entry, for example, students will research information about a specific topic to inform an audience, potentially anyone accessing the particular Wikipedia entry – again, not just the instructor. The following prompt (provided below) is contextualized in the sense that students are required to provide knowledge/information about their home town; are also engaged in interactions with the audience that invite creativity and a range of responses from the audience; and, in this case, make use of two modes of communication (visual and written), as in a real situation (Shrum & Glisan, 2015) in the final product.

Example of Wikipedia Task

You and your classmates have become aware that your home town is not well represented in Wikipedia. Although there is general information about the city, there are several landmarks of historical, cultural, political, or general interest that have not been included or properly addressed. Working in groups of three, your class will address this gap by selecting and elaborating on different points of interest.

In your group, select one landmark and develop a Wikipedia entry to enhance the content about your home town. In your entry ensure that there is a definition of the term presented. Develop the body of the entry with at least four main sections (around 1,200 words in total), each one with a clear heading that represents its content. Include four images, videos, or figures (watch out for copyright permissions!), and at least eight references.

To ensure that this is a coherent representation of your town or city, make sure that you connect your entry with those of other groups. When providing your feedback to other groups, discuss what is missing and how to make connections between sections without repeating information.

Finally, there is another characteristic of authentic assessment to remember when students are developing an authentic task: instructors need to demystify performance expectations by showing students "exemplars or models of the performance expected, together with the rubrics" (Adair-Hauck et al., 2006, p. 362). The key, as Abraham and Williams (2009) point out, "is to share the exemplars and [assessment] criteria with students *prior to* the assessment" (p. 326). Also, as previously mentioned, assessment should not be developed and implemented only by the instructor. Including L2 students in the criteria development process "help[s] students understand the objectives of the project and feel more confident about how to proceed" (Adsanatham, 2012, p. 160), and it also increases students' sense of ownership of their work when they are able to offer input about assessment criteria.

Developing Rubrics for the Digital Multimodal Text

Wiggins (1994) pointed out that authentic assessments feature "transparent or de-mystified criteria and standards" (p. 75); these are often detailed in rubrics, a set of scored guidelines for evaluation, that explicitly state what is expected from the students. *Relearning by Design* (2000), as cited by Adair-Hauck et al. (2006, p. 361),[1] suggested some questions that rubrics could pose:

- What criteria are used to judge or evaluate performance?
- Where should we look and what should we look for to judge success?
- What does a range in quality of performance look like?
- How do we determine what score should be given and what that score means?
- How are different levels of quality described and distinguished from one another?

Applying these questions to multimodal digital texts, we could assert that L2 students' performance should be evaluated in terms of how they address multimodality and other features: these include characteristics of the genre, engagement with the audience, collaboration, and L2 performance. The weighting given to these criteria will depend on the affordances of the digital tools used and the objective of the task (i.e., the extent to which some components are more prominent or significant than others for the assignment). With the help of a rubric that addresses the different modes, it is possible to narrow down criteria for evaluation to be very specific; for example, the number of words in the script, the length of the digital story, the use of implicit or literal images, or the selection of music and other aural components.

Finally, we return to the idea of connecting instruction and assessment. After defining the assessment criteria and constructing a rubric, the instructor will be able to assign the resources needed to complete, say, a digital story: these may include digital storytelling software training, analysis of other digital stories, or evaluation of suggested images. By receiving (or helping to develop) the task assessment criteria and rubric from the beginning, L2 students will be clear about what is expected of them. For instance, when working on the Wikipedia entry presented earlier, L2 students can assess each other's contributions to the accomplishment of the task in terms of multiple aspects, including all of the elements that we would expect to see happening in a collaborative environment. See example of a summative peer assessment on the next page.

Given that the development of a digital multimodal task is an ongoing process, the instructor can also include process-related grading that focuses on the different aspects of the production process (see Table 6.1).

Sample Rubric for Wikipedia Task

In this class, you completed a Wikipedia entry collaboratively to increase knowledge about your home town. Please complete the following rubric (one rubric for each group member) to assess your group members' contributions to the task:

Classmate's name: ______________________________

Name:				**Total**
	***Poor = 1**	**Fair = 2**	**Excellent = 3**	
Authorship	The Wikipedia entry barely reflects this author's intellectual contribution.	The Wikipedia entry partly reflects this author's intellectual contribution.	The Wikipedia entry reflects the author's intellectual contribution to the same extent as other collaborators.	
Communication	This author either rarely communicated or tried to impose their ideas without listening to others in the group.	Communication with this author was limited but they contributed to some extent.	This author communicated respectfully and participated in a discussion of ideas which led to a democratically created product.	
Content	This author did not add value-rich content to enhance the value and quality of the final product.	This author added some relevant content to enhance the value and quality of the final product.	This author engaged well with the project and added significant content to enhance the value and quality of the final product.	
Time Management	This author often failed to complete work, leaving more for other group members to do.	This author was often late in contributing but did complete in time to be graded.	Contributions were always on time or sometimes made ahead of time.	

*Score might change depending on the objectives and goals of the course.

Table 6.1. Example of Process-related Grading for the Wikipedia Entry (Formative Assessment)

Phase 1		
Analysis	• Examine different Wikipedia entries about cities and monuments and identify the main categories they include. • Identify elements of language use to incorporate (e.g., verb tenses, adjectives) and rhetorical structure.	15%
Phase 2		
Structure	• Define the main features of your city or town (e.g., general description, etymology, history, geography) to be included in the entry.	10%
Content	• Add information to fill out the different sections of the entry (e.g., etymology, history, geography).	20%
Images	• Select images to be included to support the information provided (watch out for copyright!). Use original images as much as possible.	15%
Phase 3		
Feedback	• Provide feedback on grammar (5 items) and content (5 comments) to another group using the wiki. • Accept or reject (explain why) the feedback provided to you.	15%
Phase 4		
Content	• Complete the city and monument entry. • Include links to the entries of the other groups.	15%
Language	• Polish the language and make sure that the vocabulary is appropriate to describe the city and monument.	15%

Developing a Multimodal Assessment: Reflecting on an Intercultural Experience

Project Background

This is a semester-long project in a second-year semester class, in which students develop a digital story about an intercultural experience that they might have had either abroad or in their own country. In line with previous research showing that assessment processes can include students' voices in the development of the grading criteria (Adsanatham, 2012; Van Kooten 2013), the instructor aims to develop an assessment tool in conjunction with students. This form of collaboration helps students to tune into the multimodal nature of today's digital learning tasks (Nelson, 2006; Yang, 2012) and have a better sense of what is expected from them when composing multimodal texts. The task follows the bridging activity framework and a task-based approach with the aim of creating a series of steps in which, after examining different types of digital stories, students progressively develop grading criteria which focus on oral, aural, gestural, and written modes, and which will later on be applied to evaluate their own work. In this way, the creation of an assessment tool mirrors the learning practices and outcomes that should be present in any assessment procedure and highlights how they complement each other. The assessment protocol illustrates and articulates clearly the process of creating a digital story.

Phase 1: Understanding the Assessment Criteria

Preparing L2 students to develop grading criteria for their digital story projects involves several scaffolding tasks (Adsanatham, 2012) in which they come to understand assessment criteria. As also seen in Oskoz and Elola (2014, 2016b), the first step consists of rhetorical viewing. Over a period of several weeks, and guided by the instructor, L2 students analyzed sample digital stories and commented on how well the authors had integrated images, text, and sounds within the digital storytelling genre with the idea of establishing the components that assessment tools should incorporate. The objective of learning through models is to view each digital story "critically and rhetorically by analyzing how images, sounds, alphabetic texts, and digital effects were used to construct and cohere – and, in some instances, detract [from] – the argument" (Adsanatham, 2012, p. 156).

While viewing and analyzing the stories, images are evaluated in terms of their level of explicitness (the literal reflection of the object presented) or implicitness (indirect relationship with the object presented) and are assessed for their underlying values or messages. Students also learn about the effects that different music styles and sounds might have on an audience. The students will further consider how the authors of digital stories use transitions to express meaning, and how they make use of textual, visual, and aural modes to create a multimodal text. When discussing images and sounds, students must be advised of the need to abide by copyright laws, and this proviso should be included in the assessment rubric.

To guide the analyzing and selection of rubric components, L2 students were provided with a set of critical analysis questions leading them to pay close attention to general rhetorical elements that might differ according to the genre (e.g., digital story, blog) and the type of text (e.g., personal digital story, historical digital story, financial blog, traveling blog). Questions that could be asked include:

- Who is the audience?
- What type of implicit and explicit images is the author using to convey the intended meaning?
- What sounds are heard first, next, and subsequently? Why are they arranged in that way?
- How do the transitions help build the story?
- What are the feelings conveyed by the pace of the story and tone of the narrator?

Phase 2: Developing Collaborative Grading Criteria

Phase 2 consists of two parts. First, once L2 students become familiar with rhetorical viewing and analysis in the L2 classroom, the instructor can assign 3 – 4 multimodal clips showing different qualities to watch over a period of five weeks. These digital stories can be either found on YouTube or can be previous works from former classes, including other subject areas. The digital stories can also represent different genres (e.g., personal stories, documentaries) with a wide range of creators, from students to professionals

Table 6.2. Schedule and Activities for Instructional Assessment Tasks

Phase	Schedule	Instructional Assessment Tasks
Phase 1	Weeks 1–2	Instructor and students • discuss and analyze the value of images, text, music, sounds, voice, and transitions to convey meaning and emotion to the audience. Instructor • addresses copyright issues.
Phase 2	Weeks 3–7	Students • watch several digital stories to start thinking about the elements to be included in the assessment criteria; • develop assessment and grading criteria; • test their criteria with digital stories. Instructor • revises, expands, and builds upon students' individual criteria to develop a common schedule of criteria for the class.
Phase 3	Week 12 Days 1	Students • upload their digital stories to the YouTube classroom channel; • introduce their stories (purpose, audience, semiotic resources use) to the class; • assess classmates' work (formative assessment) following the established criteria and rubric. Instructor • assesses students' work (formative assessment); • collects students' peer assessment rubrics.
	Week 12 Day 2	Students • upload their final version of the digital story to the YouTube channel; • assess their classmates' final work (summative assessment); • turn in their self-reflection. Instructor • assesses students' work (summative assessment); • collects students' peer assessment rubrics.

in the field. By examining vernacular digital stories, L2 students closely observe, interpret, and evaluate sample materials before composing. The key concern with this process is that L2 students should become aware of how multimodal elements function and start to think about which elements should be included in assessment criteria that correspond to the genre they are working with. This process, even if set as homework, should be constantly revisited in the classroom. That is, after viewing the digital stories at home, L2 students then, as a group, share their analysis of one of the digital stories to ensure that there is a common understanding about how semiotic resources are integrated in the development of a multimodal text.

Once L2 students have analyzed several different digital stories, they are ready to design a grading criteria sheet that can be used to assess their own work. Tempting as it may seem to let L2 students develop their own criteria, it is still necessary to provide them with some directions regarding expectations. The questions presented in Phase 1 will help L2 students think of what should be assessed in a digital story. For instance, the criteria must clearly define the "features of an effective multimodal digital project, address the usage of various modes (e.g., images, text, sounds) and digital effects (e.g., transitions, timing), specify elements of argument (including criteria for audience, context, use of evidence, etc.), and be thorough and thoughtful" (Adsanatham, 2012, p. 157). These guidelines help students to think rhetorically, to consider the relationship between modes (Odell & Katz, 2009; Sorapure, 2006), the "readerly effects" of design choices (Ball, 2006), synaesthesia (Kress, 2003), coherence (Yancey, 2004), and argument strengths (Borton & Huot, 2007). By asking them to consider all those elements, that is, to think rhetorically, students will be more likely to avoid a common pitfall in a novice multimodal composition: the incorporation of digital effects for the sake of "coolness" without regard to rhetorical purpose (Sorapure, 2006).

Once students have developed their own individual criteria, they can explore and test how they work by analyzing other digital stories, and then fine-tune them as necessary. The final criteria to be used in evaluation, however, do not rest entirely with them. We suggest that instructors consolidate all of the grading criteria provided by students into one single document because this allows instructors to revise, expand, and build on what has already been produced by the class. As Adsanatham (2012) has pointed out, students' rubrics generally are more complete and complex than instructors may have previously imagined. Asking students to develop the criteria initially also helps them to synthetize their knowledge of what a multimodal text is and is an indirect way "to assess students' understanding of multimodality and rhetorical principles" (p. 161). It could also be claimed that combining all of the criteria allows for a fairer assessment overall.

Phase 3: Show Time: Assessment Time

On completing their digital stories, students present them in class on two consecutive days. Assessment of the digital stories takes place over those two days and is provided in peer, self, and instructor form. On the first day, students upload them to the web (either to their own YouTube channel or to the instructor's channel) and present them to the class. At the time of the presentation they introduce their audiences and outline the argument they want to make in their digital story. While watching the different stories, students assess their classmates' work based on the coherence of the argument; the arrangement of the images; the order in which they appeared (logical presentation); the rhetorical appeals used; the choice and arrangement of the aural mode (music, voice-over, and sounds) and any other elements selected for assessment. In a reflective process, students then indicate what they like about the digital stories and what features they might want to emulate in their own. The instructor also provides comments about what could enhance the quality of the digital story. The instructor compiles the classmates' grading sheets and is part of the evaluation.

Table 6.3. Digital Story Rubric (Summative and Formative Assessment)

Category	*4 Points	3 Points	2 Points	1 Point
Audience Engagement	The pace fits the storyline and helps engage the audience.	The pace is occasionally too fast or too slow.	An attempt is made at pacing, but the audience is not fully engaged.	No attempt at pacing is made and the audience is lost.
Oral Narration	Narration is clear and well edited.	Narration is fairly clear.	Narration is often hard to follow.	Narration is missing.
Music/ Sound Effects	Soundtrack effects complement and do not overwhelm narration.	Soundtrack effects often overwhelm the narration.	Soundtrack is distracting.	There is no soundtrack and the story would have benefited from one.
Visuals	All images are clear (some of them even original), and there is a good mix of literal and symbolic.	A few images are unclear, and very few of them are used symbolically.	Many images are unclear, and there is no symbolism.	Most images are unclear, are literal, and/or inappropriate.
Motion and Transitions	Used at least 4 motion effects; transitions are effective.	Used at least 3 motion effects; transitions are largely effective.	Used at least 1 motion effect; some transitions are distracting.	Used no motion effects; no transitions.
Economy	Combining the different modes, the story is told with exactly the right amount of detail and is not too long or too short.	Although combining the different modes, the story is sometimes vague or includes unnecessary detail; it sometimes seems to drag.	Despite the combination of modes, meaning is only duplicated (not enhanced). The story needs more editing and is noticeably too long or too short.	The story needs extensive editing to make the most of the use of different modes.

Grammar	Wide range of L2 grammatical structures with few or insignificant errors.	Adequate range of L2 grammatical structures; overuse of simple constructions; some minor errors.	Limited range of L2 structures; poor control of grammar, with frequent errors in basic grammar.	Frequent and persistent L2 grammatical errors; text is difficult to understand.
Vocabulary	Makes full use of the L2 vocabulary of the topic being presented.	L2 vocabulary accurate but somewhat limited.	L2 vocabulary limited, with overuse of imprecise and vague terms.	Very limited L2 vocabulary; overuse of imprecise and vague terms.
Multilingual and Translingual Practices (if applicable)	Makes excellent use of several linguistic repertoires in a coherent manner.	Makes fair use of several linguistic repertoires in a coherent manner.	Makes poor use of several linguistic repertoires.	Makes confusing use of several linguistic repertoires.
Storytelling Structure	Presents the rhetorical question to be answered.	Either the rhetorical question or the answer is missing.	Rhetorical question and the answer are missing.	There is no clear narrative in the story.
Credits and Citations (Ownership)	All original and non-original images and sound are credited and cited.	Some citations and credits are missing.	Many citations and credits are missing.	There are no citations or credits.
Mechanics	The title appears at the beginning and the final credits at the end.	Part of the title or a few of the final credits are missing.	Either the title or the final credits are missing.	Both the title and the final credits are missing.
Task Completion, Following the Prompt	Students have followed the prompt, and the task is well completed.	Students have followed the prompt, and the task is almost finished.	Students did not follow the prompt closely, and the task is not finished.	Students did not follow the prompt at all, and the task is not finished.

**Score might change depending on the objectives and goals of the exercise.

On the second day and final viewing, students present again using the updated and final versions of the digital stories. At that time, classmates and instructor re-assess the digital story following the same rubric and, as in a film festival, students vote to select the best story. Finally, students also self-assess their performance in their reflections by following the rubric. In addition to including their thoughts regarding the composing process, they also address and justify why they followed or did not follow their peers' suggestions to enhance their digital story.

Conclusion

The idea of integrating instruction and assessment is not new (Conference on College Composition and Communication, 2009; Inoue, 2005; Huot, 2002) and the adoption of integrated performance assessment is a perfect example of this potential symbiosis. However, the introduction of digital multimodal texts has perhaps increased the drive to revise assessment practices to suit a changing learning environment. While remembering our prime task as L2 writing instructors, which is to develop students' linguistic knowledge, we also need to recognize the role of an audience (which might extend beyond the classroom) to understand the power of collaborative authorship, and how to construct meaning with the use of semiotic resources. As such, we must try to develop authentic tasks, those which resemble real-life experiences, to be the focus of our performance assessments. It is our hope that, with the guidelines we have proposed, we have helped L2 instructors to adopt assessment practices that accommodate digital multimodality in the L2 classroom. By including carefully designed multimodal assessments in our L2 classroom, we are finally validating our L2 students' daily digital practices.

Note

1. The previous webpage cited by Adair-Hauck et al. (2006, p. 361) as *Relearning by Design* (2000), is no longer available. The current one (https://greatnonprofits.org/org/relearning-by-design-inc) has changed and does not provide the information we cite from that source.

Ideas for Reflection and Discussion

1. Consider the digital tools available in your L2 classroom and the assessment tasks set to evaluate and grade your students' performance. To what extent do these assessment tasks and/or rubrics reflect the multimodality of classroom activities and tasks?
2. As mentioned in this chapter, an assessment task should mirror as closely as possible those situations in which L2 students will need to use language out of the classroom context (authenticity). Considering the various digital tools that we use to communicate in multimodal form, think about contextualized authentic tasks that you have used or could use in the language classroom. Discuss the assessment criteria and the rubric that would accompany this task.
3. The chapter has provided an example of assessment criteria for multimodal texts, focusing primarily in the digital story. Think of another digital genre (e.g., tweets) that you could include in the class and of the criteria you would develop to assess students' performance based on the characteristics of the genre and the tool. Think, for instance, in terms of audience, modes (visual, aural, text, oral, gestural), collaboration, remix, and reuse. Discuss why these criteria fit the genre and tool of your choice and how it differs from or compares to other genres and tools.
4. In this chapter, we have illustrated a task-based approach to the assessment of a digital story. With the digital genre that you chose in Question 3, think about how you could break

down the assessment process into manageable steps that align with instructional phases. Explain in detail how you would develop the assessment criteria with the help and insights of your students. Also include some authentic examples of the genre that you would use in the L2 classroom so that students have a sense of how to develop and fine-tune the assessment criteria.

5. In Chapter 2, we provided an example in which L2 students developed a blog and created a map to highlight and describe historical and cultural landmarks. Develop some assessment criteria and a rubric that you could use to assess these tasks.

Chapter 7

Coming to Terms with 21st Century L2 Writing and Digital Literacy

The Place of Instruction

L2 instructors' preparation has generally taken the form of tertiary-level methodology courses, conferences, and occasional workshops, offered in local or national educational settings (Lacorte, 2018). This limited access to training raises the question of how to prepare new instructors and refresh the knowledge of all who are interested in the new multiliteracies and multilingual practices that are discussed in this book. In other words, how do we prepare L2 instructors to become, as Lacorte (2018) puts it, a co-inquirer, mediator, transformation agent, designer, facilitator, and empowerer? To wear all these hats requires an understanding of how digital literacy is mediated through technology and how to apply it to fit the parameters of the classroom context. The challenges are to decide how we can make use of literacy-related technology, how technology use affects our thinking, and how to reject the notion that technology should replicate traditional classroom practices.

We hope that during this book we have addressed the concerns, insecurities, and sometimes unfounded beliefs that have hindered instructors from tackling not just the linguistic and writing conventions of multimodal texts, but also from exploring a wider realm of humanities learning that is a rich source of social, cultural, political, and historical knowledge. That is, for those who lacked a clear understanding of how digitally mediated L2 writing should be approached, we hope we have made some pathways clearer so that they can now find ways to continue developing their L2 learners' writing skills to transform the way students see themselves becoming digitally literate. For those convinced that certain kinds of digital symbols, such as the use of acronyms, emoticons, and emojis (e.g., *lol*, *tbh*, for irony ☺,) weaken the use of language because they do not adhere to normative and prescriptive views, we hope we have conveyed that these non-standard forms are essentially and purposefully communicative and valid (e.g., mitigation of an ambiguous or harsh message) rather than used out of students' ignorance of standard forms (Herring, 2001, 2003). In fact, as Kern (2015) states, "people's use of non-standard forms involves a kind of translation, from one form to another – motivated sometimes phonologically, sometimes graphically" (pp. 216–217). The reality is that the use of non-standard forms, which is often connected to the brevity and immediacy of the messages, is not as widespread as one might have thought (Baron, 2008), and is limited in practice to certain communication forms like texting. In their favor, the ability to use them requires cognitive flexibility and fluidity to handle symbols across systems (Kern, 2015). L2 instructors should be open-minded if and when their L2 students engage in this type of writing: If it is appropriate to the student's communicative message and tool, they should legitimize and support its use as valid.

To those instructors who might feel reluctant about the inclusion of digital social tools and multimodal texts because their students appear to be more skilled than they are at manipulating those tools and modes, we hope that with this book we have relieved their doubts and hesitation. The fact is that, rather than teaching how to use the tools, the role of the instructor can be geared more to helping students produce rhetorically sophisticated texts. To those who argue against the inclusion of multilingual or translingual practices in the L2 classroom, we have pointed out that multilingual students, who typically use a mesh of languages when communicating with others, have an entirely valid need to explore and express their identity and language competency. The L2 class should become a balanced space in which students are encouraged to maximize their linguistic and technological knowledge and to use it appropriately for any type of communication they are asked to explore. To those who feel unprepared to keep up with the speed of technological advances and to meet the unknown future of L2 education because "[f]or the first time in our history, we are unable to accurately anticipate the literacy requirements expected at the time of graduation for children who will enter school this year" (Leu, 2000, p. 760), we hope to have strengthened their mindset to be ready for the unknown.

As Kern (2015) explains, literacy has been altered in its surface aspects and its cultural manifestations; but at an essential level, literacy remains as it has always been. We need to understand that literacy in this time and era is about designing meaning, it is about expressing identity and affiliation, and it is about becoming socialized into particular cultures of practice (Kern, 2015). Therefore, instructors need a deeper understanding of what literacies mean today and how to approach them. Crucially, rather than asking instructors to respond reactively to new technologies, we hope that they can help students to acquire the skills to manage any new technologies they may encounter in their lives (Chun et al., 2016). Otherwise, L2 writers will have unequal experiences based on the skills of the instructor they happen to come across.

Our hope is that L2 instructors see these necessary changes in a positive light and can direct their efforts toward a more inclusive classroom in relation to the heterogeneity of the students; the multilingual nature of the students; the inclusion of multimodal texts and communication in conjunction with more traditional versions of academic work; the space for reflective identities and voices; and the historical, political and social contexts in which communication occurs. In this last chapter, we focus on several final considerations that instructors may find useful and we present a model based on a combination of relevant theoretical and pedagogical perspectives that – in conjunction with the use of emerging social digital tools – can provide a framework for L2 multiliteracies. We call for a renewed understanding of what new instructors will need to consider when taking up instructional roles in a digital future. In previous chapters, we have described several pedagogical approaches to working with L2 students in the areas of multimodality, multilingualism, multiliteracy, and identity and have described ways to explore different areas of L2 digital writing, such as genres, tasks, feedback, tools, and assessment. In this chapter, we highlight the features that we believe should stand out in L2 instructors' digital practices.

Digital Literacies: A Digital Journey

As L2 practitioners, the instructor's goal is to guide students in the understanding of how to operationalize linguistic and cultural norms in both traditional and innovative ways across different materials, media, and technologies (Chun et al., 2016). Doing so means moving beyond a superficial notion of literacy so that we do not neglect "a very large and essential proportion of how we experience, reflect upon, and navigate our world" (Ess, 2016, p. 414). At the same time, the gap between analog and digital literacies needs to be bridged in a balanced and objective way. Rather than distinguishing between "new" literacies and "old" literacies, as a simplistic dichotomy, we need to concentrate on defining the relationships between current and past literacy practices (Kern, 2015). This approach values functional reading and writing skills while also considering how multiple factors influence the way we create meaning and how digital tools re-shape our ideas about what written communication means in a social context. If L2 practitioners are to enable students to make meaning using the technologies available to them, both analog and digital technologies, then instructors should become familiar with different discourse styles and registers depending on medium, purpose, and context. This change in pedagogical foci requires instructors to take risks with multimodality and, when appropriate to the context, to engage in composing something different from the traditional essay (Graban, Charlton, & Charlton, 2013).

In allowing students to take these kinds of risks and to innovate in their writing modes, we are not asking students or instructors to set aside traditional academic practices. Just as in previous writing practices, we still want students "to be rhetorical, to think carefully about what they want and need to say, who needs to hear it, and (here comes the potentially controversial part) how those two things affect the composition that gets produced" (Graban et al., 2013, p. 258). That is, digital multimodal composing should not dilute academic requirements nor be seen to have a role only outside academia; on the contrary, this type of composing enables users to amplify and fine- tune their intended meanings. In this scenario, instructors can teach their L2 students how to communicate using digital social tools by first exposing them to new genres through reading activities (e.g., texts from blogs and tweets); then, after they are familiarized as readers, lead them to design, and finally create their own content and design (see Sauro, 2014), all the while instilling in them a necessary sense of critical reflection.

Perhaps our digital journey can start by understanding how, as Chun et al. (2016) point out, literacy practices always maintain some conventions from earlier technologies (e.g., we "scroll" our electronic texts and often use "paper" page layouts on our screens), while also adopting new non-standard conventions (e.g., inclusion of emoticons and graphic art). When we "remediate" earlier media – by, for example, reusing content, revising or altering the content itself, or remixing or redistributing content (e.g., sharing remixed copies with others) (Bolter & Grusin, 2000) – we influence the design of communication and express particular values and ideas about what communication is (Gitelman & Pingree, 2003; Manovich, 2001).

Notions of literacy change as new communication technologies develop. These transformations are part of what instructors need to understand as new types of discourses, social practices, and emerging skills (Baker, 2010; Lankshear & Knobel, 2006; Leu, Forzani, Rhoads, Maykel, Kennedy, & Timbrell, 2014). Considering these challenges, analog and digital writing activities need to be used together to encourage new literacies. Rather than repeating and reusing (even multimodal digital) genres because of instructors' and students' familiarity with them (e.g., a narrative text in the wiki), there is a need for users to engage in multimodal writing "as a normal kind of intellectual engagement, where they have to choose more selectively and reflectively" (Graban et al., 2013, p. 258) among all the multimodal digital composing possibilities, and decide on the most appropriate one for the communicative purposes to their intended audience.

The implication for instructors' instructional design, and consequently for L2 students' work, is to develop their grammar(s), vocabular(ies), pragmatics, and genre knowledge(s), and at the same time develop a disposition for culturally connecting forms, contexts, meanings, and ideologies in an array of media (Chun et al., 2016). Kern (2015) proposes a *relational pedagogy* that acknowledges the relation between formal conventions (e.g., orthography, grammar) and the social ways people creatively use language that does not conform to standard prescriptive forms of communication. L2 instructors therefore need to be reflective of the course they develop and consider the issue of whether to adopt what they have already used and adapt it, or to develop a completely new approach based on emerging technologies and literacies. Instructors need to think about the relationships among the various components and factors that define L2 digital literacies. For this reason, we propose some guiding questions L2 instructors might want to ask themselves as they develop their courses:

- How can I guide my students to reflect on genres and forms of communication we have used in the past and move them forward with new ones?

- How do I explain to my students that the words, images, or sounds used in one medium may not work the same way in a different medium?
- How can I share with my students that the syntax and pragmatics of communication vary with different types of media and the audience that will receive the message?
- To what extent should I have students access, join, and become involved in sites of interest, or to ask them to access, create, share, and remix purposeful content for language learning?

Multilingual Literacies Befriend Multilingual Competence

In the light of today's bilingual/multilingual populations of students, it might seem appropriate to adopt a multilingual approach to writing rather than the monolingual bias that has dominated in the past. It would seem reasonable then to use multicompetence perspectives (i.e., competence gained from different languages) grounded in distinct social contexts, while recognizing the significance of the writer's "agency, power, and identity" (Ortega & Carson, 2010, p. 50). Although L2 curricula have not yet adopted this approach in most educational contexts, we believe that L2 instructors should familiarize themselves with multilingual competence since the L2 curriculum is starting to find ways to include this model of competence in conjunction with better-known competence models. For instance, Kobayashi and Rinnert (2013) recommend a multicompetence model of writing development to explain the creation of L1/L2/L3 texts or other varied forms of communication. They perceived three elements in this model: students' *repertoire of knowledge* (i.e., students' L1, L2, and L3 writing knowledge), the *individual and situational factors* affecting writers' decisions, and their *written output*.

Repertoires of knowledge refer to writing conventions, rhetorical features, meta-knowledge, disciplinary writing, and linguistic knowledge, which are all developed through explicit and implicit writing instruction and writing experience across multiple languages, as well as by the acquisition of linguistic features of each language for the construction of text across languages. *Individual factors* refers to the writer's agency (when making decisions), perceptions, language proficiency, and attitudes (to mention a few), whereas *social factors* refers to task, topic, and setting. It is our writers who decide, either consciously or unconsciously, which features to choose, based on individual factors such as their language proficiency, perspectives, and recent writing experience, together with social factors that impact the writing environment, such as the classroom context. These decisions then allow them to acquire more resources and to use previously learned notions and skills efficiently across languages in new and innovative ways (Kobayashi & Rinnert, 2013). Finally, the *written output* is based on the writers' decisions about the choice of text features. This multilingual competence empowers writers in a way not available to monolingual writers. Their texts do not correspond to a single language; they present a linguistic form of hybridity that represent features of more than one language. Thus, multilingual writing will tend to be locally situated within and across languages; will be varied, even within a particular educational setting; and will be developmental, due to individual factors and the effect of increased instruction and practice. More importantly, this model lets us recognize that the notion which literacy transfers from one language to another is inadequate, since multilingual students rely "on a merged system of writing knowledge across languages, rather than transferring writing features from one language to another" (Rinnert & Kobayashi, 2016, p. 373).

Apart from linguistic decisions, the instructor also needs to consider the non-linguistic aspects of communication that will govern students' task-related decisions. For instance, the instructor needs to consider: Which visual or audio resources (corresponding to cultures that are integrated through their L1, L2, or L3) will students select? How will students mesh those resources together to enrich the linguistic expression of their text? What is the basis for the students' decisions, and how will their linguistic and cultural background affect those decisions? What form will students' intended audience take? Clearly, the challenge for L2 instructors is finding ways to integrate the social context at various levels into the development of digital writing and to neutralize the unequal power relations among languages or dialects that students and educational settings may consciously or unconsciously favor or assume and therefore perpetuate. As Ortega (2017) states, we can no longer accept studying "L2 learning as 'double monolingualism' instead of as 'emergent multilingualism' without distorting the object of study and creating validity and ethical problems" (pp. 304–305).

The multilingual competence model undoubtedly presents some caveats or considerations to bear in mind. L2 instructors cannot assume that they recognize the linguistic profiles of all of their students. Instructors need to: (a) figure out the degree to which students are multilingual by asking the right questions in the right way; (b) not assume that, by definition, language students only know and use one language; and (c) seek to align multilingual and translingual teaching with testing (Ortega, 2017). The questions below can help L2 instructors to understand their students more deeply and to then readjust their curricular objectives if necessary.

- To what extent is the acceptance of multilingual competence and its representation in texts feasible in L2 (writing) courses?
- How can globalized online spaces create new, multilingual contexts that foster L2 learning opportunities for L2 students?
- What forms of linguistic adjustments might students need to make when participating in different platforms, such Facebook or fan fiction online communities?
- To what extent do diverse communication media need to be mastered for students to express themselves in multilingual ways?
- To what extent are L2 instructors addressing L2 students' attempts to produce meaning with the incorporation of new modes of writing and communication?

Digital Tools (and Literacies) Are Not Neutral

Another element that we need to remember is the political dimension that literacies, including digital literacies, have (Chun et al., 2016). Chun et al. (2016) underscore Marvin's (1988) view that the new digital tools present themselves as new "arenas for negotiating issues crucial to the conduct of social life; among them, who is inside and outside, who may speak, who may not, and who has authority and may be believed" (p. 4). While technological advances, especially the internet and digital social tools, have led to noticeable gains for commerce and cultural diffusion, education, social inclusion, and political participation, they have also led to manipulation, domination, and exploitation. Just as social media tools have the potential to encourage intercultural dialog, they can also serve cultural imperialism and skew political causes (Chun et al., 2016). Daily we read about "fake news" and campaigns of misinformation as well as how companies have utilized and sold data for their own purposes. It is essential to foster L2 students' awareness of how "writing systems and other technologies of literacy have histories and ideologies embedded in them" (Kern, 2015, p. 244–245). It is necessary, as part of literacy education, to reflect on how the information provided can be manipulated to serve particular interests. For instance, and in line with recent events on Facebook raising concerns around privacy issues, students should be aware of how information is collected on media sites and how it is utilized and fed to their devices to prioritize, personalize, and target specific causes. L2 students should also be aware of how the default settings, for example, on Twitter or Facebook, define how and what type of information is provided to them and how their information stream can change based on the platform managers' intentions. The integration of digital tools is changing the way we collect, store, and retrieve information and students need to know what types of knowledge, extending past information, it is critical to learn.

L2 instructors know that students are not, or should not be, passive consumers and users of digital social tools. Rather, they seek to engage their students to become active participants when involved in digital practices in order to question their own and others' ideologies, language choices, and policies. When using these tools, students should also be asked to reflect on ethical questions related to power (e.g., the power of prestige linguistic forms over local dialects or the acquisition of information in areas without access to the internet). The use of these tools has implications: through their use we can promote or condemn particular types of ethical or unethical conduct (e.g., flaming, cyberbullying) (Kern, 2015). Certainly, many users are closing their Facebook or Twitter accounts because of the incendiary, denigrating, or insulting messages they are receiving. Additionally, students should be sensitive to how people from other cultures may understand and value technologies and literacy practices differently (Chun et al., 2016). Moreover, given the facility to cut and paste and to disseminate information from one text to another to produce mendacious information, the ability to analyze the source and quality of information critically is extremely important: our students need to be able to verify the authenticity of all information they retrieve and share.

The following questions are designed to encourage L2 instructors to teach the critical analysis of digital information:

- How do the digital tools my students use in the L2 classroom control what type of information is provided?
- How do students use the information collected to support their creation of texts for academic and non-academic purposes?
- How can I convey to students that the choice of information and even the use of technologies may be interpreted differently by audiences from other cultures?
- How can I initiate a discussion with students about the power that digital tools and multilingual and multimodal texts have in local and global contexts?

Closing the Digital and Translingual Divide

Multiliteracies, as Fordham and Oakes (2013) point out, are not linked to the learning of specific disciplines within the classroom setting; they are also essential skills for becoming a citizen in a pluralist, global society. Participating in a multicultural democratic society requires the capacity to navigate conceptually and communicatively within and between several rhetorical dimensions. This implies the need to create worthwhile information and to use sophisticated technologies, as well as the ability to assess individuals' rhetorical choices in relation to, for example, writing, visual images, or technological applications (Fordham & Oakes, 2013). The problem is, as Ortega (2017) points out, that there is a divide between the haves, those who are "already wealthy and technologically savvy [and who] use technology more frequently" (p. 301), and the have nots. Bridging this gap allows students from all social, historical, and economic backgrounds to successfully achieve digital literacies. Yet, what is relevant is not only that students have access to technology but that they are able to engage with it in a manner that transcends recreational uses. The goal is to provide students with access to the information and social networks that bring higher knowledge and useful ways to serve their interests and their communities. The important question is how best to educate marginalized, often multilingual students that we might find in our classroom, such as the indigenous, migrants, refugees, HL speakers, 1.5-generation speakers as well as the elite multilinguals who are labeled a "foreigner" if they do not master the L2 to the level of a native speaker (Ortega, 2017).

L2 instructors could observe and assess students' prior digital literacy competence to make sure that they are not wrongly classified based on erroneous or prejudiced suppositions (Marsh, 2016). Having a baseline of the students' literacy competence, instructors can then focus on students' digital fluency to help them improve their technical proficiency and ease them in performing and accomplishing digital tasks (e.g., create a travel itinerary using Google maps) while achieving the already set-up outcomes (e.g., utilize different semiotic resources) to create a well-crafted and appealing final product (e.g., professional travel itinerary) that usually lead them toward better socioeconomic opportunities (Briggs & Makice, 2011). Students' use of the technology, however, needs to be defined within local and contextual parameters and by the technology users themselves. To ensure that students engage in sophisticated rhetorical work in the L2 writing class, we should harmonize pedagogical decisions with anticipation of students' future needs. In this case, it makes complete sense to conduct a needs analysis of language learning as well as of technological proficiency to create appropriate technology-mediated curricula (González-Lloret, 2014). We would add that there is also a need to ensure L2 instructors are well informed about the extent of the multiliteracy needs of our L2 student population so they can guide students wisely in the development of those competencies.

When thinking of bridging the digital divide, it is equally important to consider the gap created when using multiple languages in the creation of digital texts: that is, multilingualism and translingualism. As Johnson (2013) stated, to bridge the digital gap we need to operationalize multilingual or translingual approaches to the notion of text composition. However, instructors are often ill-prepared to tackle multilingual and translingual approaches for several reasons, not all of which are under their control (Gevers, 2018). Clearly there is a need for adjustments at the institutional level, but these might not be reasonable or practical for language programs, which are already wrestling with complex educational requirements and constraints.

Instructors' expertise and willingness to facilitate students' translingual development can consider students' varying levels of linguistic proficiency, which can limit their success with translingual approaches. While detractors of translingualism do not see it as realistic or desirable for students to code-mesh, particularly with students who view themselves as monolingual or who lack proficiency in the dominant language of the target culture, some detractors still see the value of building critical awareness regarding translingualism; that is, of helping students to analyze how people use translingual texts while not encouraging code-meshing through instruction (Gevers, 2018). Horner, Lu, Royster, and Trimbur (2011), for instance, emphasize the use of descriptive teaching (e.g., in which students examine and analyze texts created in a translingual manner) and the need to expose students to different language varieties so they can be encouraged to explore linguistic variation in texts, thus drawing attention to their heterogeneity. Canagarajah (2013b), however, advocates a dialogical approach that allows for translingual experimentation if the goal is awareness building rather than explicit teaching of code-meshing strategies. The idea is to match the L2 curriculum to students' future needs. Nonetheless, L2 instructors need to acknowledge certain caveats in introducing translingual approaches to the L2 classroom. First, L2 instructors may not have the support necessary to discuss translingual practices in a way that is helpful to students (Matsuda, 2013, 2014; Tardy, 2017). Second, advanced L2 students may have the expertise to experiment with code-meshing strategies, but lower proficiency students may not; that is, students may need to develop proficiency in established language varieties and awareness of dominant discourses before being able to benefit from such an approach (Gevers, 2018).

Gevers (2018) also cautions L2 instructors that even though class activities which work with language difference can be used for developing critical awareness of translingual practices, an approach to instruction which involves code-meshing may be detrimental if students are asked to meet traditional academic learning outcomes that are not accepting of translingualism. In addition, L2 instructors need to be mindful of their bias regarding what is right or wrong and to understand that the notion of error itself can be a social construct. For example, Krall-Lanoue (2013) advises instructors to understand and negotiate their students' non-standard language use, seeing the recognition of errors as meaningful rather than problematic. Matsuda (2014) also warns against uncritically embracing translingualism and applying it in the classroom without a clear rationale. In his view, encouraging students' translingual behavior could reinforce "the ethnocentric tendency to impose an etic perspective while missing the opportunity to consider and negotiate with the emic perspective" (p. 482). He further indicates that a stress on translingualism might only reflect the interests and intellectual curiosity of certain scholars and educators.

Therefore, instructors need to consider certain factors if they want to incorporate translingual practices in their instruction (Gevers, 2018): (a) to make sure that multilingual students are in a position to and want to negotiate translingual identities as writers; (b) to consider what literacies are required of students in academia and in the workplace; (c) to ascertain that they will have institutional support; and (d) to consider whether students will benefit from putting non-standard language patterns into writing and in what contexts these practices may be most successful. Accepting or encouraging translingual hybridity in writing opens up the potential for a "third space" (Bhabha, 1994) that allows for a hypothetically empowering position of "in-betweenness" (Canagarahah, 2013b, p. 3).

In this context, questions that L2 instructors can ask are:

- Have I carefully considered if my curriculum can link the external digital world and the technological world of the classroom?
- How can I judge my students' digital expertise diplomatically, without making assumptions or making them feel uncomfortable?
- To what extent am I engaged in inclusive teaching practices that take into account the translingual nature of my students' backgrounds?
- What types of digital writing practices can I bring to the L2 classroom that could engage my students to recognize and validate their multilingual practices?

Hybridity in Our Thinking: Flexible Models for L2 Digital Writing

Real transformations in the L2 writing class imply a "philosophical change in how we see our relationship to technology" (Graban et al., 2013, p. 250) and how we recognize monolingual and prescriptive perspectives so as to avoid replicating old literacy practices with the new digital tools as we integrate multilingual practices. Incorporating flexible multilingual and transligual models means that L2 instructors would be informed of the best theoretical and pedagogical approaches for the teaching of L2 writing practice, both composing and design, when integrating digital tools. Thus, we propose to focus first on the interface of relevant theoretical perspectives which, in conjunction with emerging social media tools, are transforming the way we view the written text.

Keeping in mind that as L2 writing instructors we want to facilitate our students' language development, we have informed our practice within accepted SLA tenets (e.g., scaffolding, mediation, interaction), rhetorical tenets (e.g., genre and writing conventions), and applied linguistics tenets (e.g., L2 discourse based on writing purpose, feedback, pedagogies). In light of the qualitative changes that the use of a range of semiotic resources in conjunction with the written text bring to the composition process, we have expanded our theoretical base to consider models, such as social semiotics, that lie outside the traditional realm of L2 teaching and learning (see Figure 7.1).

Reflecting on the affordances of the digital tools at our disposal, we have examined their power to support multimodality, the expanded role of the audience, and the reconsideration of authorship and ownership. Meaningful inclusion of digital tools in the L2 classroom will enable us to expand our linguistic perspectives, to analyze the rhetorical characteristics of texts and messages, and to appreciate the inherent value of eclectic semiotic resources.

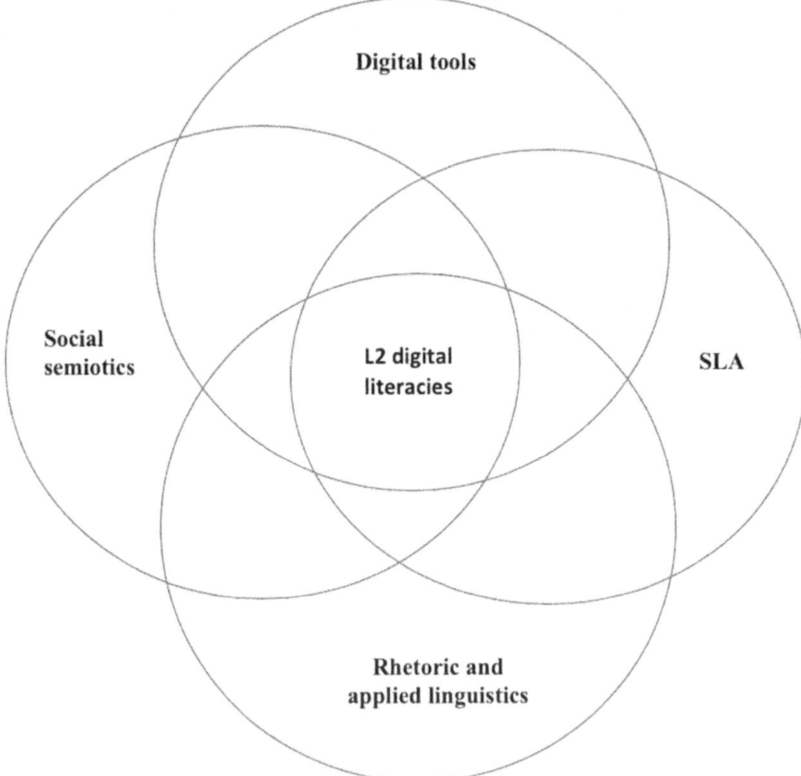

Figure 7.1. Interface of Digital Tools and Theoretical Frameworks

We are not seeking to change or eliminate teaching practices that have been successful in the past; rather, we want to encourage the cultivation of critical awareness as we help students to acquire literacies that will enable them to become informed and responsible citizens in the future.

It is doubtless a challenge for instructors to successfully apply unfamiliar theoretical frameworks in the classroom. It is also difficult to grasp the connection between the different digital tools and the literacies (e.g., information literacy, computer literacy, media literacy) that these tools support. There are a number of options for addressing these difficulties. Instructors need to identify trusted pedagogical approaches that can guide them in how to work with multiliteracies. Adopting multimodal, multilingual, and translingual practices for digital literacy requires that both language instructors and students adapt to the qualities, goals, and contexts of mediated language use and evaluate which genres and communication tools are most suitable to be included in their own L2 curricula (Thorne & Black, 2007).

Clearly, technological innovations in the area of digital social tools are constantly evolving and our practical applications may well be outdated by the time some educators read this book and learn of them. Yet the pedagogical frameworks that we advocate (see Chapter 1), which encourage analysis, critical reflection, and effective practice, will themselves suggest the tools that will offer the best support (see Figure 7.2).

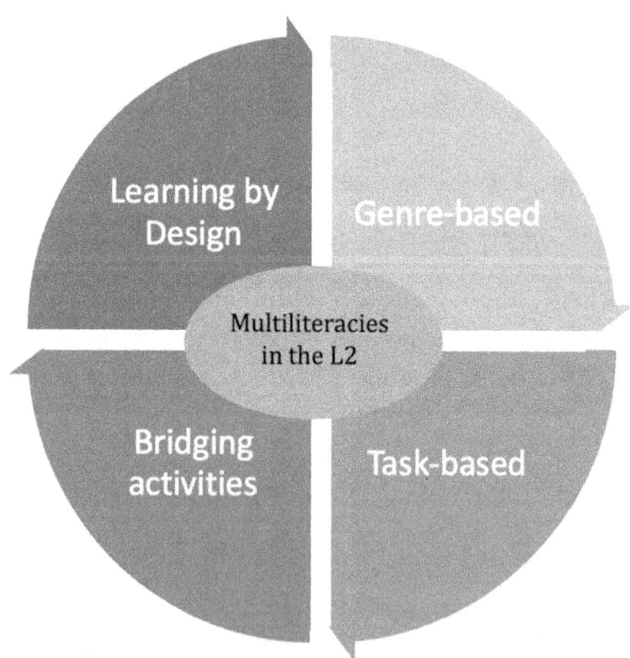

Figure 7.2. Pedagogical Frameworks

As Blake (2013) has pointed out, "No particular technology is superior to any other tool; it is all in the way the activities are implemented so as to engage and foster the student's own sense of agency" (p. xvii). In other words, whether we use wikis or blogs or whether we engage in fan fiction or Wikipedia entry-like practices, writing instructors' goals will be to provide their L2 learners with the linguistic, discursive, and analytical knowledge that will empower them to become critical participants in today's digitally mediated literacies practices. The key to successfully helping L2 students achieve these aims resides in the approach or multiple approaches that instructors select and apply, such as Learning by Design, genre-based instruction, bridging activies, and/or task-based language teaching, that they may tap into when creating a course.

In this chapter, we outline an instructional model (see Figure 7.3) that includes all of the components that we have addressed in previous chapters and that we believe are important when developing writing activities in the L2 classroom. The primary objective of this model is to articulate a sort of map that current and future L2 instructors can reflect on and use flexibly as a guide when developing a syllabus, program curriculum, or a simple task. The function of this model is not to provide a normative and fixed way of addressing multiliteracies and multilingualism, but is rather a descriptive attempt to view the elements presented in this book with the idea of seeing how they affect one another. There are other elements as influential as the ones under discussion here. Since we are largely focused on the external environment, especially of teaching and its impact on students' digital writing, it is out of our purview to recognize and operationalize constructs such as individual cognitive abilities and differences, since they function within the paradigm of internal factors of language learning; yet as L2 instructors, we must retain the capacity to tailor our tasks to a more individualized design or to provide more specific individualized feedback to trigger scaffolding learning moments.

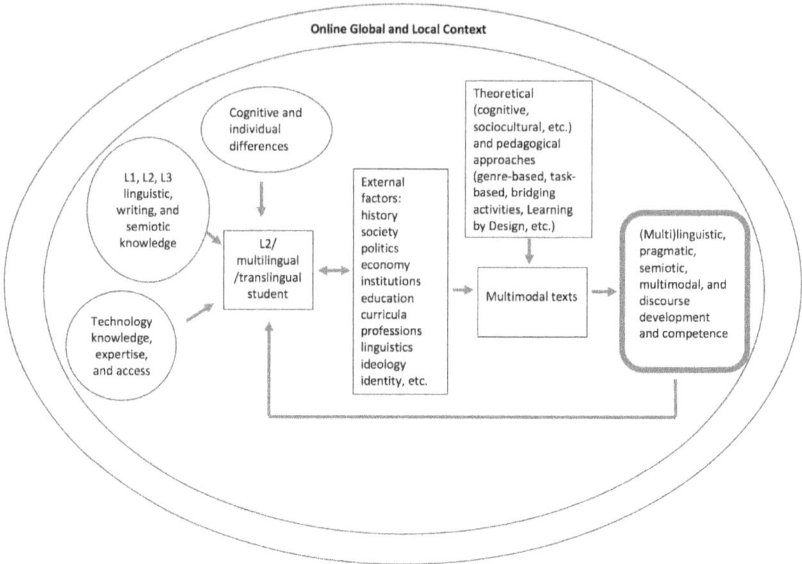

Figure 7.3. Multiliterate and Multilingual Model

To address our students needs, we need to consider a number of factors as shown in the model of Figure 7.3. First, knowledge of students' (multi)linguistic and technical knowledge, expertise, and access to technology will help us to ask the right questions to obtain an accurate and comprehensive profile of student abilities. Further, understanding the world around us and its political, educational, and economic constraints should reveal parameters that are part of the situated learning experience and help us to design a framework in which task development becomes an instrument that meets students' needs and maximizes their potential for success. The model incorporates how L2/multilingual/translingual students are affected by many internal factors, such as cognitive and individual differences; L1, L2, L3 linguistic, writing, and semiotic knowledge; technology knowledge, expertise, and access; and external factors, such as historical, social, political, and economic. Thus, when students take their first steps toward the creation of a multimodal text, whether it be L2, multilingual, or translingual text, there are numerous factors that are unconsciously or consciously triggered and that will then shape their digital writing practices. The process of text design falls within an array of theoretical (e.g., sociocultural) and pedagogical approaches (e.g., Learning by Design) that govern how well students will complete a text which meets course expectations. It is this chain of conscious and unconscious actions that ultimately supports the development and the growth of the L2 student's (multi)linguistic, pragmatic, semiotic, multimodal, and discourse development and competence.

The question that many instructors may ask is how can this model be applied in the L2 (writing) classroom? How do we frame the creation of a learning task within a theoretical view? The answer depends on the desired outcomes for the task. Because the completion of the task is one of the objectives, one expected outcome could be linguistic and semiotic development as well as an improvement in multilinguistic competence. Therefore, instructors will need to consider the various ways students can achieve these competences. For example, a sociocultural framework can be applied to address evidence of scaffolding, collaborative work, and a clear relationship between the digital tools' affordabilities and the student's work. On the other hand, instructors may use a social-semiotic perspective if the desired outcome is to increase students' expertise with various semiotic resources. Framing the task within a theoretical perspective enables the gap between theory and practice to be bridged, resulting in effective task design. From a pedagogical perspective the following example illustrates the adoption and adaptation of factors that are intrinsic to successful task design.

Setting up Our Students for Success: Applying the Model

An instructor needs to design a task that takes into account the above-mentioned components to cater to a mixed L2 cohort of students at college level, in an urban area where the dominant language is English. Thinking about the globally controversial topic of immigration, the instructor decides to create a digital multimodal writing task that helps students understand the economic, social, and political reasons for migration, the difficulties and advantages of settling in a new place, and how certain decisions will impact on all family members. To learn about the bigger picture, the students will research community views by examining the impact of immigration on the local, regional, and national economy and will discuss how the host country has responded to various groups of immigrants during its past and recent history. The instructor selects a multi-author blog as a digital tool because blogging is a flexible genre that accommodates descriptions, narrations, and argumentations. It acts as a quasi-journalistic genre, which provides students a chance to experiment with a genre related to that professional area. Students will be asked to employ different methods and tools to gather information (e.g., read, interview, and interact with families that have immigrated in the last 20 years) and create multimodal texts, all of which will allow them to develop critical digital literacy. In terms of language, the instructor encourages, but does not force, multilingual and translingual uses. Once the first series of blog entries are published, other students from the college and an audience from outside the school context will have access to read and respond to them. The steps we envision to ensure the success of the task are described below.

Step 1: Getting to Know the Students

The first goal is to get to know the students in the class. To this end, the instructor will conduct a survey to obtain biographical information and to query students' perceptions about their language(s) proficiency; current technological access and expertise, specifically regarding social tools; and last but not least, knowledge of and opinions about immigration. The background information will give the instructor a picture of the students' heritage and the languages that they know and use, and their historical and family connections to the language(s). Recognizing the linguistic diversity that our L2 students bring to the class highlights and validates their own linguistic practices; for example, whether students come from what is referred to as a primary monolingual, elite bilingual, or a marginalized bilingual (or multilingual) setting.

Obtaining information regarding students' knowledge about the topic of immigration can also be useful when deciding how to start addressing this topic in class, especially if there are conflicting ideas and opinions among the students. Regarding technology, we should consider the divide between the have and the have nots and the potential consequences of this divide for students' learning (Ortega, 2017). The instructor thus needs to be aware of the students' current uses of technology, their competence with different tools, and their degree of access to them. With the results of the survey, the instructor can collect enough information about the students to design and tailor the task based on their particular knowledge base and needs (if survey is not an initiative that appeals to the instructor, focus groups or brainstorming sessions could be alternatives).

Further, because it is usual to find variation in language and technology proficiency levels, some subtasks (or phases toward the completion of the blog in this case) may benefit from collaborative work and adjustment of linguistic feedback to scaffold students' learning more individually. The instructor will support all students equally to create an inclusive instructional atmosphere that is responsive to students' needs. This kind of classroom environment can support students' personal and cultural narratives and move away from those that are hegemonic monocultural, monolingual, or normative; thus, the class moves towards a more flexible heteroglossia in which narratives can become transcultural and translingual. As a note of caution, we are not advocating the use of translingual practices if it is not in the students' interest to do so.

Step 2: Considering the Context(s)

Once the three elements of the model – technology expertise, linguistic and semiotic knowledge, and individual differences – that will influence students' individual performance have been identified through the survey, the instructor has to think about the factors that need to be navigated in a learning task if the objective is to create a real-life authentic task that can be recognized as such by the students. A main consideration is to acknowledge the wide scope of educational and out-of-school text-based practices that the instructor can draw on. The goals of the curricular program and the institution itself will provide some parameters about the educational outcomes they want students to achieve. In addition, the instructor will need an understanding of the local and national political situation regarding topics such as immigration and language policy; social, economic, and demographic factors; and local history. Obtaining this multi-faceted knowledge will provide a sense of how the thorny topic of immigration can be addressed, and how differing views can be presented respectfully or be challenged thoughtfully. Perceptions of immigration and language policies, for instance, encourage students to position themselves in terms of their growing sense of identity as they engage in critical analysis and reflective discussion.

This kind of learning does not come in a vacuum, and the instructor needs to think of ways in which students can come to terms with their own ideologies and those of other people around them. Such critical reflections may also have an important influence on their evolving identities as they position themselves in relation to the immigration topic. Exploring the context at the local and global level provides a greater chance to get to know what people think and also to observe how critical and reflective content may shape people's perceptions and opinions. This expanded view of the topic can result in a delegitimization of dichotomous opinions (i.e., totally in favor of or against immigration) that are not always helpful as we confront the complexities of our world.

Step 3: Developing the Task

Contextualizing the task for local or global contexts can be managed in the online environment. The inquiry-based methodology will benefit from a sequenced pedagogical plan and will serve the learning goals the instructor has set up. Regardless of the chosen pedagogical approach, the important part of task design is the allocation and timing of different phases to guide students to successfully complete the task. For example, Learning by Design recommends that the instructor design a multiliteracy task in four stages: experiencing, conceptualizing, analyzing, and applying (see task outlined in Chapter 4 for more details). If applying the bridging activities framework, students will observe and collect digital texts and practices that illustrate similar blogs to the one they will produce. They will analyze a selection of texts that vary in social and lexical-grammatical aspects as well as non-linguistic aspects, and will then produce their own texts, share them, and reflect on their reception (see task in Chapter 3 for more details). Within each phase, the instructor can create particular subtasks intended to guide students to think critically and to remind them to gather relevant information before composing an entry for the class blog. An important element of the blog is also language choice. The instructor needs to decide beforehand if, apart from the target language, the use of translingualism is going to be accepted or not.

In all phases, the instructor will provide guidance in the understanding of blogging as a genre, its flexible structures, and all linguistic and non-linguistic aspects that characterize the genre: these include the selection of semiotic resources (respectful and culturally appropriate), the choice of discourse style, the distinctive voices with which the information is articulated and communicated, and the role of the blog audience. Also, the instructor needs to decide what types of feedback (see Chapter 4 for more details) will be most beneficial to student authors and modes of assessment to monitor students' progress and execution of the task at various stages of task completion (see Chapter 5 for more details).

Gathering the information for blog entries, making sure that they are effective in structure and design, and responding to the audience's comments are elements controlled by the students that will help to maintain their motivation to complete all stages of the task systematically. The essential challenge for the instructor is balancing the various pedagogical elements that come into play, such as the use of individual and collaborative work (co-authoring or otherwise cooperating), setting up short-term goals (paying attention to the readings, summarizing information, outlining the task, etc.) and not losing sight of long-term goals (creation of a final blog entry); and creating opportunities for peer and/or instructor feedback. This process approach to the creation of blog entries allows for drafting of entries and sequenced student revisions. The success of the blog task depends on information being delivered in a multimodal way and in the level of engagement with the audience and the quality and relevance of audience responses.

Outcomes

Blog completion (or its ongoing development if used as a multiyear activity) represents the final stage or achievement of the task. The ideal outcome of this organized and carefully designed task, however, is that instructors can see evidence of student improvement: this shows at linguistic, semiotic, pragmatic, discourse, and multimodal levels and also in the development of content knowledge and writing competence in general. The instructor can feel confident that her/his L2 writers have achieved valuable multilingual/translingual and multiliteracy competences. These competences support our students' growth as L2 writers and consolidate their previous knowledge, setting them up for the challenges that lie ahead of them as citizens in today's world.

Conclusion

Adjusting our roles as writing instructors to suit changing educational styles and views is one aspect of our profession that we are used to. In this chapter, we have focused on an instructional model that will help us to create courses, tasks, or programs with a very definite goal in mind: to help students become multiliterate and multilingual writers. In today's world we must see the teaching of languages and literacies as more than an extension of traditional language teaching: our aim has now shifted toward practical ways of operationalizing digital literacies and the multi/translingual phenomenon. This new approach allows L2 learners to have a voice in education and society and is capable of bridging the digital and linguistic divide. Addressing these elements will give the L2 instructor a better understanding of what students need to learn and how to teach it.

As language professionals, it is crucial for us to create and recommend a model for language teaching that serves L2 digital literacy with an emphasis on writing. We want to provide a sense that all elements of the model come into focus, implicitly or explicitly, during the process of teaching and learning. Our idea is to present the teaching model within the interface of theoretical and pedagogical frameworks in a situated social learning environment. The application of this flexible (albeit no doubt imperfect) model, allows for constant experimentation on the part of an instructor, who may adapt it from time to time and wherever necessary to suit a range of student achievement outcomes. We hope that this model helps instructors to situate their digital learning tasks within today's digital world.

Ideas for Reflection and Discussion

1. What are the main difficulties and challenges that L2 instructors may face when introducing digital social tools and digital genres into the classroom?
2. What considerations mentioned in the chapter (or others you have thought of) should you take into account in designing a multiliteracy and/or multilingual course in your institution?
3. Even if the instructor is keen to adopt new pedagogical approaches, the institution may limit such initiatives. What are some of the institutional constraints you could foresee in relation to translingualism, the digital divide, and availability of social tools?
4. This book has discussed many factors that directly or indirectly affect the way we teach languages today, and some of them are evident in the instructional model presented in this chapter. What other factors could be included in the model?
5. Lacorte (2018) suggests some roles that instructors teaching multiliteracies adopt in their L2 classrooms. What are the roles you see yourself adopting to support students with digital composing and language use?

Concluding Remarks

Trying to make predictions about emerging digital tools, and their communicative uses is always going to be a guessing game. The important point to remember is that no matter what challenges or communicative opportunities lie ahead, as L2 practitioners we will need to persist in our research efforts and continue to strengthen our teaching practice to ensure that our L2 students achieve multiliteracy. The only way for L2 instructors and researchers to navigate this unmapped journey is to be prepared to be flexible in unfamiliar situations, recognizing that constant new experience and practice will make them flexible and develop their expertise. Being adventurous and open-minded with digital technology seems to be the main characteristic we will need in the classrooms of the future. As we continue our journey into digital literacies for writing, we foresee some research avenues that will support us to become better L2 writing instructors; some of these are mentioned in this book but they need to be further explored and new ones need to be identified.

The notion of texts, as we have always known them, has changed. While tools like wikis or blogs offer spaces where L2 writers can still compose texts in academic registers, such as exposition or argumentation, other tools, such as Facebook or Twitter, ask L2 writers to focus more on other kinds of communicative messages; these are generally brief, due to the characteristics of the tools themselves, which pare the communication of information down to its essential core. As opposed to more traditional texts, these brief texts frequently create a sense of temporal immediacy, which often triggers an oral-like written discourse that has an immediate audience and is therefore interactive as the audience responds in similar style. In conjunction with different modes of communication, these texts present a form of hybridity that represents a new type of multimodality which does not always have obvious antecedents.

The newness and often disconcerting characteristics of these texts have left many L2 writing instructors with many questions; for example, how valid now is the notion of linguistic accuracy, or how should feedback be provided in this digital context? Additionally, although digital multimodality might be increasingly used in the L2 classroom, instructors are still working in a trial-and-error method of testing digital social tools and learning about multimodality as they experiment with it in the classroom. However, to maximize the potential of multimodality, and thus expand learning, Guichon and Cohen (2016) point out that knowledge of how multimodality works should be of prime importance for L2 practitioners if they want to use it effectively in the classroom. As current research has already illustrated, examining how multimodal data helps co-create meaning is not an easy task (Helm & Dooly, 2017), and teaching how the combination of different semiotic resources can be used for meaning-making is still a slippery undertaking. Further examination of these digital, multimodal texts' characteristics through research will help to refine our definitions of what constitutes best practice in terms of accuracy, feedback, genre construction, student text revision (Goldstein, 2016), assessment techniques, and other factors. The dissemination of research-based findings about best practices will increase instructors' understanding of how to integrate emerging digital tools, texts, and genres successfully in the L2 classroom.

One of the benefits of digital social tools is that they have brought writing to the forefront of communication. Our notions of text construction, authorship, ownership, collaboration, and audience have expanded and morphed to fit the new tools' affordances. But perhaps, in line with social movement in applied linguistics and sociocultural studies, digital tools have also shone a new light on our students' personal multilingual practices. Moving away from monolingual practices that treated bilingualism and multilingualism as two or more language systems working independently, new thinking has led to the questioning of monolingual, monocultural assumptions (Casanave, 2017). We now recognize that L2 students' varied backgrounds and experiences not only influence the linguistic repertoires they use to tell their stories, in both the traditional and the newer academic and non-academic genres, but also can suggest novel and exciting ways of telling them. Further research that examines the role of multiple languages (i.e., the languages in our students' repertoires) in the composing process will ultimately provide L2 practitioners with research-tested information about the many linguistic, cognitive, and social factors that interact in multilingual or translingual text construction (Manchón 2013). Consequently, we will get a better picture of factors that add to or detract from L2 learners' linguistic competencies. Applying this knowledge to L2 curricula will help L2 instructors to operate more comfortably with multilingual and translingual practices.

Of equal importance is the re-emergence of interest within academic writing in hearing writers' voices. Although writers' own voices have been widely examined in discourse analysis and identity studies, with the advent of digital social tools, we now recognize that student voices are linked to an emerging sense of self and to empowerment. The use of digital tools allows learners to participate and interact in common-bond, common-identity communities or affinity spaces. An important question, however, is not only how individual student voices are being interpreted but how digital tools have brought a focus to the representation of socially constructed meanings. There is a need for more analysis of written discourse that examines the social nature of exchanges and co-authored texts, showcasing examples of discursive features. The extent to which learners' written texts are shaped by their collaborative work with others and redirected by the comments of their audience certainly will have an implication for assessment practices; we may need new ones, given that the results of collaborative and interactive discourse are difficult to observe and measure.

In terms of collaborative practices, providing students with joint multimodal writing experiences will likely validate their digital literacy practices and prepare them for the personal and professional experiences they will encounter after school or college (Hirvela & Belcher, 2016). Yet little is known of the actual processes, decisions, and actions that take place when students embark on the composing of multimodal texts, at either the individual or collaborative level. Conducting research in these areas, with various digital tools, will guide L2 instructors to develop tasks that reflect students' digital composing processes more closely. Further, apart from the design of the task, another way of guiding L2 students to grow as multiliterate global citizens would be to study the use of electronic feedback. Until now the most prominent use of feedback, through Google Docs, MS Word, screencast recordings or chats, has revealed that feedback focuses mainly on local aspects of the language and discursive features of the text. The issue of how to provide feedback to more complex non-traditional academic digital multimodal texts is still in its infancy. Further research that examines feedback more specifically on multilingual or translingual features of the text and on areas such as the role of the audience will guide L2 instructors (and student peers) to provide more targeted feedback.

Finally, this book has shown how instructors can apply theoretical and pedagogical frameworks productively and judiciously to make the teaching of writing in the 21st century both efficient and enjoyable. Now might be the time for L2 writing specialists to expand our theoretical frameworks to address the new digital writing practices that have become part of L2 students' digital writing repertoires. As Rinnert and Kobayashi (2016) point out, perhaps other disciplinary theories, such as complex systems theory (Larsen-Freeman, 2006), which assumes a non-linear trajectory of language development in relation to the writing development of both individual and groups, might be able to better capture and express students' digital literacy practices when working with multiple and varied types of discourse.

Assuming these research possibilities bear fruit, and as experience with digital genres continues to permeate language curricula, L2 educators will be in a position to find a balance between expanding notions of genre and maintaining traditional and well-established writing genres. The future looks bright as it is becoming clear that we are living in an inspiring and dynamically changing time for education in general, and more specifically for the L2 writing curriculum. As you continue your own digital multimodal journey with and for your L2 students, we encourage you to continue navigating the uncharted or unfamiliar waters of the digital world, believing as we do that we have the potential to promote our students' learning experience in compelling and creative ways.

References

Abraham, L. B., & Williams, L. (2009). The discussion forum as a component of a technology-enhanced integrated performance assessment. In L. B. Abraham & L. Williams (eds.), *Electronic discourse in language learning and language teaching* (pp. 319–343). Amsterdam: John Benjamins. https://doi.org/10.1075/lllt.25.21abr

Abrams, Z. (2016). Exploring collaboratively written L2 texts among first-year learners of German in Google Docs. *Computer Assisted Language Learning, 29*(8), 1259–1270. https://doi.org/10.1080/09588221.2016.1270968

AbuSeileek, A., & Abualsha'r, A. (2014). Using peer computer-mediated corrective feedback to support EFL learners' writing. *Language Learning & Technology, 18*(1), 76–95.

Adair-Hauck, B., Glisan, E. W., Koda, K., Swender, E., & Sandrock, P. (2006). The integrated performance assessment (IPA): Connecting assessment to instruction and learning. *Foreign Language Annals, 39*, 359–382. https://doi.org/10.1111/j.1944-9720.2006.tb02894.x

Adair-Hauck, B., Glisan, E. W., & Troyan, F. J. (2013). *Implementing integrated performance assessment.* Alexandria, VA: ACTFL.

Adair-Hauck, B., & Troyan, F. J. (2013). A descriptive and co-constructive approach to integrated performance assessment feedback. *Foreign Language Annals, 46*(1), 23–44. https://doi.org/10.1111/flan.12017

Adams, R., & Ross-Feldman, L. (2008). Does writing influence learner attention to form? In D. Belcher & A. Hirvela (eds.), *The oral/literate connection: Perspectives on L2 speaking/writing connections* (pp. 243–267). Ann Arbor: University of Michigan Press.

Adsanatham, C. (2012). Integrating assessment and instruction: Using student-generated grading criteria to evaluate multimodal digital projects. *Computers and Composition*, *29*, 152–174. https://doi.org/10.1016/j.compcom.2012.04.002

Al-Ali, S. (2014). Embracing the selfie craze: Exploring the possible use of Instagram as a language mlearning tool. *Issues and Trends in Educational Technology*, *2*(2), 1–16. https://doi.org/10.2458/azu_itet_v2i2_ai-ali

Alcantud-Díaz, M., Ricart Vayá, A., & Gregori-Signes, C. (2014). "Share your experience": Digital storytelling in English for tourism. *Iberica*, *27*, 185–204.

Aljaafreh, A., & Lantolf, J. (1994). Negative feedback as regulation and second language learning in the zone of proximal development. *Modern Language Journal*, *78*(4), 465–483. https://doi.org/10.1111/j.1540-4781.1994.tb02064.x

Allen, M. R. (2003). This is not a hypertext, but...: A set of lexias on textuality. *CTHEORY*. Retrieved on January 1, 2020 from http://www.ctheory.net/articles.aspx?id=389.

Anderson, D., Atkins, A., Ball, C. E., Homicz Millar, K., Selfe, C., & Selfe, R. (2006). Integrating multimodality into composition curricula: Survey methodology and results from a CCCC research grant. *Composition Studies*, *34*(2), 59–84.

Andrews, R., & Smith, A. (2011). *Developing writers: Teaching and learning in the digital age*. New York: Open University Press.

Arnold, N., & Ducate, L. (2006). Future language teachers' social and cognitive collaboration in an online environment. *Language Learning & Technology*, *10*(1), 42–63.

Arnold, N., Ducate, L., & Kost, C. (2009). Collaborative writing in wikis: Insights from culture project in German class. In L. Lomicka & G. Lord (eds.), *The next generation: Social networking and online collaboration in foreign language learning* (pp. 115–144). San Marcos, TX: Texas State University.

Arnold, N., Ducate, L., & Kost, C. (2012). Collaboration or cooperation? Analyzing group dynamics and revision processes in wikis. *CALICO Journal*, *29*(3), 431–448. https://doi.org/10.11139/cj.29.3.431-448

Askehave, I., & Nielsen, A. E. (2005). Digital genres: A challenge to traditional genre theory. *Information Technology & People*, *18*(2), 120–141. https://doi.org/10.1108/09593840510601504

Atkinson, D. (2001). Reflections and refractions on the JSLW special issue on voice. *Journal of Second Language Writing, 10*, 107–124. https://doi.org/10.1016/S1060-3743(01)00035-2

Aydin, S. (2014). Foreign language learners' interactions with their teachers on Facebook. *System, 42*, 155–163. https://doi.org/10.1016/j.system.2013.12.001

Aydin, Z., & Yildiz, S. (2014). Using wikis to promote collaborative EFL writing. *Language Learning & Technology, 18*(1), 160–180.

Baerentsen, K. B., & Trettvik, J. (2002). An activity theory approach to affordance. *Proceedings of the Second Nordic Conference on Human-Computer Interaction* (pp. 51–60). Retrieved on January 1, 2020 from http://dl.acm.org/citation.cfm?id=572020.572028.

Baker, E. A. (2010). *The new literacies: Multiple perspectives on research and practice*. New York: Guilford.

Bakhtin, M. (1986). The problem of special genres. In C. Emerson & M. Holquist (eds.), *Speech genres and other late essays* (pp. 66–102). Austin: University of Texas.

Ball, C. E. (2006). Designerly = readerly: Re-assessing multimodal and new media rubrics for use in writing studies. *Convergence, 12*(4), 393–412. https://doi.org/10.1177/1354856506068366

Ball, C. E., Bowen, T. S. & Fenn, T. B. (2013). Genre and transfer in a multimodal composition class. In T. Bowen & C. Whithaus (eds.), *Multimodal literacies and emerging genres* (pp. 15–36). Pittsburgh: University of Pittsburgh Press. https://doi.org/10.2307/j.ctt6wrbkn.5

Baron, N. S. (2008). *Always on: Language in an online and mobile world.* Oxford: Oxford University Press. https://doi.org/10.1093/acprof:oso/9780195313055.001.0001

Barton, D. (2007). *Literacy: An introduction to the ecology of written language*. London: Wiley.

Bateman, J. A. (2008). Introduction: Four whys and a how. *Multimodality and genre* (pp. 1–20). London: Palgrave Macmillan. https://doi.org/10.1057/9780230582323_1

Bauer, B., de Benedette, L., Furstenberg, G., Levet, S., & Waryn, S. (2006). The cultural project. In J. A. Belz & S. L. Thorne (eds.), *Internet-mediated intercultural FL education* (pp. 31–62). Boston: Heinle & Heinle.

Bawarshi, A. S., & Reiff, M. J. (2010). *Genre: An introduction to history, theory, research, and pedagogy*. Anderson, SC: Parlor Press.

Bawden, D. (2008). Origins and concepts of digital literacy. In C. Lankshear & M. Knobel (eds.), *Digital literacies* (pp. 17–32). New York: Peter Lang.

Belcher, D. D. (2017). On becoming facilitators of multimodal composing and digital design. *Journal of Second Language Writing*, *38*, 80–85. https://doi.org/10.1016/j.jslw.2017.10.004

Bernat, E., & Gvozdenko, I. (2005). Beliefs about language learning: Current knowledge, pedagogical implications, and new research directions. *TESL-EJ*, *9*(1). Retrieved on January 1, 2020 from http://tesl-ej.org/ej33/a1.html.

Bhabha, H. K. (1994). *The location of culture*. New York: Routledge.

Birch, D., & Volkov, M. (2007). Assessment of online reflections: Engaging English second language (ESL) students. *Australasian Journal of Educational Technology*, *23*(3), 291–306. https://doi.org/10.14742/ajet.1254

Bitchener, J. (2008). Evidence in support of written corrective feedback. *Journal of Second Language Writing*, *17*(2), 102–118. https://doi.org/10.1016/j.jslw.2007.11.004

Bitchener, J. (2012). A reflection on "the language learning potential" of written CF. *Journal of Second Language Writing*, *21*, 348–363. https://doi.org/10.1016/j.jslw.2012.09.006

Bitchener, J., & Knoch, U. (2010). Raising the linguistic accuracy level of advanced L2 writers with written corrective feedback. *Journal of Second Language Writing*, *19*(4), 207–217. https://doi.org/10.1016/j.jslw.2010.10.002

Black, R. W. (2006). Language, culture, and identity in online fanfiction. *E-Learning*, *3*(2), 170–184. https://doi.org/10.2304/elea.2006.3.2.170

Black, R. W. (2009). Online fan fiction, global identities, and imagination. *Research in the Teaching of English*, *43*, 397–425.

Blake, R. J. (2000). Computer mediated communication: A window on L2 Spanish interlanguage. *Language Learning & Technology*, *4*(1), 111–125.

Blake, R. J. (2013). *Brave new digital classroom: Technology and foreign language learning* (2nd edition). Washington, DC: Georgetown University Press.

Blake, R. J. (2016). Technology and the four skills. *Language Learning & Technology*, *20*(2), 129–142.

Blattner, G., Dalola, A., & Lomicka, L. (2016a). Mind your hashtags: A sociopragmatic study of student interpretations of French native speakers' tweets. In C. Wang & L. Winstead (eds.), *Handbook of research on foreign language education in the digital age* (pp. 33–58). Hershey, PA: IGI Global. https://doi.org/10.4018/978-1-5225-0177-0.ch003

Blattner, G., Dalola, A., & Lomicka, L. (2016b). Twitter in foreign language classes: Initiating learners into contemporary language variation. In V. X. Wang (ed.), *Handbook of research on learning outcomes and opportunities in the digital age* (pp. 769–797). Hershey: IGI Global. https://doi.org/10.4018/978-1-4666-9577-1.ch034

Blattner, G., & Fiori, M. (2011). Virtual social network communities: An investigation of language learners' development of socio-pragmatic awareness and multiliteracy skills. *CALICO Journal*, *20*(1), 24–43. https://doi.org/10.11139/cj.29.1.24-43

Blin, F. (2016). Towards an "ecological" CALL theory. In F. Farr & L. Murray (eds.), *The Routledge handbook of language learning and technology* (pp. 39–54). New York: Routledge.

Blin, F., & Appel, C. (2011). Computer supported collaborative writing in practice: An activity theoretical study. *CALICO Journal*, *28*(2), 473–497. https://doi.org/10.11139/cj.28.2.473-497

Blin, F., Jalkanen, J., & Taalas, P. (2016). Sustainable CALL development. In F. Farr & L. Murray (eds.), *The Routledge handbook of language learning and technology* (pp. 223–238). New York: Routledge.

Bloch, J. (2012). *Plagiarism, intellectual property and the teaching of L2 writing*. Bristol, UK: Multilingual Matters. https://doi.org/10.21832/9781847696533

Block, D. (2013). The structure and agency dilemma in identity and intercultural communication research. *Language and Intercultural Communication*, *13*(2), 126–147. https://doi.org/10.1080/14708477.2013.770863

Blommaert, J., Collins, J., & Slembrouck, S. (2005). Spaces of multilingualism. *Language and Communication*, *25*(3), 197–216. https://doi.org/10.1016/j.langcom.2005.05.002

Blyth, C. S. (2014). Exploring the affordances of digital social 201 reading for L2 literacy: The case of eComma. In J. Guikema & L. Williams (eds.), *Digital literacies in foreign and second language education* (pp. 201–226). San Marcos, TX: CALICO.

Blyth, C. S., & Dalola, A. (2016). Translingualism as an open educational language practice: Raising critical language awareness on Facebook. *Alsic*, *19*(1), 1–24. https://doi.org/10.4000/alsic.2962

Bolter, J. D., & Grusin, R. (2000). *Remediation: Understanding new media*. Cambridge, MA: MIT Press.

Borton, S. C., & Huot, B. (2007). Responding and assessing. In C. Selfe (ed.), *Multimodal composition: Resources for teachers* (pp. 1–14). Cresskill, NJ: Hampton Press.

Bowen, T., & Whithaus, C. (2013). What else is possible?: Multimodal composing and genre in the teaching of writing. In T. Bowen & C. Whithaus (eds.), *Multimodal literacies and emerging genres* (pp. 1–12). Pittsburgh: Pittsburgh University Press. https://doi.org/10.2307/j.ctt6wrbkn

Briggs, C., & Makice, K. (2011). *Digital fluency: Building success in the digital age.* SociaLens. Retrieved on January 1, 2018 from http://www.socialens.com/blog/wp-content/uploads/downloads/2012/01/SociaLens_Digital_Fluency_Sample1.pdf. Downloadable pdf no longer available.

Brooks, F. B., & Donato, R. (1994). Vygotskyan approaches to understanding foreign language learner discourse during communication tasks. *Hispania*, *77*(2), 262–274. https://doi.org/10.2307/344508

Bucholtz, M., & Hall, K. (2005). Identity and interaction: A socio-cultural linguistic approach. *Discourse Studies*, *7*, 585–614. https://doi.org/10.1177/1461445605054407

Bump, J. (2013). Thinking outside the text box: 3-D interactive, multimodal literacy in a college writing class. In T. Bowen & C. Whithaus (eds.), *Multimodal literacies and emerging genres* (pp. 111–140). Pittsburgh: Pittsburgh University Press. https://doi.org/10.2307/j.ctt6wrbkn.9

Butler, J. P. (1990). *Gender trouble: Feminism and the subversion of identity*. New York: Routledge.

Canagarajah, A. S. (2002). *Critical academic writing and multilingual students*. Ann Arbor: University of Michigan Press. https://doi.org/10.3998/mpub.8903

Canagarajah, A. S. (2007). Lingua franca English, multilingual communities, and language acquisition. *Modern Language Journal*, *91*, 923–939. https://doi.org/10.1111/j.1540-4781.2007.00678.x

Canagarajah, A. S. (2013a). Negotiating translingual literacy: An enactment. *Research in the Teaching of English*, *48*(1), 40–67.

Canagarajah, A. S. (2013b). *Translingual practice: Global Englishes and cosmopolitan relations*. Abingdon, UK: Routledge. https://doi.org/10.4324/9780203073889

Casanave, C. P. (ed.) (2017). *Controversies in second language writing* (2nd edition). Ann Arbor, MI: University of Michigan Press. https://doi.org/10.3998/mpub.8876881

Castrillo de Larreta-Azelain, M. D. (2013). Learners attitude toward collaborative writing in e-language learning classes: A Twitter project for German as a foreign language. *Revista Española De Lingüística Aplicada, 26*, 127–138

Caws, C., & Heift, T. (2016). Evaluation in CALL: Tools, interactions, outcomes. In F. Farr & L. Murray (eds.), *The Routledge handbook of language learning and technology* (pp. 127–140). New York: Routledge.

Cenoz, J. (2013). Defining multilingualism. *Annual Review of Applied Linguistics, 33*, 3–18. https://doi.org/10.1017/S026719051300007X

Chandler, J. (2003). The efficacy of various kinds of error feedback for improvement in the accuracy and fluency of L2 student writing. *Journal of Second Language Writing, 12*(3), 267–296. https://doi.org/10.1016/S1060-3743(03)00038-9

Chen, H. I. (2013). Identity practices of multilingual writers in social networking spaces. *Language Learning & Technology, 17*(2), 143–170.

Chen, T. (2016). Technology-supported peer feedback in ESL/EFL writing classes: A research synthesis. *Computer Assisted Language Learning, 29*(2), 365–397. https://doi.org/10.1080/09588221.2014.960942

Chen, W. C., Shih, Y. C. D., & Liu, G. Z. (2015). Task design and its induced learning effects in a cross-institutional blog-mediated telecollaboration. *Computer Assisted Language Learning, 28*(4), 285–305. https://doi.org/10.1080/09588221.2013.818557

Cho, H. (2017). Synchronous web-based collaborative writing: Factors mediating interaction among second-language writers. *Journal of Second Language Writing, 36*, 37–51. https://doi.org/10.1016/j.jslw.2017.05.013

Chun, D. (2011). Developing intercultural communicative competence through online exchanges. *CALICO Journal, 28*(2), 392–419. https://doi.org/10.11139/cj.28.2.392-419

Chun, D., Kern, R., & Smith, B. (2016). Technology in language use, language teaching, and language learning. *Modern Language Journal, 100*(S1), 64–80. https://doi.org/10.1111/modl.12302

Cole, J., & Vanderplank, R. (2016). Comparing autonomous and class-based learners in Brazil: Evidence for the present-day advantages of informal, out-of-class learning. *System, 61*(1), 31–42. https://doi.org/10.1016/j.system.2016.07.007

Conference on College Composition and Communication (CCCC). (2009). Writing assessment: A position statement. Retrieved on January 1, 2020 from http://cccc.ncte.org/cccc/resources/positions/writingassessment.

Conley, R., & Gallego, M. (2012). Negotiation of meaning in e-tandems: Student perceptions of language acquisition during an intercultural exchange program. *International Journal of International Technology and Distance Learning*, *9*(5), 21–32.

Cope, B., & Kalantzis, M. (2015). The things you do to know: An introduction to the pedagogy of multiliteracies. In D. Scott & E. Hargreaves (eds.), *A pedagogy of multiliteracies* (pp. 1–36). London: Palgrave Macmillan. https://doi.org/10.1057/9781137539724_1

Cope, B., Kalantzis, M., McCarthey, S., Vojak, C., & Kline, S. (2011). Technology-mediated writing assessments: Principles and processes. *Computers and Composition*, *28*, 79–96. https://doi.org/10.1016/j.compcom.2011.04.007

Cotos, E. (2011). Potential of automated writing evaluation feedback. *CALICO Journal*, *28*(2), 420–459. https://doi.org/10.11139/cj.28.2.420-459

Crystal, D. (2008). *Txtng: The Gr8 Db8*. Oxford: Oxford University Press.

Crystal, D. (2011). *Internet linguistics: A student guide*. New York: Routledge. https://doi.org/10.4324/9780203830901

Damon, W., & Phelps, E. (1989). Strategic uses of peer interaction in children's education. In T. Berndt & G. Ladd (eds.), *Peer relationships in child development* (pp. 114–147). New York: Wiley.

Darvin, R., & Norton, B. (2014). Transnational identity and migrant language learners: The promise of digital storytelling. *Education Matters*, *2*(1), 55–66.

Dean, D. (2008). *Genre theory: Teaching, writing, and being*. Urbana, IL: National Council of Teachers of English.

De Houwer, A. (2015). Harmonious bilingual development: Young families' well-being in language contact situations. *International Journal of Bilingualism*, *19*(2), 169–184. https://doi.org/10.1177/1367006913489202

De Oliveira, L. C. (2011). *Knowing and writing school history: The language of students' expository writing and teachers' expectations*. Charlotte, NC: Information Age.

deHaan, J., Johnson, N. H., Yosimura, N., & Kondo, Y. (2012). Wiki and digital video use in strategic interaction-based experiential EFL learning. *CALICO Journal*, *29*(2), 249–268. https://doi.org/10.11139/cj.29.2.249-268

DePalma, M.-J., & Alexander, K. P. (2015). Bag full of snakes: Negotiating the challenges of multimodal composition. *Computers and Composition*, *37*, 182–200. https://doi.org/10.1016/j.compcom.2015.06.008

Domingo, M., Jewitt, C., & Kress, G. (2016). Multimodal social semiotics: Writing in online contexts. In A. Georgakopoulou & T. Spilioti (eds.), *The Routledge handbook of language and digital communication* (pp. 251–266). New York: Routledge.

Donato, R. (1994). Collective scaffolding in second language learning. In L. Lantolf & G. Apple (eds.), *Vygotskian approaches to second language research* (pp. 33–56). Westport, CT: Ablex.

Dooly, M. (2011). Divergent perceptions of telecollaborative language learning tasks: Task-as-workplan vs. task-as-process. *Language Learning & Technology*, *15*(2), 69–91.

Ducate, L., & Arnold, D. (2012). Computer-mediated feedback: Effectiveness and students' perceptions of screen-casting software vs the comment function. In G. Kessler, A. Oskoz, & I. Elola (eds.), *Technology across writing contexts and tasks* (pp. 31–55). San Marcos, TX: CALICO.

Ducate, L., & Lomicka, L. (2005). Exploring the blogosphere: Use of web logs in the foreign language classroom. *Foreign Language Annals*, *38*(3), 410–421. https://doi.org/10.1111/j.1944-9720.2005.tb02227.x

Ducate, L., & Lomicka, L. (2008). Adventures in the blogosphere: From blog readers to blog writers. *Computer Assisted Language Learning*, *21*(1), 9–28. https://doi.org/10.1080/09588220701865474

Dudeney, G., & Hockly, N. (2016). Literacies, technology and language teaching. In F. Farr & L. Murray (eds.), *The Routledge handbook of language learning and technology* (pp. 115–126). New York: Routledge.

Dudeney, G., Hockly, N., & Pegrum, M. (2013). *Digital literacies*. Harlow, UK: Pearson. https://doi.org/10.4324/9781315832913

Edasawa, Y., & Kabata, K. (2007). An ethnographic study of a key-pal project: Learning a foreign language through bilingual communication. *Computer Assisted Language Learning*, *20*(3), 189–207. https://doi.org/10.1080/09588220701489473

Ellis, E. (2013). Back to the future? The pedagogical promise of the (multimedia) essay. In T. S. Bowen & C. Whithaus (eds.), *Multimodal literacies and emerging genres* (pp. 164–182). Pittsburgh: Pittsburgh University Press.

Ellis, R. (2003). *Task-based language learning and teaching*. Oxford: Oxford University Press.

Ellis, R. (2009). A typology of written corrective feedback types. *ELT Journal*, *63*(2), 97–107. https://doi.org/10.1093/elt/ccn023

Ellis, R., Sheen, Y., Murakami, M., & Takashima, H. (2008). The effects of focused and unfocused written corrective feedback in an English as a foreign language context. *System*, *36*(3), 353–371. https://doi.org/10.1016/j.system.2008.02.001

Elola, I., & Oskoz, A. (2008). Blogging: Fostering intercultural competence development in foreign language and study abroad contexts. *Foreign Language Annals*, *41*(3), 421–444. https://doi.org/10.1111/j.1944-9720.2008.tb03307.x

Elola, I., & Oskoz, A. (2010a). Collaborative writing: Fostering foreign language and writing conventions development. *Language Learning and Technology*, *14*(3), 30–49.

Elola, I., & Oskoz, A. (2010b). A social constructivist approach to foreign language writing in online environments. In G. Levine & A. Phipps (eds.), *Critical and intercultural theory and language pedagogy* (pp. 185–201). Boston: Heinle and Heinle.

Elola, I., & Oskoz, A. (2016). Supporting second language writing using multimodal feedback. *Foreign Language Annals*, *49*(1), 58–74. https://doi.org/10.1111/flan.12183

Elola, I., & Oskoz, A. (2017). Writing with 21st century social tools in the L2 classroom: New literacies, genres, and writing practices. *Journal of Second Language Writing*, *36*, 52–63. https://doi.org/10.1016/j.jslw.2017.04.002

Elola, I., & Oskoz, A. (2019). Writing between the lines: Acquiring writing skills and digital literacies through social tools. In N. Arnold & L. Ducate (eds.), *Engaging language learners through CALL: From theory and research to informed practice* (pp. 240–266). Bristol, CT & Sheffield, UK: Equinox.

Elola, I., Padial, A., & Guerrero-Rodríguez, P. (in press). Herramientas sociales en la clase de español como lengua de herencia. In D. Pascual y Cabo & J. Torres (eds.), *Aproximaciones al estudio del español como lengua de herencia*. New York: Routledge.

Ene, E., & Upton, T. A. (2014). Learner uptake of teacher electronic feedback in ESL composition. *System*, *46*, 80–95. https://doi.org/10.1016/j.system.2014.07.011

Ene, E., & Upton, T. A. (2018). Synchronous and asynchronous teacher electronic feedback and learner uptake in ESL composition. *Journal of Second Language Writing*, *41*, 1–13. https://doi.org/10.1016/j.jslw.2018.05.005

Engeström, Y. (2001). Expansive learning at work: Toward an activity theoretical reconceptualization. *Journal of Education and Work*, *14*, 133–156. https://doi.org/10.1080/13639080020028747

Engeström, Y. (2008). *From teams to knots: Activity-theoretical studies of collaboration and learning at work*. Cambridge, UK: Cambridge University Press. https://doi.org/10.1017/CBO9780511619847

Erickson, T. (2000). Making sense of computer-mediated communication (CMC): Conversations as genres, CMC systems as genre ecologies. *Proceedings of the 33rd Hawaii International Conference on System Sciences*, 1–10. https://doi.org/10.1109/HICSS.2000.926694

Erstad, O. (2011). Citizens navigating in literate worlds. In M. Thomas (ed.), *Deconstructing digital natives, young people, technology and new literacies* (pp. 99–118). New York: Routledge.

Ess, C. (2016). Choose now! Media, literacies, identities, politics. In A. Georgakopoulou & T. Spilioti (eds.), *The Routledge handbook of language and digital communication* (pp. 412–416). London: Routledge.

Facebook. (2019). About. Retrieved on June 1, 2019 from https://www.facebook.com/pg/facebook/about/.

Farmer, B., Yue, A., & Brookes, C. (2008). Using blogging for higher order learning in large cohort university teaching: A case study. *Australasian Journal of Educational Technology*, *24*(2), 123–136. https://doi.org/10.14742/ajet.1215

Fernández-García, M., & Martínez-Arbelaiz, A. (2002). Negotiation of meaning in nonnative speaker–nonnative speaker synchronous discussions. *CALICO Journal*, *19*(2), 279–294. https://doi.org/10.1558/cj.v19i2.279-284

Ferris, D. R. (1999). The case for grammar correction in L2 writing classes: A response to Truscott *Journal of Second Language Writing*, *8*(1), 1–10. https://doi.org/10.1016/S1060-3743(99)80110-6

Ferris, D. R. (2002). *Treatment of error in second language student writing*. Ann Arbor: University of Michigan Press.

Ferris, D. R. (2006). Does error feedback help student writers? New evidence on the short- and long-term effects of written error correction. In K. Hyland & F. Hyland (eds.), *Feedback in second language writing* (pp. 81–104). Cambridge, UK: Cambridge University Press. https://doi.org/10.1017/CBO9781139524742.007

Ferris, D. R. (2010). Second language writing research and written corrective feedback in SLA. *Studies in Second Language Acquisition*, *32*(2), 181–201. https://doi.org/10.1017/S0272263109990490

Ferris, D. R. (2012). Technology and corrective feedback for L2 writers: Principles, practices, and problems. In G. Kessler, A. Oskoz, & I. Elola (eds.), *Technology across writing contexts and tasks* (pp. 7–29). San Marcos, TX: CALICO.

Ferris, D. R., & Roberts, B. J. (2001). Error feedback in L2 writing classes: How explicit does it need to be? *Journal of Second Language Writing*, *3*, 161–184. https://doi.org/10.1016/S1060-3743(01)00039-X

Ferris, F., & Hedgcock, J. (2013). *Teaching L2 composition: Purpose, process, and practice*. New York: Routledge. https://doi.org/10.4324/9780203813003

Flower, D. R., & Hayes, J. R. (1981). A cognitive process theory of writing. *College Composition and Communication*, *32*, 365–387. https://doi.org/10.2307/356600

Fordham, T., & Oakes, H. (2013). Rhetoric across modes, rhetoric across campus: Faculty and students building a multimodal curriculum. In T. Bowen & C. Whithaus (eds.), *Multimodal literacies and emerging genres* (pp. 313–335). Pittsburgh: Pittsburgh University Press. https://doi.org/10.2307/j.ctt6wrbkn.17

Fornara, F. (2018). Using Instagram to foster learners' autonomy for intercultural learning. *The FLTMAG*. Retrieved on January 1, 2020 from http://fltmag.com/using-instagram-to-foster-learners-autonomy/.

Fornara, F., Lomicka, L. (2019). Using visual social media in language learning to investigate the role of social presence. *CALICO Journal*, *36*(3), 184–203. https://doi.org/10.1558/cj.37205

Fornara, F., Lomicka, L., & Hattem, D. (2018). Using Instagram to investigate the role of social presence in intermediate-level language classes. Paper presented at the CALICO conference, May 2018. Urbana-Champaign.

García, O., & Li Wei (2014). *Translanguaging: Language, bilingualism and education*. Basingstoke, UK: Palgrave Macmillan. https://doi.org/10.1057/9781137385765

García-Pastor, M. D. (2017). Learners' identities at stake: Digital identity texts in the EFL classroom. *Language Value*, *9*(1), 36–61. https://doi.org/10.6035/LanguageV.2017.9.3

Gebhard, M., Shin, D.-S., & Seger, W. (2011). Blogging and emergent L2 literacy development in an urban elementary school: A functional perspective. *CALICO Journal*, *28*(2), 278–307. https://doi.org/10.11139/cj.28.2.278-307

Gee, J. (2003). *What video games have to teach us about learning and literacy*. New York: Palgrave Macmillan. https://doi.org/10.1145/950566.950595

Gevers, J. (2018). Translingualism revisited: Language difference and hybridity in L2 writing. *Journal of Second Language Writing*, *40*, 73–83. https://doi.org/10.1016/j.jslw.2018.04.003

Gibson, J. J. (1979). *The ecological approach to visual perception*. New York: Houghton Mifflin.

Gitelman, L., & Pingree, G. B. (eds.). (2003). *New media, 1740–1915*. Cambridge, MA: MIT Press. https://doi.org/10.7551/mitpress/5001.001.0001

Glisan, E. W., Uribe, D., & Adair-Hauck, B. (2007). Research on integrated performance assessment at the post-secondary level: Student performance across the modes of communication. *Canadian Modern Language Review*, *64*, 39–68. https://doi.org/10.3138/cmlr.64.1.039

Godwin-Jones, R. (2018). Second language writing online: An update. *Language Learning & Technology*, *22*(1), 1–15.

Goldstein, L. M. (2016). Making use of teacher written feedback. In R. M. Manchón & P. K. Matsuda (eds.), *Handbook of second and foreign language writing* (pp. 407–432). Berlin: De Gruyter. https://doi.org/10.1515/9781614511335-022

Gonzalez-Bueno, M. (1998). The effects of electronic mail on Spanish L2 discourse. *Language Learning & Technology*, *1*(2), 55–70.

González-Lloret, M. (2014). The need for needs analysis in technology-mediated TBLT. In M. González-Lloret & L. Ortega (eds.), *Technology and tasks: Exploring technology-mediated TBLT* (pp. 23–50). Philadelphia: John Benjamins. https://doi.org/10.1075/tblt.6.02gon

González-Lloret, M., & Ortega, L. (eds.). (2014). *Technology and tasks: Exploring technology-mediated TBLT*. Philadelphia: John Benjamins. https://doi.org/10.1075/tblt.6

Graban, T. S., Charlton, C., & Charlton, J. (2013). Multivalent composition and the reinvention of expertise. In T. Bowen & C. Whithaus (eds.), *Multimodal literacies and emerging genres* (pp. 248–281). Pittsburgh: Pittsburgh University Press. https://doi.org/10.2307/j.ctt6wrbkn.15

Graham, S. L. (2016). Relationality, friendship, and identity in digital communication. In A. Georgakopoulou & T. Spilioti (eds.), *The Routledge handbook of language and digital communication* (pp. 305–320). London: Routledge.

Greenfield, R. (2003). Collaborative e-mail exchange for teaching secondary ESL: A case study in Hong Kong. *Language Learning and Technology*, *7*(1), 46–70.

Gregori-Signes, C. (2008). Integrating the old and the new: Digital storytelling in the EFL language classroom. *GRETA*, *16*, 43–49.

Gregori-Signes, C., & Pennock-Speck, B. (2012). Digital storytelling as a genre of mediatized self-representations: An introduction. *Digital Education Review*, *22*. Retrieved on January 1, 2020 from http://revistes.ub.edu/index.php/der/article/view/11291/pdf.

Grosbois, M. (2016). Computer supported collaborative writing and language learning. In F. Farr & L. Murray (eds.), *The Routledge handbook of language learning and technology* (pp. 269–280). New York: Routledge.

Guichon, N., & Cohen, C. (2016). Multimodality and CALL. In F. Farr & L. Murray (eds.), *The Routledge handbook of language learning and technology* (pp. 509–521). New York: Routledge.

Guth, S., & Helm, F. (2010). *Telecollaboration 2.0: Language, literacies and intercultural learning in the 21st century*. New York: Peter Lang. https://doi.org/10.3726/978-3-0351-0013-6

Hafner, C. A. (2015). Remix culture and English language teaching: The expression of learner voice in digital multimodal compositions. *TESOL Quarterly*, *49*(3), 486–509. https://doi.org/10.1002/tesq.238

Hafner, C. A., Chik, A., & Jones, R. H. (2013). Engaging with digital literacies in TESOL. *TESOL Quarterly*, *47*(4), 812–815. https://doi.org/10.1002/tesq.136

Hafner, C. A., Chik, A., & Jones, R. H. (2015). Digital literacies and language learning. *Language Learning & Technology*, *19*(3), 1–7.

Hamp-Lyons, L., & Mathias, S. P. (1994). Examining expert judgments of task difficulty on essay tests. *Journal of Second Language Writing*, *31*(1), 49–68. https://doi.org/10.1016/1060-3743(94)90005-1

Hampel, R. (2006). Rethinking task design for the digital age: A framework for language teaching and learning in a synchronous online environment. *ReCALL*, *18*(1), 105–121. https://doi.org/10.1017/S0958344006000711

Hampel, R. (2010). Task design for a virtual learning environment in a distant language course. In M. Thomas & H. Reinders (eds.), *Task-based language learning and teaching with technology* (pp. 131–135). London: Continuum.

Hampel, R., & Hauck, M. (2006). Computer-mediated language learning: Making meaning in multimodal virtual learning spaces. *The JALT CALL Journal*, *2*(2), 3–18.

Hanna, B. E., & de Nooy, J. (2009). *Learning language and culture via public internet discussion forums*. New York: Palgrave Macmillan. https://doi.org/10.1057/9780230235823

Hanna, B. E., & de Nooy, J. (2003). A funny thing happened on the way to the forum: Electronic discussion and foreign language learning. *Language Learning & Technology, 7*(1), 71–85.

Hattem, D. (2012). The practice of microblogging. *Journal of Second Language Teaching and Research, 1*(2), 38–70.

Hattem, D. (2014). Microblogging activities: Language play and tool transformation. *Language Learning & Technology, 18*(2), 151–174.

Hayles, H. (2012). *How we think: Digital median and contemporary technogenesis*. Chicago: University of Chicago Press. https://doi.org/10.7208/chicago/9780226321370.001.0001

Helm, F., & Dooly, M. (2017). Challenges in transcribing multimodal data: A case study. *Language Learning & Technology, 21*(1), 166–185

Herring, S. C. (2001). Computer-mediated discourse. In D. Schiffrin, D. Tannen, & H. Hamilton (eds.), *The handbook of discourse analysis* (pp. 612–634). Oxford: Blackwell. https://doi.org/10.1002/9780470753460.ch32

Herring, S. C. (2003). Media and language change: Introduction. *Journal of Historical Pragmatics, 4*(1), 1–17. https://doi.org/10.1075/jhp.4.1.02her

Herring, S. C. (2004). Slouching toward the ordinary: Current trends in computer-mediated communication. *New Media and Society, 6*(1), 26–36. https://doi.org/10.1177/1461444804039906

Herring, S. C., Scheidt, L. A., Wright, E., & Bonus, S. (2005). Weblogs as a bridging genre. *Information Technology and People, 18*(1), 142–171. https://doi.org/10.1108/09593840510601513

Hessler, B., & Lambert, J. (2017). Threshold concepts in digital storytelling: Naming what we know about storywork. In G. Jamissen, P. Hardy, Y. Nordkvelle, & H. Pleasants (eds.), *The international handbook of digital storytelling in higher education* (pp. 19–35). Cham, Switzerland: Springer International. https://doi.org/10.1007/978-3-319-51058-3_3

Heyd, T. (2016). Digital genres and processes of remediation. In A. Georgakopoulou & T. Spilioti (eds.), *The Routledge handbook of language and digital communication* (pp. 87–102). New York: Routledge.

Hirvela, A., & Belcher, D. D. (2016). Reading/writing and speaking/writing connections: The advantages of multimodal pedagogy. In R. Manchón & P. K. Matsuda (eds.), *Handbook of second and foreign language writing* (pp. 587–612). Boston: De Gruyter. https://doi.org/10.1515/9781614511335-030

Ho, M., & Savignon, S. J. (2007). Face-to-face and computer-mediated peer review in EFL writing. *CALICO Journal*, *24*(2), 269–290. https://doi.org/10.1558/cj.v24i2.269-290

Hockly, N. (2012). Digital literacies. *ELT Journal*, *66*(1), 108–112. https://doi.org/10.1093/elt/ccr077

Hornberger, N. H., & Wang, S. (2008). Who are our heritage language learners? In D. M. Brinton, O. Kagan, & S. Bauckus (eds.), *Heritage language education: A new field emerging* (pp. 3–35). New York: Routledge. https://doi.org/10.4324/9781315092997-2

Horner, B., Lu, M.-Z., Royster, J. J., & Trimbur, J. (2011). Language difference in writing: Toward a translingual approach. *College English*, *73*(3), 303–321.

Horner, B., NeCamp, S., & Donahue, C. (2011). Toward a multilingual composition scholarship: From English only to a translingual norm. *College Composition and Communication*, *6*(2) 269–300.

Hourigan, T., & Murray, L. (2010). Using blogs to help language students to develop reflective learning strategies: Towards a pedagogical framework. *Australasian Journal of Educational Technology*, *26*(2), 209–225. https://doi.org/10.14742/ajet.1091

Hull, G. A., & Katz, M. L. (2006). Crafting an agentive self: Case studies of digital storytelling. *Research in the Teaching of English*, *41*(1), 43–81.

Huot, B. (2002). *(Re)Articulating writing assessment for teaching and learning*. Logan, UT: Utah State University Press.

Hyland, K. (2001). Bringing in the reader: Addressee features in academic articles. *Written Communication*, *18*(4), 549–574. https://doi.org/10.1177/0741088301018004005

Hyland, K. (2007a). *Genre and second language writing*. Ann Arbor: University of Michigan Press.

Hyland, K. (2007b). Genre pedagogy: Language, literacy and L2 writing instruction. *Journal of Second Language Writing*, *16*(3), 148–164. https://doi.org/10.1016/j.jslw.2007.07.005

Hyland, K. (2011). Learning to write: Issues in theory, research, and pedagogy. In R. M. Manchón (ed.), *Learning-to-write and writing-to-learn in an additional language* (pp. 17–35). Amsterdam: John Benjamins. https://doi.org/10.1075/lllt.31.05hyl

Instagram. (2018). About. Retrieved on May 1, 2018 from https://www.instagram.com/about/us/.

Ishida, T. (1995). E-mail for distance Japanese language learning and teacher training. In M. Warschauer (ed.), *Virtual connections: Online activities*

& projects for networking language learners (pp. 185–186). Honolulu: University of Hawai'i Press.

Inoue, A. B. (2005). Community-based assessment pedagogy. *Assessing writing, 9*, 208–238. https://doi.org/10.1016/j.asw.2004.12.001

Ivanič, R. (1998). *Writing and identity*. Amsterdam: John Benjamins. https://doi.org/10.1075/swll.5

Jamison, A. (2013). *Fic: Why fanfiction is taking over the world*. Dallas, TX: Smart Pop Books.

Jenkins, H., Clinton, K., Purushotma, R., Robison, A. J., & Weigel, M. (2009). *Confronting the challenges of participatory culture: Media education for the 21st century*. Cambridge, MA: MIT Press. https://doi.org/10.7551/mitpress/8435.001.0001

Jewitt, C. (2003). Re-thinking assessment: Multimodality, literacy and computer-mediated learning. *Assessment in Education, 10*(1), 83–102. https://doi.org/10.1080/09695940301698

Johns, A. M. (2011). The future of genre in L2 writing: Fundamental, but contested, instructional decisions. *Journal of Second Language Writing, 20*(1), 56–68. https://doi.org/10.1016/j.jslw.2010.12.003

Johnson, D. C. (2013). Positioning the language policy arbiter: Governmentality and footing in the school district of Philadelphia. In J. W. Tollefson (ed.), *Language policies in education: Critical issues* (2nd edition, pp. 116–136). New York: Routledge.

Jones, R. H., & Hafner, C. A. (2012). *Understanding digital literacies: A practical introduction*. London, UK: Routledge. https://doi.org/10.4324/9780203095317

Kabilan, M. K., Ahmad, N., & Abidin, M. J. Z. (2010). Facebook: An online environment for learning of English in institutions of higher education? *Internet and Higher Education, 13*, 179–187. https://doi.org/10.1016/j.iheduc.2010.07.003

Kalantzis, M., & Cope, B. (2008). Language education and multiliteracies. In S. May & N. H. Hornberger (eds.), *Volume 1: Language policy and political issues in education, Encyclopedia of language education* (2nd edition, pp. 195–211). New York: Springer. https://doi.org/10.1007/978-0-387-30424-3_15

Kalantzis, M., Cope, B., Chan, E., & Dalley-Trim, L. (2016). *Literacies* (2nd edition). Sydney: Cambridge University Press.

Kalantzis, M., Cope, B., & Harvey, A. (2003). Assessing multiliteracies and the new basics. *Assessment in Education, 10*(1), 15–26. https://doi.org/10.1080/09695940301692

Kanno, Y. (2003). *Negotiating bilingual and bicultural identities: Japanese returnees betwixt two worlds*. Mahwah, NJ: Erlbaum. https://doi.org/10.4324/9781410607560

Kanno, Y., & Norton, B. (2003). Imagined communities and educational possibilities: Introduction. *Journal of Language, Identity, and Education*, *2*, 241–249. https://doi.org/10.1207/S15327701JLIE0204_1

Kayi-Aydar, H. (2018). Positional identities, access to learning opportunities, and multiliteracies: Negotiations in heritage and nonheritage Spanish-speaking students' critical narratives. In G. C. Zapata & M. Lacorte (eds.), *Multiliteracies pedagogy and language learning: Teaching Spanish to heritage speakers* (pp. 149–174). Cham, Switzerland: Springer International. https://doi.org/10.1007/978-3-319-63103-5_6

Kendall, C. (1995). Individual electronic mail with native speakers. In M. Warschauer (ed.), *Virtual connections: Online activities & projects for networking language learners* (pp. 109–115). Honolulu: University of Hawai'i Press.

Kern, R. (2014). Technology as Pharmakon: The promise and perils of the internet for foreign language education. *Modern Language Journal*, *98*(1), 340–357. https://doi.org/10.1111/j.1540-4781.2014.12065.x

Kern, R. (2015). *Language, literacy, and technology*. Cambridge, UK: Cambridge University Press. https://doi.org/10.1017/CBO9781139567701

Kessler, G. (2009). Student-initiated attention to form in wiki-based collaborative writing. *Language Learning & Technology*, *13*(1), 79–95.

Kessler, G. (2016). Technology standards for language teacher preparation. In F. Farr & L. Murray (eds.), *The Routledge handbook of language learning and technology* (pp. 57–70). New York: Routledge.

Kessler, G., & Bikowski, D. (2010). Developing collaborative autonomous language learning abilities in computer mediated language learning: Attention to meaning among students in wiki space. *Computer Assisted Language Learning*, *23*(1), 41–58. https://doi.org/10.1080/09588220903467335

Kessler, G., Bikowski, D., & Boggs, J. (2012). Collaborative writing among second language learners in academic web-based projects. *Language Learning & Technology*, *16*(1), 91–109.

King, B. W. (2015). Wikipedia writing as praxis: Computer-mediated socialization of second-language writers. *Language Learning & Technology*, *19*(3), 106–123.

Klimanova, L., & Dembovskaya, S. (2013). L2 identity, discourse, and social networking in Russian. *Language Learning & Technology*, *17*(1), 69–88.

Kobayashi, H., & Rinnert, C. (2013). L1/L2/L3 writing development: Longitudinal case study of a Japanese multicompetent writer. *Journal of Second Language Writing, 22*(1), 4–33. https://doi.org/10.1016/j.jslw.2012.11.001

Kol, S., & Schcolnik, M. (2008). Asynchronous forums in EAP: Assessment issues. *Language Learning & Technology, 12*(2), 49–70.

Kost, C. R. (2011). Investigating writing strategies and revision behavior in collaborative wiki projects. *CALICO Journal, 28*(3), 606–620. https://doi.org/10.11139/cj.28.3.606-620

Krall-Lanoue, A. (2013). "And yea I'm venting, but hey I'm writing isn't I": A translingual approach to error in a multilingual context. In A. S. Canagarajah (ed.), *Literacy as translingual practice: Between communities and classrooms* (pp. 228–234). New York: Routledge.

Kramsch, C. (2009). *The multilingual subject*. Oxford: Oxford University Press.

Kramsch, C. (2014). Teaching foreign languages in an era of globalization: Introduction. *Modern Language Journal, 98*(1), 296–311. https://doi.org/10.1111/j.1540-4781.2014.12057.x

Kress, G. (2003). *Literacy in the new media age*. London: Routledge. https://doi.org/10.4324/9780203299234

Kress, G. (2009). What is a mode? In C. Jewitt (ed.), *The Routledge handbook of multimodal analysis* (pp. 54–67). Abingdon, UK: Routledge.

Kress, G. (2010). Multimodality: A social semiotic approach to contemporary communication. New York: Routledge. https://doi.org/10.4324/9780203970034

Kroll, J. F., Bobb, S. C., & Hoshino, N. (2014). Two languages in mind: Bilingualism as a tool to investigate language, cognition, and the brain. *Current Directions in Psychological Science, 23*(3), 159–163. https://doi.org/10.1177/0963721414528511

Kuiken, F., & Vedder, I. (2008). Cognitive task complexity and written output in Italian and French as a foreign language. *Journal of Second Language Writing, 17*(1), 48–60. https://doi.org/10.1016/j.jslw.2007.08.003

Kumagai, Y., & López-Sánchez, A. (2016). Advancing multiliteracies in world language education. In Y. Kumagai, A. López-Sánchez, & S. Wu (eds.), *Multiliteracies in world language education* (pp. 1–27). New York: Routledge. https://doi.org/10.4324/9781315736143

Kurek, M., & Hauck, M. (2014). Closing the digital divide: A framework for multiliteracy training. In J. P. Guikema & L. Williams (eds.), *Digital literacies in foreign language education* (pp. 119–140). San Marcos, TX: CALICO.

Kuutti, K. (1996). Activity theory as a potential framework for human-computer interaction research. In B. A. Nardi (ed.), *Context and consciousness: Activity theory and human-computer interaction* (pp. 17–44). Cambridge, MA: MIT Press.

Lacorte, M. (2018). Multiliteracies pedagogy and heritage language teachers: How a practice-situated intervention promoted multiliteracy. In G. C. Zapata & M. Lacorte (eds.), *Multiliteracies pedagogy and language learning* (pp. 197–226). Cham, Switzerland: Springer International. https://doi.org/10.1007/978-3-319-63103-5_8

Lam, W. S. E. (2000). L2 literacy and the design of the self: A case study of a teenager writing on the Internet. *TESOL Quarterly*, *34*(3), 457–482. https://doi.org/10.2307/3587739

Lam, W. S. E. (2004). Second language socialization in a bilingual chat room: Global and local considerations. *Language Learning & Technology*, *9*(3), 44–65.

Lam, W. S. E. (2006). Re-envisioning language, literacy, and the immigrant subject in new mediascapes. *Pedagogies: An International Journal*, *1*(3), 171–195. https://doi.org/10.1207/s15544818ped0103_2

Lambert, J. (2012). *Digital storytelling: Capturing lives, creating community* (4th edition). Berkeley: Digital Diner. https://doi.org/10.4324/9780203102329

Lankshear, C., & Knobel, M. (2006). *New literacies: Everyday practices and classroom learning* (2nd edition). Maidenhead, UK: Open University Press.

Lankshear, C., & Knobel, M. (2008). Introduction: Digital literacies–Concepts, policies and practices. In C. Lankshear & M. Knobel (eds.), *Digital literacies: Concepts, policies and practices* (pp. 1–16). New York: Peter Lang.

Lantolf, J. P. (2006). Sociocultural theory and second language learning: State of the art. *Studies in Second Language Acquisition*, *28*(1), 67–109. https://doi.org/10.1017/S0272263106060037

Lantolf, J. P., & Thorne, S. (2006). *Sociocultural theory and the genesis of L2 development*. Oxford: Oxford University Press.

Lantolf, J. P., & Thorne, S. (2007). Sociocultural theory. In B. Van Patten & J. Williams (eds.), *Theories in second language acquisition: An introduction* (pp. 170–195). Mahwah, NJ: Lawrence Erlbaum Associates.

Larsen-Freeman, D. (2006). The emergence of complexity, fluency, and accuracy in the oral and written production of five Chinese learners of English. *Applied Linguistics*, *27*(4), 590–619. https://doi.org/10.1093/applin/aml029

Lave, J., & Wenger, E. (1991). *Situated learning: Legitimate peripheral participation*. New York: Cambridge University Press. https://doi.org/10.1017/CBO9780511815355

Lavolette, E., Polio, C., & Kahng, J. (2015). The accuracy of computer-assisted feedback and students' responses to it. *Language Learning & Technology*, *19*(2), 50–68.

Lee, C. (2016). Multilingual resources and practices in digital communication. In A. Georgakopoulou & T. Spilioti (eds.), *The Routledge handbook of language and digital communication* (pp. 118–132). London: Routledge.

Lee, L. (2009). Promoting intercultural exchanges with blogs and podcasting: A study of Spanish–American telecollaboration. *Computer Assisted Language Learning*, *22*(5), 425–443. https://doi.org/10.1080/09588220903345184

Lee, L. (2010a). Exploring wiki-mediated collaborative writing: A case study in an elementary Spanish course. *CALICO Journal*, *27*(2), 260–272. https://doi.org/10.11139/cj.27.2.260-276

Lee, L. (2010b). Fostering reflective writing and interactive exchange through blogging in an advanced language course. *ReCALL*, *22*(2), 212–222. https://doi.org/10.1017/S095834401000008X

Lee, L. (2012). Engaging study abroad students in intercultural learning through blogging and ethnographic interviews. *Foreign Language Annals*, *45*(1), 7–21. https://doi.org/10.1111/j.1944-9720.2012.01164.x

Lee, M. K. (2015). Peer feedback in second language writing: Investigating junior secondary students' perspectives on inter-feedback and intra-feedback. *System*, *55*, 1–10. https://doi.org/10.1016/j.system.2015.08.003

Leh, A. S. (1999). Computer-mediated communication and foreign language learning via electronic mail. *Interactive Multimedia Electronic Journal of Computer-Enhanced Learning*, *1*(2), 149–164. https://doi.org/10.1080/14759399900200058

Lehtonen, T. (2017). You will certainly learn English much faster at work than from a textbook. *System*, *68*, 50–59. https://doi.org/10.1016/j.system.2017.06.013

Leja, H. (2007). Improving writing skills in foreign language classes. In M. Camilleri, P. Ford, H. Leja, & V. Sollars (eds.), *Blogs: Web journal in language education* (pp. 27–34). Graz, Austria: European Centre for Modern Languages, Council of Europe.

Leontiev, A. N. (1978). *Activity, consciousness and personality*. Englewood Cliffs, NJ: Prentice Hall.

Leontiev, A. N. (1981). *Problems of the development of the mind.* Moscow: Progress Publishers. Originally published in Russian, *Problemy razvitiia psikhiki* (Moscow: Moscow State University, 1959).

Leppänen, S. (2007). Youth language in media contexts: Insights into the functions of English in Finland. *World Englishes*, *26*(2), 149–169. https://doi.org/10.1111/j.1467-971X.2007.00499.x

Leppänen, S. (2008). Cybergirls in trouble? Fan fiction as a discursive space for interrogating gender and sexuality. In C. R. Caldas-Coulthard & R. Iedema (eds.), *Identity trouble: Critical discourse and contested identities* (pp. 156–179). Houndsmills, UK: Palgrave Macmillan. https://doi.org/10.1057/9780230593329_9

Leu, D. J. (2000). Literacy and technology: Deictic consequences for literacy education in an information age. In M. L. Kamil, P. B. Mosenthal, P. D. Pearson, & R. Barr (eds.), *Handbook of reading research* (Vol. III, pp. 743–770). Mahwah, NJ: Lawrence Erlbaum.

Leu, D. J., Forzani, E., Rhoads, C., Maykel, C., Kennedy, C., & Timbrell, N. (2014). The new literacies of online research and comprehension: Rethinking the reading achievement gap. *Reading Research Quarterly*, *50*, 37–59. https://doi.org/10.1002/rrq.85

Levine, G. (2011). *Code choice in the language classroom*. Bristol, UK: Multilingual Matters. https://doi.org/10.21832/9781847693341

Li, M., & Storch, N. (2017). Second language writing in the age of CMC: Affordances, multimodality, and collaboration. *Journal of Second Language Writing*, *37*, 1–5. https://doi.org/10.1016/j.jslw.2017.05.012

Li, M., & Zhu, W. (2013). Patterns of computer-mediated interaction in small writing groups using wikis. *Computer Assisted Language Learning*, *26*(1), 61–82. https://doi.org/10.1080/09588221.2011.631142

Li, M., & Zhu, W. (2017a). Explaining dynamic interactions in wiki-based collaborative writing. *Language Learning & Technology*, *21*(2), 96–120.

Li, M., & Zhu, W. (2017b). Good or bad collaborative wiki writing: Exploring links between group interactions and writing products. *Journal of Second Language Writing*, *35*, 38–53. https://doi.org/10.1016/j.jslw.2017.01.003

Li, S. (2010). The effectiveness of corrective feedback in SLA: A meta-analysis. *Language Learning*, *60*(2), 309–365. https://doi.org/10.1111/j.1467-9922.2010.00561.x

Li Wei & Ho, W. Y. (2018). Language learning sans frontiers: A translanguaging view. *Annual Review of Applied Linguistics*, *38*, pp. 33–59. https://doi.org/10.1017/S0267190518000053

Liao, H. C. (2016). Enhancing the grammatical accuracy of EFL writing by using an AWE-assisted process approach. *System*, *62*, 77–92. https://doi.org/10.1016/j.system.2016.02.007

Liaw, M., & Master, S. B. (2010). Understanding telecollaboration through an analysis of intercultural discourse. *Computer Assisted Language Learning*, *23*(1), 21–40. https://doi.org/10.1080/09588220903467301

Lin, A. Y. M. (2015). Agency, language learning, and creative digital content production. Paper presented at the American Association of Applied Linguistics conference, March 2015. Toronto. Cited from Sauro (2017).

Liou, H.-C. (2016). CALL tools for reading and writing In F. Farr & L. Murray (eds.), *The Routledge handbook of language learning and technology* (pp. 478–490). New York: Routledge.

Lomicka, L., & Lord, G. (2011). Podcasting – Past, present and future: Applications of academic podcasting in and out of the language classroom. In B. R. Facer & M. Abdous (eds.), *Academic podcasting and mobile assisted language learning: Applications and outcomes* (pp. 1–20). Hershey, PA: IGI Global. https://doi.org/10.4018/978-1-60960-141-6.ch001

Lomicka, L., & Lord, G. (2012). A tale of tweets: Analyzing microblogging among language learners. *System*, *40*(1), 48–63. https://doi.org/10.1016/j.system.2011.11.001

Lomicka, L., & Lord, G. (2016). Social networking and language learning. In F. Farr & L. Murray (eds.), *The Routledge handbook of language learning and technology* (pp. 255–268). New York: Routledge.

Long, M. H., & Crookes, G. (1992). Three approaches to task-based language teaching. *TESOL Quarterly*, *26*(1), 27–56. https://doi.org/10.2307/3587368

Lotherington, H., & Jenson, J. (2011). Teaching multimodal and digital literacy in L2 settings: New literacies, new basics, new pedagogies. *Annual Review of Applied Linguistics*, *31*, 226–246. https://doi.org/10.1017/S0267190511000110

Lotherington, H., & Ronda, N. (2014). 2B or not 2B? From pencil to multimodal programming: New frontiers in communicative competencies. In J. Guikema & L. Williams (eds.), *Digital literacies in foreign language education* (pp. 9–28). Calico Monograph Series, Vol. 12. San Marcos, TX: CALICO.

Lotherington, H., & Sinitskaya Ronda, N. (2012). Multimodal literacies and assessment: Uncharted challenges in the English classroom. In C. Leung & B. Street (eds.), *English – A changing medium for schooling* (pp. 104–128). Clevedon, UK: Multilingual Matters. https://doi.org/10.21832/9781847697721-008

Lu, M. Z., & Horner, B. (2016). Introduction: Translingual work. *College English 78*(3), 207–18.

Lunsford, A., & Ede, L. (2009). Among the audience: On audience in an age of new literacies. In M. E. Weiser, B. M. Fehler, & A. M. González (eds.), *Engaging audience: Writing in an age of new literacies* (pp. 42–73). Urbana, IL: National Council of Teachers of English.

Luzón, M. J., Ruiz-Madrid, M. N., & Villanueva, M. L. (eds.) (2010). *Digital genres, new literacies and autonomy in language learning*. Newcastle, UK: Cambridge Scholars.

Mahfouz, S. (2010). A study of Jordanian university students' perceptions of using email exchanges with native English keypals for improving their writing competency. *CALICO Journal*, *27*(2), 393–408. https://doi.org/10.11139/cj.27.2.393-408

Maingueneau, D. (2010). Types of genres, hypergenre and internet. In M. J. Luzón, N. Ruiz-Madrid, & M. L. Villanueva (eds.), *Digital genres, new literacies and autonomy on language learning* (pp. 25–42). Newcastle, UK: Cambridge Scholars.

Manchón, R. M. (ed.) (2011). *Learning-to-write and writing-to-learn in an additional language*. Amsterdam: John Benjamins. https://doi.org/10.1075/lllt.31

Manchón, R. M. (2013). Writing. In F. Grosjean and P. Li (eds.), *The psycholinguistics of bilingualism* (pp. 100–115). Oxford: Blackwell.

Manovich, L. (2001). *The language of new media*. Cambridge, MA: MIT Press.

Marsh, J. (2016). The digital literacy skills and competences of children of pre-school age. *Media Communication*, *7*(2), 197–214.

Martin, A. (2005). DigEuLit – a European framework for digital literacy: A progress report. *Journal of eLiteracy*, *2*, 130–136.

Martin, J. R. (1992). *English text: System and structure*. Amsterdam: John Benjamins. https://doi.org/10.1075/z.59

Martin, J. R. (1993). A contextual theory of language. In B. Cope & M. Kalantzis (eds.), *The powers of literacy. A genre approach to teaching writing* (pp. 116–136). London: Falmer Press.

Martin, J. R., & Rose, D. (2008). *Genre relations: Mapping culture*. Bristol, CT & Sheffield, UK: Equinox.

Marvin, C. (1988). *When old technologies were new: Thinking about electric communication in the late nineteenth century*. New York: Oxford University Press.

Marwick, A. E. (2015). Instafame: Luxury selfies in the attention economy. *Public Culture*, *27*(175), 137–160. https://doi.org/10.1215/08992363-2798379

Matsuda, P. K. (2001). Voice in Japanese written discourse: Implications for second language writing. *Journal of Second Language Writing*, *10*, 35–53. https://doi.org/10.1016/S1060-3743(00)00036-9

Matsuda, P. K. (2013). It's the wild West out there: A new linguistic frontier in U.S. college composition. In A. S. Canagarajah (ed.), *Literacy as translingual practice: Between communities and classrooms* (pp. 128–138). New York: Routledge.

Matsuda, P. K. (2014). The lure of translingual writing. *PMLA*, *129*(3), 478–483. https://doi.org/10.1632/pmla.2014.129.3.478

Matsuda, P. K., & Jeffery, J. (2012). Voice in student essays. In K. Hyland & C. Sancho Guinda (eds.), *Stance and voice in written academic genres* (pp. 151–165). New York: Palgrave Macmillan. https://doi.org/10.1057/9781137030825_10

McFarland, M. (2017). What is Twitter, as explained by its evolving tagline. *The Washington Post*. September 12, 2014. Retrieved on May 1, 2020 from https://www.washingtonpost.com/news/innovations/wp/2014/09/12/what-is-twitter-as-explained-by-its-evolving-tagline/?noredirect=on&utm_term=.5db68fb88272.

McGrail, E., & Behizadeh, N. (2017). K–12 multimodal assessment and interactive audiences: An exploratory analysis of existing frameworks. *Assessing Writing*, *31*, 24–28. https://doi.org/10.1016/j.asw.2016.06.005

McLoughlin, C., & Lee, M. J. W. (2007). Social software and participatory learning: Pedagogical choices with technology affordances in the Web 2.0 era. *Proceedings of Ascilite Singapore 2007* (pp. 664–675). Retrieved on January 1, 2020 from http://citeseerx.ist.psu.edu/viewdoc/download?doi=10.1.1.471.2008&rep=rep1&type=pdf.

Melo-Pfeifer, S. (2015). Blogs and the development of plurilingual and intercultural competence: Report of a co-actional approach in Portuguese foreign language classroom. *Computer Assisted Language Learning*, *28*(3), 220–240. https://doi.org/10.1080/09588221.2013.818556

Merchant, G. (2006). Identity, social networks and online communication. *E-Learning*, *3*(2), 235–244. https://doi.org/10.2304/elea.2006.3.2.235

Meyers, K. A. (2003). Face-to-face versus threaded discussions: The role of time and higher-order thinking. *Journal of Asynchronous Learning Networks*, *7*(3), 55–65. https://doi.org/10.24059/olj.v7i3.1845

Mikulski, A., Elola, I., Padial, A., & Berry, G. (2019). *Revista Española de Lingüística Aplicada/Spanish Journal of Applied Linguistics, 32*(2), 542–571. https://doi.org/10.1075/resla.18018.mik

Miller-Cochran, S. (2017). Understanding multimodal composing in an L2 writing context. *Journal of Second Language Writing, 38*, 88–89. https://doi.org/10.1016/j.jslw.2017.10.009

Mills, N. (2011). Situated learning through social networking communities: The development of joint enterprise, mutual engagement, and a shared repertoire. *CALICO Journal, 28*(2), 326–344. https://doi.org/10.11139/cj.28.2.345-368

Miyazoe, T., & Anderson, T. (2010). Learning outcomes and students' perceptions of online writing: Simultaneous implementation of a forum, blog and wiki in an EFL blended learning setting. *System, 38*, 185–199. https://doi.org/10.1016/j.system.2010.03.006

Moore, A. H., Fowler, S. B., & Watson, C. E. (2007). Active learning and technology: Designing change for faculty, students, and institutions. *Educause Review, 42*(5), 42–61.

Morris, F. (2005). Child-to-child interaction and corrective feedback in a computer mediated L2 class. *Language Learning & Technology, 9*, 29–45.

Müller, K. (2011). Genre in the design space. *Computers and Composition, 28*, 186–194. https://doi.org/10.1016/j.compcom.2011.07.007

Munday, P., Delaney, Y. A., & Bosque, A. M. (2016). #InstagramELE: Learning Spanish through a social network. Digital presentation at the L2DL/AZCALL conference 2016. University of Arizona, Tucson. Cited from Fornara, Lomicka, & Hatten (2018).

Murray, E. A., Sheets, H. A., & Williams, N. A. (2009). The new work of assessment: Evaluating multimodal compositions. *Computers and Composition Online*. Retrieved on January 1, 2020 from http://cconlinejournal.org/murray_etal/index.html.

Murray, L., & Hourigan, T. (2006). Using micropublishing to facilitate writing in the foreign language. In L. Ducate & N. Arnold (eds.), *Calling on CALL: From theory to research to new directions in foreign language teaching* (pp. 149–179). San Marcos, TX: CALICO.

Murray, L., Hourigan, T., & Jeanneau, C. (2007). Blog writing integration for academic language learning purposes: Towards an assessment framework. *Iberica, 14*, 9–32.

National Council of Teachers of English. (2003). The NCTE definition of 21st century literacies. Retrieved on May 1, 2018 from http://www.ncte.org/positions/statements/21stcentdefinition.

Nelson, M. E. (2006). Mode, meaning, and synaesthesia in multimedia L2 writing. *Language Learning and Technology*, *10*(2), 56–76.

New London Group. (1996). A pedagogy of multiliteracies. *Harvard Educational Review*, *66*(1), 60–93. https://doi.org/10.17763/haer.66.1.17370n67v22j160u

New Media Consortium. (2005). A global imperative: The report of the 21st century literacy summit. Retrieved on January 1, 2020 from https://library.educause.edu/-/media/files/library/2005/10/21stcentliteracy.pdf.

Newell, G. E., Beach, R., Smith, J., & VanDerHeide, J. (2011). Teaching and learning argumentative reading and writing: A review of research. *Reading Research Quarterly*, *46*, 273–304.

Newman, D. R., Johnson, C., Cochrane, C., & Webb, B. (1996). An experiment in group learning technology: Evaluating critical thinking in face-to-face and computer-supported seminars. *Interpersonal Computing and Technology*, *4*, 57–74.

Nielson, K. B. (2014) Evaluation of an online, task-based Chinese course. In M. González-Lloret & L. Ortega (eds.), *Technology and tasks: Exploring technology-mediated TBLT* (pp. 295–322). Philadelphia: John Benjamins. https://doi.org/10.1075/tblt.6.11nie

Nitta, R., & Baba, K. (2014). Task repetition and L2 writing development: A longitudinal study from a dynamic systemics perspective. In H. Byrnes & R. M. Manchón (eds.), *Task-based language learning insights from and for L2 writing* (pp. 107–136). Philadelphia: John Benjamins. https://doi.org/10.1075/tblt.7.05nit

Norris, J. M. (2009). Task-based teaching and testing. In M. H. Long & C. J. Doughty (eds.), *Handbook of language teaching* (pp. 578–594). Malden, MA: Wiley/Blackwell. https://doi.org/10.1002/9781444315783.ch30

Norton, B. (2000). *Identity and language learning: Gender, ethnicity and educational change*. Harlow, UK: Longman/Pearson Education.

Odell, L., & Katz, S. (2009). “Yes, a t-shirt!”: Assessing visual composition in the “writing” class. *College Composition and Communication*, *6*(1), W197–W216.

Ortega, L. (2017). New CALL-SLA research interfaces for the 21st century: Towards equitable multilingualism. *CALICO Journal*, *34*(3), 285–316. https://doi.org/10.1558/cj.33855

Ortega, L., & Carson, J. (2010). Multicompetence, social context, and L2 writing research praxis. In T. Silva & P. K. Matsuda (eds.), *Practicing theory in second language writing* (pp. 48–71). West Lafayette, IN: Parlor Press.

Oskoz, A. (2009). Learners' feedback in online chats: What does it reveal about students learning? *CALICO Journal*, *27*(1), 48–68. https://doi.org/10.11139/cj.27.1.48-68

Oskoz, A. (2013). Developing a community of inquiry in a foreign language blended course. In Z. Akyol & R. Garrison (eds.), *Educational communities of inquiry: Theoretical framework, research and practice* (pp. 267–294). Hershey, PA: IGI Global. https://doi.org/10.4018/978-1-4666-2110-7.ch013

Oskoz, A., & Elola, I. (2012). Understanding the impact of social tools in the FL classroom: Activity theory at work. In G. Kessler, A. Oskoz, & I. Elola (eds.), *Technology across writing contexts and tasks* (pp. 131–153). San Marcos, TX: CALICO.

Oskoz, A., & Elola, I. (2013). Beyond the FL writing classroom: Social tools at work. In N. Estévez Fuerte & B. Clavel Arroitia (eds.), *Adquisición de segundas lenguas en el marco del nuevo milenio* (pp. 211–228). Valencia, Spain: Universitat de València.

Oskoz, A., & Elola, I. (2014). Promoting FL collaborative writing through the use of Web 2.0 tools. In M. González-Lloret & L. Ortega (eds.), *Technology and tasks: Exploring technology-mediated TBLT* (pp. 115–147). Philadelphia: John Benjamins. https://doi.org/10.1075/tblt.6.05osk

Oskoz, A., & Elola, I. (2016a). Digital stories in L2 education: Overview. *CALICO Journal*, *33*(2), 157–173. https://doi.org/10.1558/cj.v33i2.29295

Oskoz, A., & Elola, I. (2016b). Digital stories: Bringing multimodal texts to the Spanish writing classroom. *ReCALL*, *28*(3), 326–342. https://doi.org/10.1017/S0958344016000094

Otto, S. E. (2017). From past to present: A hundred years of technology for L2 learning. In C. Chapelle & S. Sauro (eds.), *The handbook of technology and second language teaching and learning* (pp. 10–25). New York: John Wiley & Sons. https://doi.org/10.1002/9781118914069.ch2

Pai, C. W. & Liou, H. C. (2009). Comparison of synchronous and asynchronous computer-mediated peer reviews of EFL college students. Paper presented at the CALICO conference, March 2009. Arizona State University, Tempe, AZ. Cited from Liou (2016).

Papacharissi, Z. (2006). Audiences as media producers: Content analysis of 260 blogs. In M. Tremayne (ed.), *Blogging, citizenship, and the future of media* (pp. 21–38). New York: Routledge.

Pasfield-Neofitou, S. (2011). Online domains of language use: Second language learners' experiences of virtual community and foreignness. *Language Learning & Technology*, *15*(2), 92–108.

Pavlenko, A., & Blackledge, A. (eds.). (2004). *Negotiation of identities in multilingual contexts*. Clevedon, UK: Multilingual Matters. https://doi.org/10.21832/9781853596483

Pellet, S. H. (2012). Wikis for building content knowledge in the foreign language classroom. *CALICO Journal*, *29*(2), 224–248. https://doi.org/10.11139/cj.29.2.224-248

Pennycook, A. (2001). *Critical applied linguistics: A critical introduction*. Mahwah, NJ: Erlbaum. https://doi.org/10.4324/9781410600790

Pérez-Sabater, C., & Montero-Fleta, B. (2015). ESP vocabulary and social networking: The case of Twitter. *Iberia*, *29*, 129–154.

Pettitt, T. (2007). *Opening the Gutenberg parenthesis: Media in transition in Shakespeare's England*. Paper presented at the Media in Transition 5 conference, April 2007. Cambridge, MA. Retrieved on January 1, 2020 from https://www.academia.edu/4169782/Opening_the_Gutenberg_Parenthesis_Media_in_Transition_in_Shakespeare_s_England.

Polio, C. (2012). The relevance of second language acquisition theory to the written error correction debate. *Journal of Second Language Writing*, *21*(4), 375–389. https://doi.org/10.1016/j.jslw.2012.09.004

Prensky, M. (2001). Digital natives, digital immigrants: A new way to look at ourselves and our kids. *Horizon*, *9*(5), 1–6. Retrieved on May 1, 2018 from https://www.marcprensky.com/writing/Prensky%20-%20Digital%20Natives,%20Digital%20Immigrants%20-%20Part1.pdf. https://doi.org/10.1108/10748120110424816

Prensky, M. (2009). H. Sapiens digital: From digital immigrants to digital natives to digital wisdom. *Innovate: Journal of Online Education*, *5*(3). Retrieved on January 1, 2020 from https://nsuworks.nova.edu/innovate/vol5/iss3/1.

Prior, P. (2007). From Voloshinov and Bakhtin to mediated multimodal genre systems. In A. Bonini, D. de Carvalho Figueriedo, & F. J. Rauen (eds.), *Proceedings of the 4th International Symposium on Genre Studies* (pp. 270–286). Santa Catarina, Brazil: University of Southern Santa Catarina.

Purnama, A. D. (2017). Incorporating memes and Instagram to enhance student's participation. *LLT Journal*, *20*(1), 1–14. https://doi.org/10.24071/llt.2017.200101

Rance-Roney, J. (2008). Digital storytelling for language and culture learning. *Essential Teacher*, *5*(1), pp. 29–31. Retrieved on January 1, 2020 from https://www.tesol.org/docs/pdf/12830.pdf?sfvrsn=380931b9_2.

Reinhardt, J., & Thorne, S. L. (2011). Beyond comparisons: Frameworks for developing digital L2 Literacies. In N. Arnold & L. Ducate (eds.), *Present and future promises of CALL: From theory and research to new directions in language teaching* (pp. 257–280). San Marcos, TX: CALICO.

Reinhardt, J., Warner, C., & Lange, K. (2014). Digital games as practices and texts: New literacies and genres in an L2 German classroom. In J. P. Guikema & W. Lawrence (eds.), *Digital literacies in foreign and second language education* (pp. 159–178). San Marcos, TX: CALICO.

Reinhardt, J., & Zander, V. (2011). Social networking in an intensive English program classroom: A language socialization perspective. *CALICO Journal*, *28*(2), 326–344. https://doi.org/10.11139/cj.28.2.326-344

Reiss, D., & Young, A. (2013). Multimodal composing, appropriation, remediation, and reflection: Writing, literature, and media. In T. S. Bowen & C. Whithaus (eds.), *Multimodal literacies and emerging genres* (pp. 164–182). Pittsburgh: Pittsburgh University Press. https://doi.org/10.2307/j.ctt6wrbkn.11

Reyes Torres, A., Pich Ponce, E., & García Pastor, M. D. (2012). Digital storytelling as a pedagogical tool within a didactic sequence in foreign language teaching. *Digital Education Review*, *22*, 1–18.

Rinnert, C., & Kobayashi, H. (2016). Multicompetence and multilingual writing. In R. M. Manchón, & P. K. Matsuda (eds.), *Handbook of second and foreign language writing* (pp. 365–385). Boston: De Gruyter. https://doi.org/10.1515/9781614511335-020

Ritchie, M., & Black, C. (2012). Public internet forums: Can they enhance argumentative writing skills of second language learners? *Foreign Language Annals*, *45*(3), 349–361. https://doi.org/10.1111/j.1944-9720.2012.01203.x

Roberts, B. J. (1999). *Can error logs raise more than consciousness? The effects of error logs and grammar feedback on ESL students' final drafts*. Unpublished Master's thesis. California State University, Sacramento.

Robin, B. (2006). The educational uses of digital storytelling. In C. Crawford, R. Carlsen, K. McFerrin, J. Price, R. Weber & D. Willis (eds.), *Proceedings of SITE 2006—Society for Information Technology & Teacher Education International Conference* (pp. 709–716). Orlando: Association for the Advancement of Computing in Education (AACE).

Robinson, P. (2001). Task complexity, task difficulty, and task production: Exploring interactions in a componential framework. *Applied Linguistics*, *22*, 27–57. https://doi.org/10.1093/applin/22.1.27

Rowsell, J., Kosnik, C., & Beck, C. (2008). Fostering multiliteracies pedagogy through preservice teacher education. *Teaching Education*, *19*(2), 109–122. https://doi.org/10.1080/10476210802040799

Russell, D. R. (1997). Rethinking genre in school and society: An activity theory analysis. *Written Communication*, *14*, 504–554. https://doi.org/10.1177/0741088397014004004

Samaniego, M., & Warner, C. (2016). Designing meaning in inherited languages: A multiliteracies approach to HL instruction. In M. Fairclough & S. Beaudrie (eds.), *Innovative strategies for heritage language teaching: A practical guide for the classroom* (pp. 191–213). Washington, DC: Georgetown University Press.

Samburskiy, D., & Quah, J. (2014). Corrective feedback in asynchronous online interaction: Developing novice online language instructors. *CALICO Journal*, *31*(2), 158–178. https://doi.org/10.11139/cj.31.2.158-178

Samuda, V., & Bygate, M. (2008). *Tasks in second language learning*. Basingstoke, UK: Palgrave Macmillan. https://doi.org/10.1057/9780230596429

Sánchez, E. L. (2017). *I am not your perfect Mexican daughter*. New York: Alfred A. Knopf.

Sauro, S. (2001). *The success of task type in facilitating oral language production in online computer mediated collaborative projects*. Unpublished Master's thesis. Department of English, Iowa State University.

Sauro, S. (2009). Computer-mediated corrective feedback and the development of L2 grammar. *Language Learning & Technology*, *13*(1), 96–120.

Sauro, S. (2011). SCMC for SLA: A research synthesis. *CALICO Journal*, *28*(2), 369–391. https://doi.org/10.11139/cj.28.2.369-391

Sauro, S. (2014). Lessons from the fandom: Task models for technology-enhanced language learning. In M. González-Lloret & L. Ortega (eds.), *Technology-mediated TBLT: Researching technology and tasks* (pp. 239–262). Amsterdam: John Benjamins. https://doi.org/10.1075/tblt.6.09sau

Sauro, S. (2016). Does CALL have an English problem? *Language Learning & Technology*, *20*(3), 1–8.

Sauro, S. (2017). Online fan practices and CALL. *CALICO Journal*, *34*(2), 131–146. https://doi.org/10.1558/cj.33077

Sauro, S., & Sundmark, B. (2016). Report from Middle Earth: Fan fiction tasks in the EFL classroom. *ELT Journal*, *70*(4), 414–423. https://doi.org/10.1093/elt/ccv075

Sauro, S., & Zourou, K. (2017). CALL for papers for "CALL in the Digital Wilds" special issue. *Language Learning & Technology*, *21*(1), 186.

Savignon, J., & Roithmeier, W. (2004). Computer-mediated communication: Texts and strategies. *CALICO Journal*, *21*(2), 265–290. https://doi.org/10.1558/cj.v21i2.265-290

Schmidt, R. (1990). The role of consciousness in second language learning. *Applied Linguistics*, *11*, 129–158. https://doi.org/10.1093/applin/11.2.129

Schmidt, R. (2001). Attention. In P. Robinson (ed.), *Cognition and second language instruction* (pp. 3–32). Cambridge, UK: Cambridge University Press. https://doi.org/10.1017/CBO9781139524780.003

Schwämmlein, E., & Wodzicki, K. (2012). "What to tell about me?" Self-presentations in online communities. *Journal of Computer-Mediated Communication*, *17*(4), 387–407. https://doi.org/10.1111/j.1083-6101.2012.01582.x

Sengupta, S. (2001). Exchanging ideas with peers in network-based classrooms: An aid or a pain? *Language Learning & Technology*, *5*(1), 103–134.

Shang, H. F. (2007). An exploratory study of e-mail application on FL writing performance. *Computer Assisted Language Learning*, *20*(1), 79–96. https://doi.org/10.1080/09588220601118479

Sheen, Y. (2007). The effect of focused written corrective feedback and language aptitude on ESL learners' acquisition of articles. *TESOL Quarterly*, *41*, 255–283. https://doi.org/10.1002/j.1545-7249.2007.tb00059.x

Sheen, Y. (2010). The role of oral and written corrective feedback in SLA. *Studies in Second Language Acquisition*, *32*(2), 169–179. https://doi.org/10.1017/S0272263109990489

Shiffman, B. G. (1997). Grading student writing: The dilemma from a feminist perspective. In L. Allison, M. Hourigan, & L. Bryant (eds.), *Grading in the post-process classroom: From theory to practice* (pp. 58–72). Portsmouth, NH: Boynton/Cook.

Shih, R. C. (2011). Can Web 2.0 technology assist college students in learning English writing? Integrating Facebook and peer assessment with blended learning. *Australasian Journal of Educational Technology*, *27*(5), 829–845. https://doi.org/10.14742/ajet.934

Shin, D.-S., & Cimasko, T. (2008). Multimodal composition in a college ESL class: New tools, traditional norms. *Computers and Composition, 25*(4), 376–395. https://doi.org/10.1016/j.compcom.2008.07.001

Shin, J. K. (2008). *Building an effective community of inquiry for EFL professionals in an asynchronous online discussion board*. Unpublished Doctoral dissertation. University of Baltimore, Baltimore County.

Shintani, N., & Aubrey, S. (2016). The effectiveness of synchronous and asynchronous written corrective feedback on grammatical accuracy in a computer-mediated environment. *Modern Language Journal*, *100*(1), 296–319. https://doi.org/10.1111/modl.12317

Shrum, J. L., & Glisan, E. W. (2015). *Teacher's handbook: Contextualized language instruction* (5th edition). Boston: Cengage Learning.

Sinclair, G. (2010). Exploring Canada's digital future. Paper presented at the featured "Big Thinking" lecture at the Congress of the Humanities and Social Sciences, May 2010. Concordia University, Montréal. Cited from Lotherington & Jensen (2011).

Siyanova-Chanturia, A. (2015). Collocation in beginner learner writing: A longitudinal study. *System*, *53*, 148–160. https://doi.org/10.1016/j.system.2015.07.003

Sollars, V. (2007). Writing experiences in a second/foreign language classroom: From theory to practice. In M. Camilleri, P. Ford, H. Leja, & V. Sollars (eds.), *Blogs: Web journal in language education* (pp. 15–24). Strasbourg, France: Council of Europe.

Sorapure, M. (2006). Between modes: Assessing student new media compositions. *Kairos*. Retrieved on January 1, 2020 from http://technorhetoric.net/10.2/coverweb/sorapure/.

St. John, E., & Cash, D. (1995). Language learning via e-mail: Demonstrable success with German. In M. Warschauer (ed.), *Virtual connections: Online activities and projects for networking language learners* (pp. 191–197). Honolulu: Second Language Teaching & Curriculum Center, University of Hawai'i.

Statista. (2019). Number of monthly active Twitter users worldwide from 1st quarter 2010 to 1st quarter 2019 (in millions). Retrieved on June 1, 2019 from https://www.statista.com/statistics/282087/number-of-monthly-active-twitter-users/.

Stickler, U., & Hampel, R. (2011). CyberDeutsch: Language production and user preferences in a Moodle virtual learning environment. *CALICO Journal*, *28*(1), 49–73. https://doi.org/10.11139/cj.28.1.49-73

Storch, N. (2002). Patterns of interaction in ESL pair work. *Language Learning*, *52*(1), 119–158. https://doi.org/10.1111/1467-9922.00179

Storch, N. (2005). Collaborative writing: Product, process, and students' reflections. *Journal of Second Language Writing*, *14*(3), 153–173. https://doi.org/10.1016/j.jslw.2005.05.002

Storch, N. (2016). Collaborative writing. In R. M. Manchón & P. K. Matsuda (eds.), *Handbook of second and foreign language writing* (pp. 387–406). Boston: De Gruyter. https://doi.org/10.1515/9781614511335-021

Storch, N., & Wigglesworth, G. (2010). Learners' processing, uptake, and retention of corrective feedback on writing: Case studies. *Studies in Second Language Acquisition*, *32*(2), 303–334. https://doi.org/10.1017/S0272263109990532

Strobl, C. (2014). Affordances of Web 2.0 technologies for collaborative advanced writing in a foreign language. *CALICO Journal*, *31*(1), 1–18. https://doi.org/10.11139/cj.31.1.1-18

Strobl, C. (2017). The potential of automated corrective feedback to remediate cohesion problems in advanced students' writing. In K. Borthwick, L. Bradley, & S. Thouësny (eds.), *CALL in a climate of change: Adapting to turbulent global conditions – Short papers from EUROCALL 2017* (pp. 294–299). Research-publishing.net. https://doi.org/10.14705/rpnet.2017.eurocall2017.729

Sun, Y.-C. & Chang, Y.-J. (2012). Blogging to learn: Becoming EFL academic writers through collaborative dialogues. *Language Learning & Technology*, *16*(1), 43–61. http://dx.doi.org/10125/44274

Sundqvist, P., & Sylvén, L. K. (2014). Language-related computer use: Focus on young L2 English learners in Sweden. *ReCALL*, *26*(1), 3–20. https://doi.org/10.1017/S0958344013000232

Swain, M. K. (1985). Communicative competence: Some roles of comprehensible input and comprehensible output in its development. In S. M. Gass & C. G. Madden (eds.), *Input in second language acquisition* (pp. 235–253). Rowley, MA: Newbury House.

Swain, M. K. (2001). Examining dialogue: Another approach to content specification and to validating inferences drawn from test scores. *Language Testing*, *18*, 275–302. https://doi.org/10.1177/026553220101800302

Swain, M. K., & Lapkin, S. (1995). Problems in output and the cognitive processes they generate: A step towards second language learning. *Applied Linguistics*, *16*(3), 371–391. https://doi.org/10.1093/applin/16.3.371

Swales, J. M. (1990). Genre analysis: English in academic and research settings. Cambridge, UK: Cambridge University Press.

Swales, J. M. (2004). *Research genres: Explorations and applications*. Cambridge, UK: Cambridge University Press. https://doi.org/10.1017/CBO9781139524827

Sykes, J., Oskoz, A., & Thorne, S. L. (2008). Web 2.0, immersive environments, and the future of language education. *CALICO Journal*, *25*(3), 528–546. https://doi.org/10.1558/cj.v25i3.528-546

Tagg, C., & Seargeant, P. (2016). Facebook and the discursive construction of the social network. In A. Georgakopoulou & T. Spilioti (eds.), *The Routledge handbook of language and digital communication* (pp. 323–353). London: Routledge.

Tai, H. C., Lin, W. C., & Yang, S. C. (2015). Exploring the effects of peer review and teachers' corrective feedback on EFL students' online writing performance. *Journal of Educational Computing Research*, *53*(2), 284–309. https://doi.org/10.1177/0735633115597490

Takayoshi, P., & Selfe, C. L. (2007). Thinking about multimodality. In C. L. Selfe (ed.), *Multimodal composition: Resources for teachers* (pp. 1–12). Cresskill, NJ: Hampton Press.

Tardy, C. M. (2005). "It's like a story": Rhetorical knowledge development in advanced academic literacy. *Journal of English for Academic Purposes*, *4*(4), 325–338. https://doi.org/10.1016/j.jeap.2005.07.005

Tardy, C. M. (2009). *Building genre knowledge*. West Lafayette, IN: Parlor Press.

Tardy, C. M. (2016). *Beyond convention: Genre innovation in academic writing*. Ann Arbor: University of Michigan Press. https://doi.org/10.3998/mpub.5173647

Tardy, C. M. (2017). Crossing, or creating, divides? A plea for transdisciplinary scholarship. In B. Horner & L. Tetrault (eds.), *Crossing divides: Exploring translingual writing pedagogies and programs*. Logan, UT: Utah State University Press. https://doi.org/10.7330/9781607326205.c010

Terantino, J. (2013). Facebook comparison research: Faculty and student perceptions of social media for foreign language courses. In B. Zou, M. Xing, Y. Wang, M. Sun, & C. H. Xiang (eds.), *Computer-assisted foreign language teaching and learning: Technological advances* (pp. 91–103). Hershey, PA: IGI Global. https://doi.org/10.4018/978-1-4666-2821-2.ch006

Thomas, E. E., & Stornaiuolo, A. (2016). Restorying the self: Bending toward textual justice. *Harvard Educational Review*, *86*(3), 313–338. https://doi.org/10.17763/1943-5045-86.3.313

Thorne, S. L. (2003). Artifacts and cultures-of-use in intercultural communication. *Language Learning and Technology*, *7*(2), 38–67.

Thorne, S. L. (2013). Digital literacies. In M. Hawkins (ed.), *Framing languages and literacies: Socially situated views and perspectives* (pp. 192–218). New York: Routledge.

Thorne, S. L., & Black, R. W. (2007). Language and literacy development in computer-mediated contexts and communities. *Annual Review of Applied Linguistics*, *27*, 133–160. https://doi.org/10.1017/S0267190508070074

Thorne, S. L., & Black, R. W. (2011). Identity and Interaction in internet-mediated contexts. In C. Higgins (ed.), *Identity formation in globalizing contexts* (pp. 257–278). New York: De Gruyter Mouton. https://doi.org/10.1515/9783110267280.257

Thorne, S. L., Black, R. W., & Sykes, J. M. (2009). Second language use, socialization, and learning in internet interest communities and online gaming. *Modern Language Journal*, *93*(S1), 802–821. https://doi.org/10.1111/j.1540-4781.2009.00974.x

Thorne, S. L., & Reinhardt, J. (2008). "Bridging activities," new media literacies, and advanced foreign language proficiency. *CALICO Journal*, *25*(3), 558–572. https://doi.org/10.1558/cj.v25i3.558-572

Truscott, J. (1996). The case against grammar correction in L2 writing classes. *Language Learning*, *46*(2), 327–369. https://doi.org/10.1111/j.1467-1770.1996.tb01238.x

Truscott, J., & Hsu, A. Y.-P. (2008). Error correction, revision, and learning. *Journal of Second Language Writing*, *17*, 292–305. https://doi.org/10.1016/j.jslw.2008.05.003

Tseng, S. C., & Tsai, C. C. (2007). On-line peer assessment and the role of the peer feedback: A study of high school computer course. *Computers & Education*, *49*(4), 1161–1174. https://doi.org/10.1016/j.compedu.2006.01.007

Tuzi, F. (2004). The impact of e-feedback on the revisions of L2 writers in an academic writing course. *Computers and Composition*, *21*(2), 217–235. https://doi.org/10.1016/j.compcom.2004.02.003

Twitter. (2019). About. Retrieved on June 1, 2019 from https://about.twitter.com/en_us/company.html.

Ullrich C., Borau, K., Stepanyan K. (2010). Who students interact with? A social network analysis perspective on the use of twitter in language learning. In M. Wolpers, P. A. Kirschner, M. Scheffel, S. Lindstaedt, & V. Dimitrova (eds.), *Sustaining TEL: From innovation to learning and practice*. EC-TEL 2010. Lecture Notes in Computer Science, Vol. 6383 (432–437). Berlin/Heidelberg Springer. https://doi.org/10.1007/978-3-642-16020-2_33

Ushioda, E. (2011). Language learning motivation, self and identity: Current theoretical perspectives. *Computer Assisted Language Learning*, *24*(3), 199–210. https://doi.org/10.1080/09588221.2010.538701

Valdés, G. (1997). The teaching of Spanish to bilingual Spanish-speaking students: Outstanding issues and unanswered questions. In M. C. Colombi & F. X. Alarcón (eds.), *La enseñanza del español a hispanohablantes* (pp. 8–44). Boston: Houghton Mifflin.

Van den Branden, K. (2006). Training teachers: Task-based as well? In K. Van den Branden (ed.), Task-based language education: From theory to practice (pp. 217–73). Cambridge, UK: Cambridge University Press. https://doi.org/10.1017/CBO9780511667282.011

Van de Branden, K., Bygate, M., & Norris, J. M. (2009). *Task-based language teaching: A reader*. Amsterdam: John Benjamins. https://doi.org/10.1075/tblt.1

Van Handle, D. C., & Corl, K. A. (1998). Extending the dialogue: Using electronic mail and the internet to promote conversation and writing in intermediate-level German language courses. *CALICO Journal*, *15*(1–3), 129–143. https://doi.org/10.1558/cj.v15i1-3.129-143

Van Kooten, C. (2013). Toward a rhetorically-sensitive assessment model for new media composition. In H. McKee & D. N. DeVoss (eds.), *Digital writing assessment and evaluation*. Logan, UT: Computers and Composition Digital Press/Utah State University Press.

van Lier, L. (2000). From input to affordance: Social-interactive learning from an ecological perspective. In P. J. Lantolf (ed.), *Sociocultural theory and second language learning* (pp. 245–259). Oxford: Oxford University Press.

Vandergriff, I. (2016). *Second-language discourse in the digital world. Linguistic and social practices in and beyond the networked classroom*. Amsterdam: John Benjamins. https://doi.org/10.1075/lllt.46

Villamil, O. S., & de Guerrero, M. C. M. (1996). Peer revision in the L2 classroom: Social-cognitive activities, mediating strategies, and aspects of social behavior. *Journal of Second Language Writing*, *5*(1), 51–75. https://doi.org/10.1016/S1060-3743(96)90015-6

Villamil, O. S., & de Guerrero, M. C. M. (1998). Assessing the impact of peer revision in L2 writing. *Applied Linguistics*, *19*(4), 491–514. https://doi.org/10.1093/applin/19.4.491

Vinagre, M. (2005). Fostering language learning via e-mail: An English–Spanish exchange. *Computer Assisted Language Learning, 18*(5), 369–388. https://doi.org/10.1080/09588220500442749

Vinagre, M., & Lera, M. (2008). The role of error correction in online exchanges. In F. Zhang & B. Barber (eds.), *Handbook of research on computer-enhanced language acquisition and learning* (pp. 326–341). Hershey, PA: IGI Global. https://doi.org/10.4018/978-1-59904-895-6.ch019

Vinagre, M., & Maíllo, C. (2007). Focus on form in on-line projects: Linguistic development in email tandem exchanges. In C. Periñán (ed.), *Revisiting language learning resources* (pp. 91–112). Cambridge, UK: Cambridge Scholars.

Vinagre, M., & Muñoz, B. (2011). Computer-mediated corrective feedback and language accuracy in telecollaborative exchanges. *Language Learning & Technology, 15*(1), 72–103.

Vinogradova, P. (2014). Digital stories in heritage language education: Empowering heritage language learners through a pedagogy of multi literacies. In T. G. Wiley, J. K. Peyton, D. Christian, S. C. K. Moore, & N. Liu (eds.), *Handbook of heritage, community, and native American languages in the United States research, policy, and educational practice* (pp. 314–323). New York: Routledge.

Vurdien, R. (2013). Enhancing writing skills through blogging in an advanced English as a foreign language class in Spain. *Computer-Assisted Language Learning, 26*(2), 126–143. https://doi.org/10.1080/09588221.2011.639784

Vygotsky, L. (1978). *Mind in society*. Cambridge, MA: Harvard University Press.

Walther, J. B. (2012). Interaction through technological lenses: Computer-mediated communication and language. *Journal of Language and Social Psychology, 31*, 397–414. https://doi.org/10.1177/0261927X12446610

Wang, S., & Vasquez, C. (2012). Web 2.0 and second language learning: What does the research tell us? *CALICO Journal, 29*(3), 412–430. https://doi.org/10.11139/cj.29.3.412-430

Wanner, A. (2008). Creating comfort zones of orality in online discussion forums. In S. S. Magnan (ed.), *Mediating discourse online* (pp. 125–149). Amsterdam: John Benjamins. https://doi.org/10.1075/aals.3.09wan

Ward, J. M. (2004). Blog-assisted language learning (BALL): Push button publishing for the pupils. *TEFL Web Journal, 3*(1), 1–16.

Ware, P., & O'Dowd, R. (2008). Peer feedback on language form in telecollaboration. *Language Learning & Technology, 12*(1), 43–63.

Warschauer, M., & Grimes, D. (2007). Audience, authorship, and artifact: The emergent semiotics of Web 2.0. *Annual Review of Applied Linguistics*, *27*(1), 1–23. https://doi.org/10.1017/S0267190508070013

Werstch, J. V. (1991). *Voices of the mind*. Cambridge, MA: Harvard University Press.

Whiddon, J. (2016). Instafrench: investigating the use of social media and student-selected images to support l2 writing. Unpublished Master's thesis. Georgia State University.

Whithaus, C. (2005). *Teaching and evaluating writing in the age of computers and high-stakes testing*. Mahwah, NJ: Erlbaum. https://doi.org/10.4324/9781410613691

Wiggins, G. (1994). Toward more authentic assessment of language performances. In C. Hancock (ed.), *Teaching, testing, and assessment: Making the connection* (pp. 69–85). Lincolnwood, IL: National Textbook Co.

Wiggins, G., & McTighe, J. (2005). *Understanding by design* (Expanded 2nd edition). Alexandria, VA: Association for Supervision and Curriculum Development.

Willingham, D. T. (2009). *Why don't students like school? A cognitive scientist answers questions about how the mind works and what it means for the classroom*. San Francisco: Jossey-Bass. https://doi.org/10.1002/9781118269527

Wilson, G., & Stacey, E. (2004). Online interaction impacts on learning: Teaching the teachers to teach online. *Australasian Journal of Educational Technology*, *20*(1), 33–48. https://doi.org/10.14742/ajet.1366

Winke, P. M. (2014). Formative, task-based oral assessment in an advanced Chinese-language class. In M. González-Lloret & L. Ortega (eds.), *Technology and tasks: Exploring technology-mediated TBLT* (pp. 263–294). Philadelphia: John Benjamins. https://doi.org/10.1075/tblt.6.10win

Wolff, W. I. (2013). Interactivity and the invisible: What counts as writing in the age of Web 2.0. *Computers and Composition*, *30*, 211–225. https://doi.org/10.1016/j.compcom.2013.06.001

Woo, Y., & Reeves, T. C. (2007). Meaningful interaction in web-based learning: A social constructivist interpretation. *The Internet and Higher Education*, *10*(1), 15–25. https://doi.org/10.1016/j.iheduc.2006.10.005

Wood, D., Bruner, J., & Ross, G. (1976). The role of tutoring in problem solving. *Journal of Child Psychology and Psychiatry*, *17*, 89–100. https://doi.org/10.1111/j.1469-7610.1976.tb00381.x

Wu, A. (2003). Supporting electronic discourse: Principles of design from a social constructivist perspective. *Journal of Interactive Learning Research*, *14*(2), 167–184.

Wu, W., & Lee, W. (2008). Adopting e-learning platform under pen-pal setting to enhance EFL students' writing motivation and performance. In K. McFerrin, R. Weber, R. Carlsen, & D. A. Willis (eds.), *Proceedings of Society for Information Technology and Teacher Education International Conference 2008* (pp. 3610–3616). Chesapeake, VA: Association for the Advance of Computing in Education.

Yancey, K. B. (2004). Looking for sources of coherence in a fragmented world: Notes toward a new assessment design. *Computers and Composition*, *21*(1), 89–102. https://doi.org/10.1016/j.compcom.2003.08.024

Yang, S.-H. (2009). Using blogs to enhance critical reflection and community of practice. *Educational Technology & Society*, *12*, 11–21.

Yang, S. J., & Yi, Y. (2017). Negotiating multiple identities through eTandem learning experiences. *CALICO Journal*, *34*(1), 97–114. https://doi.org/10.1558/cj.29586

Yang, Y.-F. (2012). Multimodal composing in digital storytelling. *Computers and Composition*, *29*(3), 221–238. https://doi.org/10.1016/j.compcom.2012.07.001

Yates, J., & Orlikowski, W. J. (1992). Genres of organizational communication: A structurational approach to studying communication and media. *The Academy of Management Review*, *17*(2), 299–326. https://doi.org/10.5465/amr.1992.4279545

Yeh, H.-C. (2014). Exploring how collaborative dialogues facilitate synchronous collaborative writing. *Language Learning & Technology*, *18*(1), 23–37.

Yen, Y.-C., Hou, H.-T., & Chang, K. E. (2015). Applying role-playing strategy to enhance learners' writing and speaking skills in EFL courses using Facebook and Skype as learning tools: A case study in Taiwan. *Computer Assisted Language Learning*, *28*(5), 383–406. https://doi.org/10.1080/09588221.2013.839568

Yi, Y. (2009). Adolescent literacy and identity construction among 1.5 generation students: From a transnational perspective. *Journal of Asian Pacific Communication*, *19*(1), 100–129. https://doi.org/10.1075/japc.19.1.06yi

Yi, Y. (2017). Establishing multimodal literacy research in the field of L2 writing: Let's move the field forward. *Journal of Second Language Writing*, *38*, 90–91. https://doi.org/10.1016/j.jslw.2017.10.010

Yu, S., & Lee, I. (2016). Exploring Chinese students' strategy use in a cooperative peer feedback writing group. *System*, *58*, 1–11. https://doi.org/10.1016/j.system.2016.02.005

Zapata, G. C. (2018). A match made in heaven: An introduction to *Learning by Design* and its role in heritage language education. In G. C. Zapata & M. Lacorte (eds.), *Multiliteracies pedagogy and language learning* (pp. 1–26). Cham, Switzerland: Palgrave Macmillan. https://doi.org/10.1007/978-3-319-63103-5_1

Zhang, T. L., & Cassany, D. (2016). Fansubbing del español al chino: Organización, roles y normas en las escritura colaborativa. *BiD: Textos Universitaris de Biblioteconomia i Documentació*, *37*. Retrieved on January 1, 2020 from http://bid.ub.edu/es/37/tian.htm.

Zhung, B., & Warschauer, M. (2017). Epilogue: Second language writing in the age of computer-mediated communication. *Journal of Second Language Writing*, *36*, 61–67. https://doi.org/10.1016/j.jslw.2017.05.014

Author Index

Z

Subject Index

www.ingramcontent.com/pod-product-compliance
Lightning Source LLC
LaVergne TN
LVHW010443080826
844660LV00026B/1208
* 9 7 8 1 7 8 1 7 9 6 9 3 1 *